CHRONIC ILLNESS ACROSS THE LIFE SPAN

CHRONIC ILLNESS ACROSS THE LIFE SPAN

Margaret Dimond, R.N., Ph.D.

Associate Professor of Nursing
College of Nursing
University of Utah
Salt Lake City, Utah

Susan Lynn Jones, R.N., Ph.D.

Professor of Nursing
School of Nursing
Kent State University
Kent, Ohio

APPLETON-CENTURY-CROFTS/Norwalk, Connecticut

Copyright © 1983 by APPLETON-CENTURY-CROFTS
A Publishing Division of Prentice-Hall, Inc.

83 84 85 86 87 / 10 9 8 7 6 5 4 3 2 1

Prentice-Hall International, Inc., London
Prentice-Hall of Australia, Pty. Ltd., Sydney
Prentice-Hall of India Private Limited, New Delhi
Prentice-Hall of Japan, Inc., Tokyo
Prentice-Hall of Southeast Asia (Pte.) Ltd., Singapore
Whitehall Books Ltd., Wellington, New Zealand
Editora Prentice-Hall do Brasil Ltda., Rio de Janeiro

Library of Congress Cataloging in Publication Data

Dimond, Margaret.
    Chronic illness across the life span.

    Bibliography: p.
    Includes index.
    1. Chronic diseases—Nursing. 2. Chronic diseases—
Social aspects. 3. Chronic diseases—Psychological
aspects. 4. Long-term care of the sick. I. Jones,
Susan L. II. Title. [DNLM: 1. Chronic disease—Nursing.
WY 152 D582c]
RT120.C45D55 1983   362.1   82-11424
ISBN 0-8385-1122-8

Cover design: Lynn M. Luchetti
Text Design: Gloria Moyer

PRINTED IN THE UNITED STATES OF AMERICA

To our families

Contents

Foreword   ix
Preface   xi

Part 1
**THEORETICAL PERSPECTIVES ON
CHRONIC ILLNESS**
Chapter 1   Disease, Illness, and Sickness   3
Chapter 2   Chronic Illness   31
Chapter 3   Overview of Human Development   53
Chapter 4   The Family in Health and Illness   93

Part 2
**FUNDAMENTAL CONCEPTS
IN CHRONIC ILLNESS**
Chapter 5   Career   115
Chapter 6   Social Support   145
Chapter 7   Identity   165
Chapter 8   Personal Control   193

Part 3
MAJOR ISSUES IN CHRONIC ILLNESS
Chapter 9   Ethics and the Quality of Life
               in Chronic Illness   221
Chapter 10   Research Issues in Chronic Illness   237

               Index   251

Foreword

Along with many other changes in the twentieth century came an increase in long-term diseases not amenable to cure. The same miraculous technological changes that brought major improvements in living for large numbers of people also made it possible for chronic diseases to increase both in number and diversity of form.

Yet, recognition of the impact of chronic disease on peoples' lives has been slow to emerge. This is partly because the modern health care system has evolved around a model of medical treatment for acute illness and injury and active biotechnical intervention to remove the causative factors. The disease-centered orientation of the biomedical model has had a powerful influence on the perspectives of health care providers and the public. Its appeal led to a system of services built around an organizing conceptual framework of disease with diagnosis, treatment and eradication of disease as primary goals.

This book is a timely reminder that the impact of disease on human beings is more than biological. The authors provide evidence that illness is a complex human experience with many personal, familial, and social implications. Drawing heavily on the work of social and behavioral scientists, they argue persuasively that understanding long-term illness and sickness requires an orientation that takes account of the personal and interpersonal dimensions of these experiences. They believe that health-care services for and research about chronic illness need conceptual and theoretical frameworks that incorporate ethical principles and behavioral concepts relevant to the multidimensional and social character of chronic illness. The book offers much food for thought for the many health-care disciplines providing services to people living with the disabilities associated with chronic disorders. Its perspective has special relevance for practitioners, investigators and teachers in the field of nursing.

The practice of nursing has a long history of concern for the health needs of people with chronic illness. Yet often nurses plan treatment based on implicit models of care without clearly distinguishing among disease, illness, and sickness as major concepts that affect professional definitions of the meaning of care. This book provides direction for the creation of explicit models of nursing practice built on conceptualizations that incorporate the personal and social dimensions of chronic illness at different stages of human development. Its guidelines orient newcomers to nursing to the humanitarian and transactional nature of the nursing enterprise in long-term care. It also should stimulate further inquiry and research into what has become a profoundly important area of human experience in our time.

Jeanne Quint Benoliel
Professor of Nursing
Community Health Care Systems Department
School of Nursing
University of Washington
Seattle, Washington

Preface

The practice of nursing has long been identified with the care and comfort of persons with chronic illness. Community and public health nursing has a proud history of providing the kind of care associated with maintaining health, teaching, and preventing complications for persons with long-term illnesses. To some extent, however, the role and function of nursing in chronic illness has been overshadowed by the drama of caring for the acutely ill in practice and in curriculum content. In recent times the focus has returned to the concept of wellness-oriented care and the maintenance and promotion of health among those with long-term illness. Additionally, the care of the chronically ill has become a multidisciplinary endeavor. The health needs of the chronically ill are diverse and complex and no single discipline is prepared to address all of these needs. An interdisciplinary approach to the management of chronic illness is essential. This text is therefore addressed to health care professionals from many disciplines.

Chronic Illness Across the Life Span provides a unique and integrated approach to teaching, practice, and research in the area of chronic illness. Our intent is to provide a broad conceptual framework for the study of chronic illness and to stimulate thinking about chronic illness from many perspectives. Although implications for care are an integral part of this text, this not intended to be a "how to care for the chronically ill" book. We assume that our readers have a sophistiated undertanding of chronic illness. Thus, the purpose of this text is to enlarge the scope of care to the chronically ill by broadening the base from which care is planned. We hope that the elaboration of the concepts of disease, illness, sickness, and chronicity, as well as issues of family, ethics, quality of life, and research will make this a comprehensive text and one which will contribute substantially to the literature on chronic illness.

The authors intend to fill a gap in the available literature on chronic illness by providing substantive material for *faculty* teaching at senior levels in baccalaureate programs, as well as for those who teach graduate students. In addition to serving as a required text for long-term care courses, this text will also be useful for graduate seminars focusing on issues in chronic illness. *Researchers* are the second group for whom the book will be interesting. The concepts discussed, the illustrative material provided on chronic illness at various life-stages, the examination of theoretical and operational definitions of concepts, and the status of research all combine to provide a rich source of ideas for investigative endeavors. Finally, our book will appeal to *practitioners* who are searching for bases for their practice that transcend the medical model. The case studies that illustrate how concepts of chronic illness can be used to enhance and expand the role of the practitioner will particularly appeal to this group.

Chronic Illness Across the Life Span is divided into three parts. Part I provides the theoretical basis for identifying a philosophy of care for the chronically ill. Chapter One is an overview of the social evolution of the concepts of *disease, illness,* and *sickness.* We show that understanding the distinction between these terms makes the assumptions that determine whether a philosophy of care for the chronically ill is based upon the more restrictive medical model, or upon a broader humanistic model explicit. Chapter Two is a discussion of the concept of *chronicity* and provides a basis for understanding the multidimensionality of chronic illness so critical to the development of comprehensive approaches to health care and research. Chapter Three reviews and critiques several major *developmental* perspectives: infancy to old age. This chapter sets the stage for the life span focus of the text. Chapter Four examines *family theory* and provides the basic framework for understanding the critical role of the family in long-term illness.

Part II contains four chapters, each dealing with a specific concept relevant to chronic illness: Career, Social Support, Identity, and Personal Control. Each chapter provides a theoretical analysis of the concept, a review of research findings relating to chronic illness and two case studies which illustrate the application of the concept to clinical practice. The case studies in each chapter describe the impact of the illness at different developmental stages.

In Part III we turn to a discussion of *ethics, quality of life,* and *research.* Chapter Nine focuses on the issues of quality of life and the ethical dilemmas inherent in the care of persons with chronic illness. We show that the assumptions of society about the importance of life quality and the way society resolves ethical issues of the implementation of technology have a direct impact on the clinical care provided to those with long-term illness. Chapter Ten summarizes the text, identifies important research questions, and discusses methodological issues inherent in the study of chronic illness across the life span.

The pronouns "he" and "him" are used in the generic sense throughout the text. The decision was made by the authors to facilitate a smooth flow of wording. It is not intended to denote a sexist bias.

The authors wish to acknowledge the following individuals for their support, encouragement and tangible assistance throughout the preparation of this manuscript: Paul Jones, Renata von Glehn and Elizabeth Warner.

Margaret Dimond R.N., Ph.D.
Salt Lake City, Utah

Susan Lynn Jones R.N., Ph.D.
Kent, Ohio

CHRONIC ILLNESS ACROSS THE LIFE SPAN

Part 1

Theoretical Perspectives On Chronic Illness

Chapter 1

Disease, Illness, and Sickness

CONCEPTUAL DEFINITIONS OF HEALTH, DISEASE, ILLNESS, AND SICKNESS

The terms "disease," "illness," and "sickness" are considered in everyday language to designate the same phenomena; consequently, they are used interchangeably. However, the experience of disease, illness, and sickness has various levels of meaning from the standpoint of social science. In the first part of the chapter we shall examine these levels of meaning.

Disease
The concept of disease refers to objective phenomena. The human body is composed of cells, tissues, and organs that must function adequately to ensure biological continuity. "Disease" denotes a state of nonhealth, or a state in which the body is suffering from a malfunctioning of one or more parts. The major disciplines concerned with the human being as a biological entity are biology and medicine. Biology is concerned with the organic and intraorganic relationships of living things; medicine is concerned with intervention into these relationships in order to increase the level of functioning and to forestall death. Biology is the science on which medicine is based.

The diagnosis of disease is within the purview of medicine and consists of correlating the observable signs or reported symptoms of a person with theoretical (biological) knowledge about the structure and functioning of the human organism. Exactly what theoretical approach should be used to relate the signs and symptoms within biological parameters, however, is far from settled. Kosa and Robertson (1969) identified four ideas that have been developed in modern medicine since the time of Louis Pasteur. These include the germ theory of disease, epidemiological theory, the cellular concept of disease, and the mechanistic concept. The first of these provided the basis for conquering infectious disease; the second is the cornerstone of public health; and the last provides the structure for surgical interventions. The cellular concept of disease has been instrumental in research and practice in chronic and degenerative diseases.

The diagnosis of disease is a complicated matter because we cannot "see into the body" with the naked eye. In general, two types of indicators give a physician clues regarding diagnosis. First are "signs," which are *observable* indicators. Signs include, for example, a skin rash, an elevated blood pressure, or an open wound. Second are "symptoms," which are *unobservable* to the naked eye. Symptoms include reported feelings such as pain, nausea, or a headache. If signs or symptoms are present, a person is considered not to be healthy or in a state of disease.

Signs and symptoms are studied against the background of biological knowledge about the way the human body is made and functions. Because this body of knowledge has become systematized, we refer to it as a science; and because medical interventions are based on biological science, we can speak of medicine as a science, distinguishing it from the folklore or "art" of treating persons in past centuries.

There is no doubt that the diagnostic process is imprecise; yet we have moved a long way in modern medicine from the folklore treatment of the past. The signs and symptoms of a disease have been found to be patterned, so that their appearance may be related to other events known about the disease. Coe (1978, p. 99) gives the example of what lay people call poison ivy and what medical science describes as an "inflammation . . . accompanied by erythema, swelling, vesicles, bullae and a serous discharge when the lesions rupture" (Ormsby & Montgomery, 1954, p. 205). This rash may appear on the skin a few hours or a few days after the skin has come into contact with *Rhus toxicodendron,* the poison ivy plant. If complications do not occur, the rash will remain for one to three weeks and will be very itchy. The physician who has learned to recognize this peculiar skin rash as an indicator of poison ivy can diagnose the problem, predict some events that will be associated with it, and prescribe a treatment.

Illness

In contrast with the objective concept of disease, "illness" denotes phenomena that are apparent to the ill person only. Illness is an altered state of perception (Coe, 1978; Twaddle & Hessler, 1977). When a patient is describing the symptoms of his disease (that which he is experiencing because of altered biological processes), he is explaining his feelings of illness. Such experiences as pain, nausea, and headache fall into this category.

Most frequently, disease is considered to be the cause of illness, and it is the threat of disease that brings a person to a health care professional for treatment. However, disease can exist in the absence of illness, and illness can occur in the absence of disease. Disease exists without illness when a person does not recognize the symptoms of the disease, as in the case of a disease process with an insidious onset. Sometimes, even when a person feels ill, he does not associate his feelings with a disease. For example, an individual may associate persistent fatigue with working too hard. Occasionally, a disease such as cancer will be diagnosed and the patient told that he has had the disease for some time. Cardiovascular diseases, cancer, and diabetes have particularly insidious onsets.

It is also possible for a person to feel ill or have an illness when there is no organic disease. Psychological or social stress can induce perceived symptoms. People are more apt to express psychological distress through physical language—illness—if they come from cultural groups in which the expression of emotional distress is prohibited (Mechanic, 1978, p. 267). Even though such people may face serious difficulties and social stress, their subculture does not allow the legitimate expression of suffering. Their pleas for emotional support are ignored; consequently, they dwell on bodily complaints. Such people are apt to be insecure, or they may be inactive, which gives them more time to dwell on their bodily complaints. Their physical symptoms may be interpreted as a plea for help in dealing with their emotional distress.

Shontz's (1975, p. 102) two-way diagram shows how the distress process and feelings of being ill may be either correlated or independent of one another. The first dimension of the diagram distinguishes between people who are diseased and those who are not diseased. The second dimension distinguishes between those who consult a physican ("feel ill") and those who do not. An adaptation of Shontz's diagram is presented in Figure 1. The two-dimensional figure results in four combinations, which are represented by cells: people who consult a physician and are objectively diseased (A); people who consult a physician and are not objectively diseased (B); people who do not consult a physician but are objectively diseased (C); and people who do not consult a

	Diseased	Not diseased
Consults physician	A	B
Does not consult physician	C	D

FIGURE 1. Relations between illness and help seeking. *Adapted from Shontz (1975, p.102)*

physician and are not objectively diseased (D). A person's actions are appropriate in two cells (A and D). In cell C, a person may not consult a physician because he does not recognize the symptoms of the disease, as discussed above. In cell B, a person may consult a physician because he feels ill even though no objective disease is involved. The physical complaints may be representative of psychological distress.

Not only can psychological and social distress be expressed in physical symptoms; the distress can *produce* disease processes, as in the case of psychosomatic diseases. A peptic ulcer is a common psychosomatic disease. For years, scientists have argued that peptic ulcers are influenced by psychological and social factors, even though the exact influence is not clear (Mechanic, 1978, p. 206). It appears that in several industrialized countries, for example, there has been an extensive change in the distribution of peptic ulcers. In the late nineteenth century there were more women than men who suffered from this disorder; this pattern has reversed in the twentieth century (MacMahon & Pugh, 1970). There is no evidence that the physiological mechanisms of men and women changed substantially during this period, but extensive social changes occurred in the respective male and female roles. For example, the divorce rate has risen steadily; both spouses usually work, and competition for scarce employment opportunities has increased. These changes may account for the high incidence of psychosomatic diseases in men and women.

Sickness
"Illness" denotes a personal event since it refers to the subjective perception of a symptom and the evaluation of that symptom. Illness becomes sickness when it becomes a social phenomenon, that is, when it becomes visible to others or is communicated to others. Once the illness becomes social, the social interactions of the ill person and those around him are modified. He is treated differently because he is

sick, and he responds to others differently because he is considered sick. Thus, disease is a biological concept; illness is a social-psychological concept, and sickness is a social concept.

Illness may become sickness in one or both of two ways (Coe, 1978). First, one may observe a change in an ill person's actions on a day-to-day basis, or one may observe that a person looks sick. Second, an ill person may communicate to others around him that he is sick. Different social situations provide different opportunities for observation and communication of an illness (Coe, 1978, p. 103). Those who are in some evaluation role in relation to the ill person are most apt to notice a change in behaviors, that is, signs of illness. These people include mothers, employers, and spouses. Those in more intimate and prolonged social contact with the ill person are more likely to be told by the ill person that he is ill. Usually a family member or a close friend is the first to be told of the feelings of ill health.

Most frequently, sickness is considered to be reflective of a disease and the feeling of being ill to be the symptom of the disease. However, sickness can occur independently of disease, illness, or both. A person may *feel ill*, whether or not he has a disease, and communicate this feeling to those around him so that he is labeled sick and treated as if he occupied the sick role; or a person may *not feel ill*, but may be observed to be sick and treated as if he occupied the sick role.

In a study of older married men in Providence, Rhode Island, Twaddle (1969) found that with the first appearance of a symptom the individual usually consulted a spouse. If there was agreement that an important deviation from normal health existed, a physician was usually contacted immediately. If, on the other hand, there was disagreement between the individual and his spouse or the spouse's opinion was not valued, consultation was initiated with other family members, neighbors, or friends. When someone who was regarded as authoritative, either because of a similar prior illness experience or because of special training, suggested seeing a physician, a physician was usually consulted without delay.

Before discussing further the interrelationships of disease, illness, and sickness, we shall present various conceptualizations of "health." It is important to clarify the concept of health because a person may be healthy or nonhealthy on each of the previously discussed levels: disease, illness, or sickness.

Conceptualizations of Health

It is possible to conceptualize health and nonhealth in a variety of ways. One popular and simplistic conceptualization is that used by the medical profession, which Antonovsky (1979. p. 43) terms the "dichotomous model." The distinctions represented by this model are

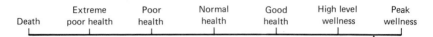

FIGURE 2. Health-illness continuum. *Adapted from Roy (1976, p. 18)*

Not sick   Sick
(healthy)   (not healthy)

FIGURE 3. The hypothesis that health is the opposite (or absence) of illness. *Adapted from Shontz (1975, p. 118)*

made on the basis of disease. If a person becomes hospitalized, he is in a state of disease; if he has not become hospitalized, he is in a state of nondisease, or health. Health is the absence of disease. Medical personnel are well served by this definition since it is the physician's task to cure disease. When he has cured a disease, his job is finished and the patient is healthy (Shontz, 1975, p. 118).

A second unidimensional model of health and nonhealth is that of Roy (1976). In this model (Fig. 2) all possible states are considered to be different states of health; death is the lowest level of health, and peak wellness is the highest.

These two conceptualizations of health and nonhealth have the disadvantage of describing the state of a person only in terms of the objective disease level outlined in the previous section; and, as explained above, a person's feelings and his social behavior may or may not be associated with the objective state of that person as a biological organism.

Shontz (1975) outlines what he considers a two-dimensional view of health (Fig. 3). At the left end of the continuum, a person is in a state of not being sick, or of being healthy; at the right end, a person is in a state of sickness, or of not being healthy. Presenting health on a two-dimensional level allows for a discussion of the independence and dependence of these dimensions. However, a further examination of Shontz's outline shows that he considers both health and sickness to be *feeling states,* which are analogous to the definition of illness outlined above. For example, Shontz states that health and sickness are dependent on one another in that they are inversely correlated. If the feeling of health is strong, the feeling of sickness is weak; conversely, if the feeling of sickness is strong, the feeling of health is weak. This hypothesis is represented in Figure 4. Lines *AB* and *BC*

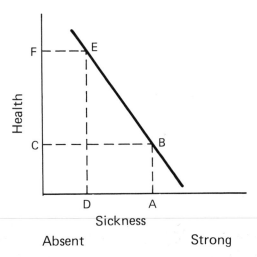

FIGURE 4. The hypothesis that health and sickness are inversely related. *Adapted from Shontz (1975, p. 119)*

show that a strong experience of sickness *(A)* is associated with a weak experience of health *(C)*. Lines *DE* and *EF* show that a strong experience of health *(F)* is associated with a weak experience of sickness *(D)*.

Shontz also believes that sickness and health, as he conceptualizes them, are independent of one another. Sickness and health are personal identities and frequently are either–or phenomena. A person feels either healthy or sick. Only *if* a person is sick does it make sense to ask *how* sick he feels. Similarly, only *if* a person is healthy does it make sense to ask *how* healthy he feels. In sum, Shontz's model conceptualizes health and nonhealth in terms of "feeling states" analogous to the definition of illness outlined above. In this sense, the model is unidimensional. Feeling healthy means feeling nonsick; feeling sick means feeling nonhealthy. One may feel either sick or healthy, or one may feel various degrees of health and sickness at the same time. Placing sickness at one end of a continuum and health at the other allows for a fuller description of the feeling state, in that feeling "sick" is more descriptive than feeling "nonhealthy." However, this does not explain health and nonhealth in terms of a three-dimensional view of disease, illness, and sickness.

As seen in Figure 1 above, Shontz distinguishes between the objective disease level and the "feeling state" associated with this level. Thus, he does present a two-dimensional view representing the disease and illness levels. On the illness level, one might feel either healthy or sick, or various degrees of each.

In the following paragraphs, we present three conceptualizations of health in which the biological (disease), social–pyschological (illness), and social (sickness) dimensions are represented. These are derived from the work of Susser (1974), Belloc, Breslow, and Hochstim (1971), and Twaddle (1974). Susser (1974) outlines an organic, functional, and social level of health. The organic level denotes physiological disorder (disease); the functional is considered to be a subjective state of psychological awareness (illness); and the social level involves a state of social functioning (sickness).

Susser (1974) believes that all three levels involve a continuum of normal to abnormal states based on three criteria. By the pathological criterion, normal and abnormal are dichotomous states of disease and nondisease, respectively. By the statistical criterion, normality is defined from its modal distribution within the population. By the social criterion, normality is defined by the values of the majority within the population. The overall point of Susser's outline of health and nonhealth is to show that the values and social structure of a person's environment are very instrumental in shaping what is considered health and nonhealth.

The World Health Organization (WHO) gives a second three-dimensional definition of health as "a state of complete physical, mental, and social well-being and not merely the absence of disease or infirmity." Breslow and his colleagues (Belloc et al., 1971) attempted to construct a single tool that would measure all three of these dimensions (Breslow, 1972, p. 350). Their final instrument was composed of three scales, which measured an individual's physical, mental, and social well-being.

The third tripartite conceptualization of health is Twaddle's (1974). Overall, Twaddle defines health as an ideal toward which people are oriented but which no one actually attains. The ideal consists of three levels. From a biological standpoint, perfect health is a state in which all the cells of the body are functioning at optimum capacity and in perfect harmony with each other. Psychologically, perfect health is a state in which an individual feels that he is in perfect harmony with his environment and capable of meeting any obligations. Socially, perfect health is a state in which an individual's capacities for task and role performance are optimized. Nonhealth, or sickness, is defined on the biological level by signs and symptoms, on the psychological level by a feeling of depression, and on the social level by a reduced capacity for role performance.

Twaddle's (1974) definition of health and nonhealth is the most comprehensive and useful for our purposes since it allows us to describe health on each of the three dimensions discussed and to demonstrate the dependence and independence of the levels. Even though we have a comprehensive definition, however, the task of defining who is healthy and who is not healthy is difficult. The criteria for health on each level differ from one social group to another, as well as among individuals within one social group. That is, no one attains perfect health, and not everyone is sick. According to Twaddle (1974, p. 30), therefore, there are a range of less than perfect health states that might be defined as normal (Fig. 5).

Because definitions of health and nonhealth differ from one group to another, normal health and ill health overlap and can exist side by side, as seen in the central section of Figure 5. As Mechanic (1978, p. 26) states, "Health and sickness depend upon the cultural context within which human problems are defined." Many diseases are not defined as such by particular groups because they occur so frequently. In some tropical countries, "yaws," an infectious disease with skin eruptions, was once so common that individuals did not regard it as a disease. Dyschromic spirochetosis, a disease of the skin, was so common in a South American tribe that Indians who did not have it were considered abnormal.

Two other examples can be given to show that conceptions of health and nonhealth are culturally bound. Obesity is a desirable condition in some countries; in the United States it is sometimes considered to be a physical and emotional disease. The epileptic is considered to have supernatural powers in some countries; in the United States epilepsy is considered to be a disease that carries a certain degree of stigma.

Definitions of health and nonhealth differ not only among social groups, but also within social groups, depending on one's status within a group. An individual who is required to have a high degree of proficiency is considered sick if there is even a small deviation from perfect health. Conversely, an individual who does not have an occupation (e.g., a retired person) can have a large deviation from normal health and still be classified within the normal limits.

Finally, definitions differ depending on which dimension of health

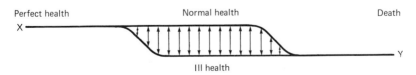

FIGURE 5. Relationships among perfect health, normal health, Ill health, and death. *Reprinted with permission From Twaddle (1974, p. 131)*

(disease, illness, or sickness) one is considering. A person who has leukemia is considered to have a disease; yet he may feel relatively healthy while the disease is in remission. Those who know about the leukemia will consider him sick; those who do not know will consider him healthy. Similarly, an athlete who has a minor sprained ankle may not be objectively diseased. However, because he is an athlete, he may feel intensely ill and be considered sick by those around him.

In the last analysis, evaluations of health and nonhealth depend implicitly on the value orientations and life situations of the people involved. Illness to one person is not necessarily illness to another. Dubos (1965) notes that health and disease are not entities but simply describe a process of adaptation to the changing demands of life and the changing meanings we give to living.

THE INTERRELATIONSHIPS OF HEALTH, DISEASE, ILLNESS, AND SICKNESS

Social Behavior in Response to Symptoms

Thus far, we have discussed disease as a biological concept. Associated with this concept are three health statuses: health, illness, and sickness. Various behaviors are considered to be manifestations of these statuses, and each behavior is linked to the concept of disease. "Health behavior" is defined by Kasl and Cobb (1966, p. 246) as any activity undertaken by a person believing himself to be healthy for the purpose of preventing disease or detecting it in an asymptomatic state. "Illness behavior" is any activity undertaken by a person who feels ill to define the state of health and to discover a suitable remedy. Mechanic and Volkart (1961, p. 52) emphasize that most important in illness behavior is the ill person's evaluation of the symptom. Complaining and seeking consultation from relatives, friends, or professionals are the principal activities of illness behavior. Finally, "sick role behavior" is any activity undertaken by a person who considers himself ill for the purpose of getting well. Receiving treatment from appropriate professionals and assuming a dependent role are the principal activities of the sick role.

To examine the interrelationships of health, illness, and sick role behaviors, we shall discuss them in relation to health and disease. We shall begin by considering health or disease as the casual variable and social behaviors as the dependent variables. The interrelationships are shown schematically in Figure 6.

Health behavior is a response to feelings of being healthy, whereas illness behavior and sick role behavior are responses to feel-

FIGURE 6. Relationships between health/disease and social behaviors.

ings of disease. An extensive amount of research and theorizing has been undertaken to explain social behaviors in response to feelings of health and disease. For example, recognition of a symptom may be necessary to motivate a person to seek help (illness behavior), but it is not in itself sufficient for a person to define himself as ill. A person is more apt to seek help if the symptoms are obvious, such as in the case of appendicitis. In many cases, however, the symptoms are more ambiguous, such as in the early stages of cancer, so that interpretation and evaluation of the symptoms are of prime importance.

From whatever source and in whatever combination, various interpretations of disease symptoms influence the way in which ill people define their situation and seek help from professionals. Thus, any set of symptoms may result in different types of illness behavior or sick role behavior for different people or sometimes for the same person. In an attempt to understand the "help-seeking process," investigators have used cultural and social variables that seem to be associated with different patterns of help seeking in response to symptoms. Much of this research has involved the study of patterns of health service utilization. It is beyond the scope of this text to review this literature. The reader is referred to selected citations that demonstrate findings related to age, sex, marital status, ethnicity, and socioeconomic status (Anderson & Anderson, 1972, pp. 386–406; Bellin & Geiger, 1972; Bice, Eichhorn, & Fox, 1972; Feldman, 1966; Galvin & Fan, 1973; Jones, Halliday & Jones, 1979; Koos, 1954; Monteiro, 1973; Sparer & Okada, 1974; Suchman, 1965a; Susser & Watson, 1971; Wan & Soiffer, 1974; Wilson, 1970; Zborowski, 1952, 1969; Zola, 1966). In the following section we review several models of help-seeking behavior.

Models of Help-Seeking Behavior. Not only have sociocultural variables been linked to variations in social behaviors as a response to illness, but models of help-seeking behavior have been constructed that attempt to explain the variables involved. Five of these models will be reviewed: those of Mechanic (1978), Rosenstock (1974) and Becker (1974), Suchman (1965b), Fabrega (1973), and Parsons (1951).

The starting point for Mechanic's model of help-seeking is the distinction between "self-defined" illness and "other-defined" illness

(Mechanic, 1978). Self-defined illness involves the individual's perception of symptoms, whereas other-defined illness involves attempts by other people to impose a definition of sickness on the individual. In other-defined conditions a person tends to resist the definition imposed by others, so that it may be necessary to bring him into treatment under pressure, as in the case of a psychotic individual.

Mechanic outlines ten dimensions that he considers important in the social process of seeking help. He considers each dimension from the self- and other-defined points of view.

1. *Salience of symptoms:* The more visible are the symptoms and the more frightening, the more likely it is that a person will recognize the symptoms in himself and the more likely it is that another person will intervene in a situation of assumed mental illness.

2. *Perceived seriousness:* A symptom must be perceived to be serious before action is taken by another person or the ill person himself. Several obvious deviations go unnoticed because they are not seen to be dangerous, as in the case of a natural "comic" or "clown" who is acting abnormally. Deviation that is considered dangerous to the person (e.g., potential suicide) or to others (e.g., potential homicide) will elicit action on the part of others.

3. *Extent of disruption of activities:* Perceived seriousness and disruption of activities are highly correlated from the other-defined viewpoint. Symptoms that are disruptive are much more likely to be defined as illness. Mechanic (1978; p. 279) gives the example of a heavy drinker; if he drinks at home and does not make a social nuisance of himself, he is much less likely to be defined as ill than if he drinks in public and is obnoxious. Someone with symptoms that are disruptive in everyday life is also more likely to be defined as ill from the self-defined viewpoint (Apple, 1960). Trivial symptoms will be taken seriously if they interfere with normal activities of life. A sprained ankle is a serious condition to a person who is planning to go to a formal dance.

4. *Frequency and persistence of symptoms:* The more frequently a behavior occurs, the more likely it is that a person will be defined as ill. If a man gets drunk only occasionally, he is less likely to be defined as an alcoholic than is one who gets drunk with regularity. Similarly, the more persistently ill a person *feels*, other factors remaining constant, the more likely he is to seek medical attention.

5. *Tolerance thresholds:* Families differ greatly in their

tolerance of deviant behaviors, and it is difficult to pinpoint exactly the factors that lead to a differential tolerance of symptoms. Tolerance toward deviant behavior is highly correlated with a person's general expectation levels of others. Research shows that middle-class people have higher performance expectations than do working-class people. Parents are more tolerant than spouses of mental patients, and members of the working class are more tolerant than those of the middle class. Single people are more tolerant than those who are married. From the self-defined viewpoint, people differ in the amount of pain they are willing to tolerate. Their tolerance depends on the amount of pain they have become accustomed to and the meaning they attribute to the painful event.

6. *Bases of appraisal:* The information, knowledge, and cultural values of the evaluator influence what behaviors will be seen as illness. In general, higher-class individuals are more knowledgeable about psychiatric symptomatology and therefore seek help for aberrant behavior more readily before a crisis occurs. These people are also more knowledgeable about how to seek help and arrange for psychiatric intervention. In the case of disruptive psychotic behavior, middle-class people are more likely to call a physician, whereas working-class people are more likely to call the police. Knowledge and values also affect the way in which people recognize and act on symptoms within themselves. Koos (1954) found wide variations in people's interpretations of symptoms such as lumps in the breast or abdomen and fainting spells. Similarly, there were wide variations in the extent to which people acted on the symptoms.

7. *Needs for denial:* Family members need to deny aberrant behavior in other family members since these disorders are stigmatized, disruptive, and carry implicit guilt. From the self-defined viewpoint, anxiety and fear also influence a person not to recognize symptoms within himself. It appears that low levels of anxiety or fear lead to early seeking of care, whereas high levels lead to delayed seeking of care.

8. *Competing needs:* Behavior takes place within a context in which motives compete with one another. Health motives are not always the most central, particularly when a person is in a state of relatively good health. One of Koos's respondents stated: "I wish I really knew what you mean about being sick. Sometimes I've felt so bad I could curl up and die, but had to go on because the kids had to be taken care of, and

besides, we didn't have the money to spend for the doctor—
how could I be sick?" (Koos, 1954, p. 30).

9. *Alternative interpretations:* Normalization of behavior
means that people interpret or explain aberrant behavior
within acceptable "normal" frames of reference. If the
challenge of the aberrant behavior is not sufficiently strong,
the individual will give the behavior an alternative explanation rather than recognize it as a psychiatric symptom.
Again, a symptom that is seen to be dangerous, such as an
attempt to hurt oneself or someone else, is less likely to be
given an alternative explanation.

10. *Accessibility of treament:* The greater are the barriers to a
health care facility, the more likely it is that another source
of care will be sought. Barriers include economic costs, time,
effort, and embarrassment. Stigma and humiliation are associated with certain psychiatric conditions so that seeking of
help may be delayed.

Mechanic outlines the variables of each dimension separately;
however, he emphasizes that, in real situations, these variables interact with one another. Some variables are highly correlated; others
are relatively independent. He gives the following example to show
how the ten dimensions might interact (Mechanic, 1978, p. 288):

> ... consider the person who experiences an occasional
> stomach pain. He may notice it but attribute it to something he
> ate or to missing a meal, or he may just pay no attention to it. If
> the pain persists or occurs more frequently, he is more likely to
> become attentive to it. The more frequently the pain bothers him,
> the more likely it will be perceived as serious and will disrupt his
> plans and activities. He becomes less tolerant of the symptom now
> that it bothers him more often, and finds that such alternative
> definitions as having eaten a meal that does not agree with him
> are no longer tenable as an interpretation of the symptom. He may
> thus see the symptom as a medical one and, if it is sufficiently
> severe, seek medical attention.

A second social–psychological model that was developed to explain the variables involved in the decision to seek help is the health
belief model of Rosenstock (1974) and Becker (1974). When these
authors originally formulated the model in the 1950s, they were concerned with explaining only health behavior, primarily because the
Public Health Service wanted them to determine why the public
responded so poorly to programs of preventive medicine such as tuberculosis screening and immunizations. Subsequently, the model was ex-

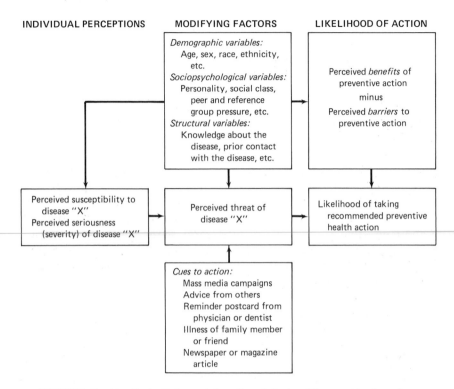

INDIVIDUAL PERCEPTIONS   MODIFYING FACTORS   LIKELIHOOD OF ACTION

FIGURE 7. Health belief model. *Reprinted with permission from Rosenstock (1974, p. 334)*

panded to include sociocultural and environmental variables in predicting illness behavior as well as health behavior (Rosenstock, 1974).

Figure 7 outlines the elements of the health belief model. The dependent variable is the probability that an individual will take appropriate action either to prevent illness or to recover health. It is influenced by individual perceptions, which in turn are influenced by a host of modifying factors. Thus, in order for an individual to take action to avoid disease he has to believe (a) that he is personally susceptible to it ("I can be affected") or (b) that it is severe ("It could disrupt some component of my life"). These beliefs are influenced by such modifying factors as an individual's age, sex, race, and social class. They are also modified by the social and physical environment, which includes mass media campaigns, advice from others, the physician's actions, and illness in a friend or family member. In reaching a state of readiness to act, an individual weighs the potential benefits against the social and economic costs of alternative courses of action. To the degree that benefits are considered superior to costs, the

probability of appropriate health, illness, or sick role behavior increases.

Whereas Mechanic and Rosenstock outline variables involved in
the decision to seek help, Suchman (1965b) has attempted to construct
a model that encompasses health behavior, illness behavior, and sick
role behavior. His model is organized around the chronological stages
of the help-seeking process. Suchman (1965b) analyzes behavior in
terms of social patterns that accompany the decision to find and
undergo medical care. He distinguishes four principal elements in
these patterns: (a) the content, (b) the sequence, (c) the spacing, and (d)
the variability of behavior during different phases of medical care. By
combining several types of content and arrangement of content, he has
devised several concepts that he considers useful, such as "shopping"
(trying multiple sources of medical care), "fragmentation of care"
(being treated by a variety of medical practitioners at a single source
of medical care), and "procrastination" (delay in seeking care following
the recognition of symptoms).

To study social patterns, Suchman (1965b) divides the sequence of
help-seeking events into five stages, which represent major transition
points for making decisions in the process of seeking medical care:

1. *Symptom experience stage:* This is the decision that something is wrong. Suchman distinguishes three analytical
   aspects of the symptom experience: (a) the physical experience
   by which some discomfort or change of appearance is actually
   felt; (b) the cognitive interpretation of the felt experience and
   evaluation of its meaning; and (c) the emotional response of
   fear or anxiety based on the evaluation. Generally speaking,
   the responses range from the denial of illness, or "flight into
   health," to assumption of the sick role; intermediate between
   the two extremes is delay in seeking and securing treatment.
   A person may also attempt self-treatment for the relief of
   symptoms.
2. *Assumption of the sick role:* This is the decision that one is
   sick and needs professional care. Here, a potential patient
   begins to seek alleviation of symptoms, information and
   advice, and temporary acceptance of his condition by his
   family and friends. The illness now becomes a social
   phenomenon because the sick person seeks agreement from
   significant others that he is sick and should be excused from
   regular duties. Contacts are often made by the sick person,
   initially with others with whom he has close ties, usually a
   spouse, family, or good friend. These individuals comprise the
   "lay referral system," and the action taken by the sick person

depends greatly on how the lay consultants react to the symptoms and the extent to which they accept any interference with the sick person's social functioning. The range of decisions here may be broad. At one extreme, the lay consultants may reject the person's claim to the sick role, and the person must resume normal obligations or experience more symptoms. At the other extreme, the individual's family may concede that he is sick, and the request for the sick role is provisionally granted. The provisional aspect of validation acknowledges the strong belief in our society that only a physician can really tell whether a person is sick and decide what should be done about it.

3. *Medical care contact stage:* This is the decision to leave the lay referral care system and enter the professional care system. Here, the individual seeks authoritative validation for his claim to the sick role as well as treatment for the disease. This stage may be prolonged if the sick individual refuses to accept the initial diagnosis or course of treatment recommended by the professional. He may then begin a lay search for another source of care. He may visit other physicians until the desired diagnosis is obtained, a phenomenon known as "shopping."

4. *Dependent-patient role:* This is the decision to transfer control to the physician and to accept the prescribed treatment. At this stage, the sick person becomes a patient. Most frequently, the patient role is viewed with ambivalence. Although a person may wish to avoid it, he may see it as the only way of eventually returning to a healthy role. It is here that the patient must deal with the possible need for childlike dependence on the physician. Other variables, such as the meaning of the illness, the prognosis for recovery, and reactions of the family, complicate the situation.

5. *Recovery and rehabilitation:* This is the decision to relinquish the patient role. The sick role stops when the patient is dismissed or withdraws from active medical care and is expected either to resume his old role as a healthy individual or to adopt a new role as a chronic invalid or long-term rehabilitee.

Several investigators modified Suchman's original model (Geersten, Klauber, Rindflesh, Kane, & Gray, 1975) in order to provide alternative explanations of the motives involved in the help-seeking process. One of the most sophisticated attempts to extend Suchman's model was that of Fabrega (1973). Whereas Suchman described and temporarily ordered the possible events and processes associated with illness, Fabrega (1973) tried to present these events in a theoretically abstract, systematic, and logically consistent manner. He attempted to model "logical" time or "decision-making" time rather than chronological events. Fabrega conceptualized stages that were bound by key events (information-processing events); these were ordered in a logical plan or program and could be independent of the chronological time elapsed. Fabrega also expanded the number of stages from five to nine, which he believed more precisely explained the behavior. In sum, Fabrega combined the "analytical" approach of Mechanic and Rosenstock with the "stage" approach of Suchman to formulate the analytical stages involved in the help-seeking process. He then attempted to quantify the probability that certain actions would be taken over other actions in this process (Fabrega, 1974, pp.171–175).

1. *Illness recognition and labeling:* Like Suchman's, Fabrega's model begins with a stage in which the illness problem is labeled. Every person has a finite set of illness categories called his taxonomy of illness. A person judges himself vulnerable to each illness in this taxonomy. When self-evaluations lead to recognition of certain deviations that approximate one of the illness categories, a person judges himself to be in a particular illness state.
2. *Illness disvalues:* The seriousness of the problem is evaluated on the basis of past and current information.
3. *Treatment plans:* Potentially available treatment plans are considered.
4. *Assessment of treatment plans:* The effectiveness of each potential treatment is assessed.
5. *Treatment benefits:* The potential benefits of each treatment plan are considered.
6. *Treatment costs:* The potential costs of each treatment plan are considered.
7. *Net benefits or utility:* The cost of each treatment plan is subtracted from the potential benefits to yield residual benefit or residual cost quantified.
8. *Selection of treatment plan:* On the basis of the results of stage 7, a treatment plan is selected.
9. *Setup for recycling:* The output of stage 8 constitutes new information that yields an updated personal history so that stage 1 may be entered again at any time.

Because the model is a "decision-making" model based on logical time, the chronological length of time at each stage may vary considerably. Moreover, a person's progression from one stage to another is not necessarily linear; rather, there is an ebb and flow between stages. The variables outlined by Mechanic and Rosenstock would determine how long a person remained in each of the stages of Fabrega's model. For example, if the symptoms were obvious, persistent, or dangerous to the individual, the first stage (identification) might be relatively short. However, if the symptoms were ambiguous, this stage might be more protracted.

The models of health, illness, and sick role behavior presented thus far are social–psychological in that they analyze the social and individual psychological variables that influence a person's evaluation of illness symptoms and the decision to seek help. Parsons (1951) takes a more strictly sociological approach by considering the sick role to be a state of social deviance. This deviance is distinguished from criminal behavior in that it is assumed that a criminal does not *want* to conform to social norms whereas a sick person is not *able* to conform to the norms. Parsons assumes that health is a state of normality; in this state a person has normal (and adequate) physiological and mental capacities so that he can participate in social activities and fulfill social obligations. In essence, he is able to conform to the social norms of society. The sick role is a deviant state in which a person has abnormal (and inadequate) physiological and mental capacities and is thus unable to participate fully in social activities and to fulfill social obligations. He is not able to conform to the social norms of society.

From this sociological perspective, deviance is a stable and objective state, not within an individual, but within a dynamic social system. The deviance (illness) is considered dysfunctional because it threatens to interfere with the stability of the social system. The medical profession functions to offset the dysfunctional aspects of illness by curing and preventing disease. Hence, medical practice is a social mechanism that seeks to control the illness of its deviant sick by returning them to a "normal" functioning state. Parsons (1951) outlines two rights and two obligations of the sick role:

1. The sick person is exempt from "normal" social roles. The extent of his exemption depends on the severity and nature of the illness. The exemption is legitimized by the physician's diagnosis and treatment since the physician is considered to be the authority. Legitimation by a physician guards against malingering by the sick person.
2. The sick person is not responsible for his condition. The illness is beyond his control and thus he is not expected to recover without professional help.
3. The sick person should try to get well, and he must view the

sick status as undesirable. Exemption from normal obligations is temporary and conditional upon the desire to regain
normal health.

4. The sick person should seek technically competent help and
   cooperate with the medical regimen. This second obligation
   explicitly acknowledges the complex nature of modern
   medicine and the need for expert advice when a person oc-
   cupies the sick role.

The two rights of the sick role occupant are designed to relieve him
of normal duties that he could perform only with great effort, if at all.
The exemption from normal social obligations is temporary, however,
and has broad implications for people with chronic illnesses (see Chapter 2 for a critique of Parsons's sick role in chronic illness). The obligations of the sick role occupant reduce the likelihood that patients
will enjoy their state of being ill or receive "secondary gains" from
being sick (Parsons, 1951).

Social Construction of Illness

In the previous section we discussed social behavior (health, illness,
and sick role behavior) as a response to physiological symptoms of
disease. The starting point for this analysis was the physiological
state of health or disease. A second approach to the interrelationship
of health, disease, illness, and sickness is to use social behavior as the
starting point for analysis. The problem then is not the etiology of
some social state or behavior so much as the etiology of the meaning of
that state or social behavior (Freidson, 1970, p. 215). For example, how
does social behavior come to be considered deviant or sick? How does
social behavior come to be considered one kind of deviance rather than
another? Is there a pattern in the way in which social behavior comes
to be imputed as sick? How does the imputation of a particular kind of
deviant social behavior affect the interaction between interested
parties? Freidson (1970, p. 215) terms such an approach the "social
construction of illness." Like Parsons, Freidson uses a deviance framework for analysis. However, unlike Parsons, he argues that medicine
not only can legitimize a sick state, but can also *create* the social
possibilities for acting sick. In this sense, medicine's monopoly includes the right to create illness as an official social role. In our
analysis, represented schematically in Figure 8, we shall examine the
work of two major writers: Freidson (1970) and Scheff (1966, 1967,
1975).

Models of the social construction of illness. Following the theoretical vein of Lemert (1951), Freidson (1970, p. 217) distinguishes

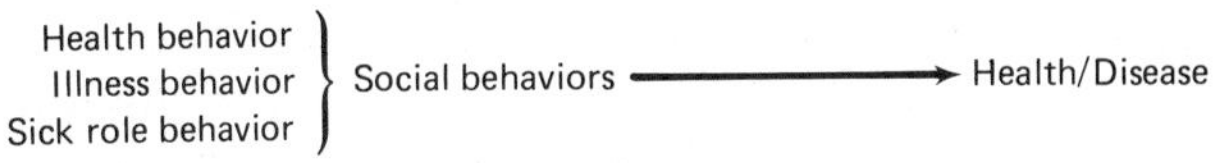

FIGURE 8. Relationships between social behaviors and health/disease.

between two forms of deviance: primary and secondary. Primary deviance includes a person's idiosyncracies that distinguish him from others but that do not interfere with the way in which he performs his socially acceptable "normal" role. Freidson gives the example of a businessman who may perform his role in an obnoxious manner but who, even though unpopular (and deviant), is still a businessman. Secondary deviance, on the other hand, itself becomes a social role and part of the social structure. In this analysis, significant deviance is of the second type. It becomes socially organized, as deviance rather than as mere idiosyncrasy, into a specifically deviant role that helps one to define oneself or to attack or adapt to the problems posed by the reactions of others to one's primary deviance. In adopting such a role, individuals must reorganize their view of themselves, others, and their relation to them. Often they must find a specific subculture and social organization that can facilitate their adaptation.

Basic to the distinction between primary and secondary deviance is that the latter is a function of others' responses to oneself. One's characteristics are of less importance in producing and forming deviance than are the social responses to them and their labeling. Thus, social control must be viewed as a cause rather than an effect of the magnitude and variable forms of primary deviation (Lemert, 1964, p. 82). Following this logic, secondary deviance can be produced when an individual is not himself motivated to adopt the deviance and when there is no objective (disease) or real primary deviation in the first place. The important point is the imputation of deviance to one individual by significant others, including himself, followed by the creation of a deviant role for the individual. Whether he is actually deviant is not relevant. The point is that, through the system of social control, a person is labeled a deviant. Social deviance is then imputed, but true deviance does not necessarily exist (Freidson, 1970, p. 222).

Crucial to the social construction of illness is the distinction between the biological concept of disease and the social conception of illness (Freidson, 1970, p. 223):

> While illness as a biophysical state exists independently of human knowledge and evaluation, illness as a social state is created and shaped by human knowledge and evaluation.

If a veterinarian diagnoses a cow's condition, he does not change the behavior of the cow because the cow merely experiences illness as a biophysical state. However, a medical doctor changes a person's behavior by the mere act of diagnosing. That is, a social state is added to a biophysical state when the meaning of illness is assigned to the disease. It is in this sense that the physician creates illness, for the physical state is defined as ill whether disease processes are present or are not present. As a kind of social deviance, the etiology of illness (or help-seeking behavior) is not biological but social, stemming from current social conceptions of disease, limited by the few biological facts that are universally recognized, and ordered by organizations and occupations devoted to defining, uncovering, and managing illness. As social deviance, illness may be expected to vary in its content and organization quite independently of biological (disease) processes.

Freidson (1970, p. 237) outlines a classification of illness that is based on Parson's four elements of the sick role. The notion of legitimacy provides the basis for the classification. Legitimacy is important in Parsons's analysis since it distinguishes the criminal deviant from the sick deviant. Furthermore, it is the conditional nature of legitimacy that motivates the sick to seek care and/or return to a state of normality. If the imputed illness is considered to be incurable or chronic, however, its legitimacy can no longer be conditional. When stigmatized illness is imputed, it always is illegitimate since it is not an acceptable form of illness. Freidson (1970, p. 238) outlines three different kinds of legitimacy: (a) conditional, whereby deviants are temporarily exempted from normal obligations and gain some extra privileges on the condition that they seek the help necessary to rid themselves of the deviance; (b) unconditional, whereby deviants are exempted permanently from normal obligations and obtain additional privileges because their deviance is considered hopeless; and (c) illegitimacy, whereby deviants are exempted from some normal obligations by virtue of the deviance for which they are not held technically responsible but gain few if any privileges and take on some handicapping new obligations.

The classification scheme proposed by Freidson and several examples are shown in Table 1. Freidson cautions that these labels are assigned from the viewpoint of middle-class America and could vary from one culture to another and from one social group to another within a culture or from time to time within a given culture.

An important distinction is made in this table between minor and serious deviations. Differences in intensity are crucial since they take into account the empirical differences in strength of response to an attribute. They also underscore the analytical distinction between deviance that is allowed to remain an individual attribute (primary

TABLE 1. TYPES OF DEVIANCE FOR WHICH THE INDIVIDUAL IS NOT HELD RESPONSIBLE, BY IMPUTED LEGITIMACY AND SERIOUSNESS.

Imputed Seriousness	Illegitimate (Stigmatized)	Conditionally Legitimate	Unconditionally Legitimate
Minor deviation	Cell 1: stammer Partial suspension of some ordinary obligations; few or no new privileges; adoption of a few new obligations	Cell 2: a cold Temporary suspension of few ordinary obligations; temporary enhancement of ordinary privileges; obligation to get well	Cell 3: pockmarks No special change in obligations or privileges
Serious deviation	Cell 4: epilepsy Suspension of some ordinary obligations; adoption of new obligations; few or no new privileges	Cell 5: pneumonia Temporary release from ordinary obligations; addition to ordinary privileges; obligation to cooperate and seek help in treatment	Cell 6: cancer Permanent suspension of many ordinary obligations; marked addition to privileges

Reprinted with permission from Freidson (1970, p. 239).

deviance) and that which becomes organized into a special role (secondary deviance) so that it dominates all other roles.

In cell 1, stigma spoils a person's ordinary identity but does not replace this identity. In cells 2 and 3, the illness or impairment qualifies as deviant but does not replace ordinary roles since the deviance is minor. Only in cell 5 do we find the sick role outlined by Parsons. In cell 4 are stigmatized roles, and in cell 6 are chronic sick or dying roles occupied by individuals for whom nothing more can be done by experts.

Each of the above-described analytical varieties of deviance implies quite different consequences for the individual and his social system. In each case the deviant is managed differently by those in social control, and in each case he responds differently.

Scheff's (1966, 1967, 1975) view of illness as a social construction created by individuals in society is similar to Freidson's. However, Scheff applies his labeling theory of illness specifically to mental illness. His argument rests on the notion of "residual rules," which are basic to middle-class Western societies. Mental illness is a violation of these rules and is termed "residual rule breaking." Residual rule breaking is a minor deviation that each of us learns in childhood. Most of this deviant behavior goes unnoticed and does not elicit punishment. However, residual rule breaking is sometimes labeled mental illness, depending on societal reaction to it. Scheff outlines nine hypotheses that comprise the model for his labeling process of mental illness (Scheff, 1975, pp. 9–10):

1. Residual rule breaking arises from fundamentally diverse sources (that is, organic, psychological, stressful, volitional acts of innovation or defiance).
2. Relative to the rate of treatment of mental illness, the rate of unrecorded residual rule breaking is extremely high.
3. Most residual rule breaking is denied and is of transitory significance.
4. Stereotyped imagery of mental disorder is learned in early childhood.
5. The stereotypes of insanity are continually reaffirmed, inadvertently, in ordinary social interactions.
6. Labeled deviants may be rewarded for playing the stereotyped deviant role.
7. Labeled deviants are punished when they attempt to return to conventional roles.
8. In the crisis occurring when a residual rule breaker is publicly labeled, the deviant is highly suggestible and may accept the label.
9. Among residual rule breakers, labeling is the most important cause of careers of residual deviance.

According to Scheff, concepts about mental illness are not scientifically precise, nor are they value free. Because mental illness is a violation of a basic cultural norm, it is stigmatized. If the label of mental illness is denied or normalized by the rule breaker, the label will be temporary. However, the deviant may be rewarded for playing the deviant role (hypothesis 6) even though he is stigmatized and isolated; and when he tries to return to a normal role, he is punished (hypothesis 7) through the stigma associated with past situations. For example, he will have difficulty finding employment because of his past record of "acting out," or he will have difficulties in his personal affairs because he has occupied the role of mental illness. It is not uncommon now for mental patients to deny that they are sick or to claim that they have improved sufficiently to return to their normal life situation; however, their protests are simply taken as further evidence that they are not really well. Their previous deviant status creates suspicions in the eyes of others, creating a vicious circle that they cannot escape.

SUMMARY AND DISCUSSION

In the first section of this chapter we distinguished between disease (a biological concept), illness (a social-psychological concept), and sickness (a social concept). We then presented several distinctions along a health continuum to show that differences in health and non-health may be apparent on a biological, social-psychological, or social level. Distinctions on each level may be highly correlated or may be relatively independent.

In the second section we discussed behaviors associated with various health statuses in an effort to examine the interrelationship of health, disease, illness, and sickness. We first considered social behaviors associated with the health/disease status as a response to the biological health/disease status. We then considered the health/disease status as a result of the various social behaviors. This analysis involved a review of seven models describing the process and behaviors by which people from a healthy to nonhealthy status on a biological, social-psychological, and social level. A comparison of the first five models is presented in Table 2.

The five models differ in three respects. First, they differ as to whether they are analytical or whether they outline stages of behavior that influence a person's response to symptoms. The analytical variables may be social (socioeconomic status or culture), they may be associated with the disease process itself (visibility of symptoms), or they may define the individual (sex, age, race). Second, the models vary in the extent to which they focus on one or more of the three concepts: health, illness, and sickness. Mechanic's main focus is illness be-

TABLE 2.   A COMPARISON OF MODELS OF
HEALTH/DISEASE————————➤SOCIAL BEHAVIORS

Model	Format	Concepts	Approach
Mechanic	Analytical variables	Illness behavior	Social-psychological
Rosenstock/ Becker	Analytical variables	Health behavior	Social-psychological
Suchman	Chronological stages	Health, illness, sick role	Social-psychological
Fabrega	Analytical stages	Health, illness, sick role	Social-psychological
Parsons	Analytical	Health, illness, sickness	Sociological

TABLE 3.   A COMPARISON OF MODELS OF
SOCIAL BEHAVIORS —————▸HEALTH/DISEASE

Model	Format	Concepts	Approach
Friedson	Analytical Variables	Health, illness, sick role	Sociological
Scheff	Analytical Variables	Health, illness, sick role	Sociological

havior, whereas that of Rosenstock and Becker is health behavior. Parsons focuses primarily on sickness. Suchman and Fabrega incorporate all three concepts into their stage analysis of help-seeking. Finally, the models differ in their level of analysis of help-seeking behavior. Parsons is unique in that his approach is strictly sociological, whereas the others take a social–psychological approach.

Despite their differences, these models are similar in that the starting point for analysis in each is the health/disease status. The questions for analysis then become: Why does one person follow preventive health behavior, whereas another person does not? What variables are involved in this response (Mechanic, Suchman, Fabrega)? What are the social consequences of the deviant state of sick role and the legitimation of this sick role by the medical profession (Parsons)?

The two models that consider health/disease to be a result of social behaviors are compared in Table 3. In both of these models analytical variables are involved in the labeling process; both incorporate health, illness, and sickness concepts; and both use a sociological perspective. The two models differ in that Freidson uses the concepts of seriousness and legitimacy as determinants of the labeling process, whereas Scheff outlines nine hypotheses in which residual rule breaking is punished and labeled as mental illness.

REFERENCES

Anderson, O. W., & Anderson, R. M. Patterns of use of health services. In H. Freeman, S. Levine, & L., Reeder (eds.), *Handbook of medical sociology*. Englewood Cliffs, N.J.: Prentice-Hall, 1972.

Antonovsky, A. *Health, Stress, and Coping*. San Francisco: Jossey–Bass Publishers, 1979.

Apple, D. How laymen define illnesses. *Journal of Health and Human Behavior*, 1960, 1, 291–295.

Becker, M. H. The health belief model and personal health behavior. *Health Education Monographs*, 1974, 2, 326–327.

Bellin, S. S. & Geiger, J. H. The impact of neighborhood health center on a patient's behavior and attitudes relating to health care: A study of low income housing. *Medical Care,* 1972, **10**, 224–239.

Belloc, N. B., Breslow, L., & Hochstim, J. R. Measurement of physical health in a general population survey. *American Journal of Epidemiology,* 1971, **93**, 328–336.

Bice, T. W., Eichhorn, R. L., & Fox, P. D. Socioeconomic status and use of physician services: A reconsideration. *Medical Care,* 1972, **10**, 261–171.

Breslow, L. A quantitative approach to the WHO definition of health: Physical, mental, and social well-being. *International Journal of Epidemiology,* 1972, **1**, 347–355.

Coe, R. M. *Sociology of medicine.* New York: McGraw-Hill, 1978.

Dubos, R. *Man adapting.* New Haven, Conn.: Yale University Press, 1965.

Fabrega, H. Toward a model of illness behavior. *Medical Care,* 1973, **6**, 470–484.

Fabrega, H. *Disease and social behavior: An interdisciplinary perspective.* Cambridge, Mass.: MIT Press, 1974.

Feldman, J. *The dissemination of health information.* Chicago: Aldine, 1966.

Freidson, E. *Profession of medicine: A study of the sociology of applied knowledge.* New York: Dodd, Mead, 1970.

Galvin, M., & Fan, M. The utilization of physician's services in Los Angeles County. *Journal of Health and Social Behavior.* 1973, **16**, 75–94.

Geersten, R., Klauber, M., Rindflesh, M., Kane, R., & Gray, R. A reexamination of Suchman's views on social factors in health care utilization. *Journal of Health and Social Behavior,* 1975, **16**, 226–237.

Jones, P., Halliday, H. L., & Jones, S. L. Prediction of neonatal death or need for interhospital transfer by prenatal risk characteristics of mother. *Medical Care,* 1979, **17**, 796–806.

Kasl, S., & Cobb, S. "Health behavior, illness behavior, and sick role behavior." *Archives of Environmental Health,* 1966, **12**, 246–266; 531–541.

Koos, E. *The health of regionville.* New York, Columbia University Press, 1954.

Kosa, J., & Robertson, L. The social aspects of health and illness. In J. Kosa, A. Antonovsky, & I. Zola (Eds.), *Poverty and health.* Cambridge, Mass.: Harvard University Press, 1969.

Lemert, E. *Social pathology.* New York: McGraw-Hill, 1951.

Lemert, E. Social structure, social control and deviation. In Marshall Clinard (Ed.), *Anomie and deviant behavior.* New York: Free Press, 1964.

MacMahon, B. & Pugh, T. *Epidemiology: Principles and Methods.* Boston: Little, Brown & Co., 1970.

Mechanic, D. *Medical sociology* (2nd ed.). New York: Free Press, 1978.

Mechanic, D. & Volkart, E. Stress, illness behavior, and the sick role. *American Sociological Review,* 1961, **26,** 51–58.

Monteiro, L. Expense is no object. . .: Income and physician visits reconsidered. *Journal of Health and Social Behavior,* 1973, **14,** 99–115.

Ormsby, O. S., & Montgomery, H. *Diseases of the skin* (8th ed.). Philadelphia: Lea & Febinger, 1954.

Parsons T. *The social system.* New York: Free Press, 1951.

Rosenstock, I. M. Historical origins of the health belief model. *Health Education Monographs,* 1974, **2,** 328–335.

Roy, Sister Callista. *Introduction to nursing: An adaptation model.* Englewood Cliffs, N. J.: Prentice-Hall, 1976.

Scheff, T. *Being mentally ill: A sociological theory.* Chicago: Aldine, 1966.

Scheff, T. *Mental illness and social processes.* New York: Harper, 1967.

Scheff, T.(Ed.) *Labeling madness.* Englewood Cliffs, N.J.: Prentice-Hall, 1975.

Shontz, F. C. *The psychological aspects of physical illness and disability.* New York: Macmillan, 1975.

Sparer, G., & Okada, L. M. Chronic conditions and physician use patterns in ten urban poverty areas. *Medical Care,* 1974, **12,** 549–560.

Suchman, E. A. Social patterns of illness and medical care. *Journal of Health and Human Behavior,* 1965, **6,** 2–16. (a)

Suchman, E. A. Stages of illness and medical care. *Journal of Health and Human Behavior,* 1965, **6,** 114–128. (b)

Susser, M. Ethical components in the definition of health. *International Journal of Health Services,* 1974, **4,** 539–548.

Susser, M. W., & Watson, W. *Sociology in medicine* (2nd ed.). New York: Oxford University Press, 1971.

Twaddle, A. Health decisions and sick role variations. *Journal of Health and Social Behavior,* 1969, **10,** 105.

Twaddle, A. & Hessler, R. The concept of health status. *Social Science and Medicine,* 1974, **8,** 29–38.

Twaddle, A. & Hessler, R. *A sociology of health.* St. Louis: Mosby, 1977.

Volkart, E. H. Man, disease, and the social environment. *Stanford Medical Bulletin,* 1960, **18,** 29–33.

Wan, T., & Soifer, S. Determinants of physician utilization: A casual analysis. *Journal of Health and Social Behavior,* 1974, **15,** 100–108.

Wilson, R. N. *The sociology of health.* New York: Random House, 1970.

Wolff, H. G. *Stress and disease.* Springfield, Ill.: Thomas, 1953.

Zborowski, M. Cultural components in response to pain. *Journal of Social Issues,* 1952, **8,** 16–30.

Zborowski, M. *People in pain.* San Francisco: Jossey–Bass, 1969.

Zola, I. Culture and symptoms. *American Sociological Review,* 1966, **31,** 615.

Chapter 2

Chronic Illness

HISTORICAL AND DEFINITIONAL PERSPECTIVES ON CHRONIC ILLNESS

The study of chronic illness in the twentieth century is more meaningful if we examine the societal and personal responses to long-term illness in the past. It is also important to understand the terminology used to describe chronic illness, for differences in terms are often indicative of differences in beliefs about the causes and prognosis of illness as well as about the individuals who have chronic illnesses. The first part of this chapter provides a historical perspective of chronic illness as well as a delineation and examination of the terminology used to describe chronic illness.

Historical Perspective

Throughout the recorded history of all cultures and societies, the sick and disabled have received special attention. In some instances this has meant social and/or physical ostracism, whereas in other instances disability has been attributed to special favor by a deity. Safilios-Rothschild (1970) describes a number of factors that influence societal response to the sick and disabled. When considered within selected historical and cultural parameters, these factors illustrate the types of prejudice, both positive and negative, that have surrounded the chronically ill.

One of the most well-known factors is a society's beliefs about the origin of disability. In ancient Hebrew culture a disabled individual was believed to be responsible for his illness because of some sin that he or someone in his family had committed, and in early Greek times diminished physical capacity was attributed to social inferiority. In both instances the individual was ostracized and treated as an outcast. With the advent of Christianity the concepts of kindness and care of the sick elicited different societal responses to the ill. Religious men and women dedicated their lives to the care and comfort of the ill, and a substantial number of people believe that sickness and suffering were indicative of God's special favor.

Although charitable concern was more desirable than social ostracism, inherent in the Christian perspective was a kind of institutionalized custodial care, a dimension not wholly positive in its effect on recipients. The so-called Age of Science gave rise to the notion that illness is caused by natural conditions beyond the control or influence of the afflicted person and that it is therefore inappropriate to place blame on the afflicted individual. Current societal response to disabled persons is an amalgamation of the Hebrew, Greek, Christian, and scientific perspectives (Safilios-Rothschild, 1970).

A second factor influencing response to disability is the extent of a country's socioeconomic development and its rate of unemployment (Safilios-Rothschild, 1970, p. 4). In agrarian societies able bodies are essential; the sick and disabled have no function in economic survival and are most likely to be perceived negatively. In more diversified and technologically oriented societies, less physically and mentally competent individuals are able to contribute to economic welfare. However, in modern Western societies the functionalistic work ethic is firmly embedded, and there is in fact prejudicial treatment of the less competent. It is interesting that the rehabilitation industry is a multimillion-dollar enterprise sustained by the goal of making all participants in the social and economic system productive.

The third factor, which is closely associated with socioeconomic development, is a society's beliefs about the origins of poverty and the role of government in alleviating it (Safilios-Rothschild, 1970, p. 5). If poverty is considered to be caused by laziness, immorality, or lack of motivation, disabled people (usually poor) either have been left to shift for themselves or have been rounded up and placed in institutions funded by the government for the purpose of reform and training. The practice of institutionalizing the poor was prevalent in the seventeenth and eighteenth centuries.

The fourth factor is stigma. The degree of stigma depends on the part of the body affected, on whether the problem is physical or emotional, visible or invisible, curable, or incurable, and on the extent to which the disabled person embarrasses or otherwise creates discomfort in others.

Lobbying efforts and media coverage of the plight of certain disabling conditions constitute a fifth factor influencing societal response. Early action by veteran groups after World War I resulted in a large-scale effort, overseen by the Veterans Administration, to rehabilitate and integrate disabled veterans into society. As a result of these efforts, war veterans have been successful in obtaining special privileges and opportunities. However, the extent to which a nation supports specialized programs depends on the merits of the situation giving rise to increased disability. The Vietnam War is a case in point. Returning veterans of this unpopular war were treated with considerably less respect and gratitude than those returning from more popular wars. Whether this has resulted in diminished benefits is debatable, but disabled Vietnam veterans have no doubt experienced the stigma of participating in such a controversial war.

Efforts to make the public aware of disabilities began with the March of Dimes (for poliomyelitis) and have since come to include other conditions, such as multiple sclerosis, cystic fibrosis, cerebral palsy, blindness, retinitis pigmentosis, and deafness. Television and satellite telecommunication have greatly enhanced these efforts. Most recently, legislation has been passed to eliminate architectural barriers to the disabled in public buildings. Although money-raising telethons and legislative activities on behalf of the disabled and chronically ill are laudable, they do not necessarily affect the way in which these individuals are received in social settings. This is likely a function of attitudes, which may in part be a reflection of definitions and labels.

Clarification of Terminology

Many terms have been used to refer to illness that is of long-term duration, is not curable, and/or has some residual features that impose limitations on an individual's functional capabilities. It is important to define and clarify the most common of these and to consider the implications of the definitions. The way in which a condition is defined has an impact on the way in which an individual responds to the condition. In addition, definitions influence the response of health care and social service providers as well as the way in which family and other significant people interact with an individual with a chronic illness.

Common terminology. The classic definition of *chronic disease* was proposed by the Commission on Chronic Illness (1956, p. 1) as "all impairments or deviations from normal which have one or more of the following characteristics: are permanent, leave residual disability, are caused by non-reversible pathological alteration, require special training of the patient for rehabilitation, and/or may be expected to require a long period of supervision, observation or care." This definition of chronic illness can be applied to many situations and has some merit because of its generality. It is also problematic. One problem is the implicit emphasis on physiological abnormalities. There are numerous situations in which there is demonstrable pathology but no evidence of deviations from or limitations in daily life functions (e.g., controlled diabetes mellitus). As noted in Chapter 1, "disease" refers to a sociobiological process and does not necessarily include the sociopsychological process. Another problem is the ambiguity of certain terms in the above definition. For example, "deviation from normal" is open to interpretation since there is no general definition of "normal." Similarly, the term "impairment" requires further explication. Thus, although the terminology employed by the commission is general, it is too narrowly confined to biological abnormalities and too ambiguous to provide a comprehensive framework for a study of long-term conditions.

A second term found in the literature is *impairment* (Daitz, 1965; Haber, 1967; Nagi, 1966; Ruesch & Brodsky, 1968). There are many variations on this term, but there is a general tendency to apply it to physiological or anatomical abnormalities. Ruesch and Brodsky (1968) distinguish among physical, psychological, and social impairments. However, the definitional vagueness of the latter two render them useful only as a starting point for discussion. An important contribution made by Ruesch and Brodsky (1968) is the recognition that physical impairment has rather universally accepted norms, whereas psychological and social impairments have very subtle variations due to age, sex, geographic region, and culture. Both Haber (1967) and Daitz (1965) make the important distinction between so-called intrinsic residuals and extrinsic residuals of impairments. Intrinsic residuals result from the disease process itself and generally are recognized as the outcome of tissue destruction. This distinction has important implications for caregivers. Indicators of residuals that may be partly or totally accounted for by the management of certain conditions include contractures, decreased range of motion, confusion, emotional lability, dependent edema, pneumonia, atelectasis, bladder infections, constipation, and bed sores (Daitz, 1965, pp. 529–530). "Impairment" has considerable potential as a unifying theme for the study of long-term conditions.

A third term that refers to aspects of long-term conditions is *functional limitations.* This term has been used to denote decreases in individuals' abilities to carry out their daily activities and expected roles (Nagi, 1966, p. 102) and losses or restrictions in individuals' capacities for activity that are due to tissue damage (Haber, 1967).

Closely related to the concept of functional limitation is a fourth term: *handicap*. Handicaps presuppose the existence of an impairment of structure or function but not necessarily a functional limitation. The implication of the term is that rehabilitation efforts have not eradicated a disease residual, and thus an individual has some activity limitation (Haber, 1967; Wright, 1960). There is a declining use of the term "handicap" in current literature. Instead, functional assessment (functional limitation) is becoming the important criterion for evaluating the effectiveness of rehabilitative and health services.

The last term to be discussed is *disability*. Like other terms, "disability" has been defined in several ways. Melvin and Nagi (1970, p. 552) describe it as a pattern of behavior that results when impairments actually do, or are perceived to, impose limitations. Similarly, "disability" has been defined as behavior resulting from the loss of ability to perform expected role activities (Haber & Smith, 1971, p. 88). Other definitions include the inability to respond to behavioral expectations (Haber, 1967) and disorganization or inability to cope with the multiple demands of the environment (Daitz, 1965; Reusch & Brodsky, 1968).

The concept of disability can be used to advantage in the responses to chronic illness throughout the life span. The major advantage is the reference to behavior without implying specific disease entities. For clinicians and investigators this is important, because it is possible to identify constellations of behavioral responses that can be formulated as part of a general framework for the understanding of and intervention in a variety of chronic illness conditions. A second advantage is derived from the term "pattern of behavior," which suggests that responses to chronic illness may have recurring aspects. If this is the case clinicians and investigators can direct efforts at identifying patterns and modifying these for specific conditions. A third advantage is derived from the term "behavior expectations." Expectations may come from self and/or from others. This suggests that responses to chronic illness may be internally organized but are likely to be a function of others' expectations as well. Thus, the behaviors resulting from disability may be conceptualized as part of a social process to which an individual attempts to adapt through negotiation with others.

Implications of Definitions
As noted above, definitions influence the ways in which chronically ill individuals respond, as well as the ways in which family, friends, and health care, legal, and social service providers respond. These responses are not necessarily planned or conscious but are often gradually formulated through repeated experiences with long-term

illness. In the following subsections, we discuss three definitional perspectives, each of which has implications for the behavior of clients as well as caregivers in situations of chronic illness.

Clinical definitions. Clinical definitions of long-term illness are made on the basis of anatomical or physiological manifestations. This type of definition raises a question: At what point does disability or altered behavior become manifest? There are significant instances in which anatomical or physiological disturbances may be present without placing any limitation on the capacity of the individual to function. As Melvin and Nagi (1970) note, impairment of function can be addressed at several levels: molecular, cellular, tissue, organ system, and whole organism. The level of pathology will influence the manifestation of impairment and disability.

Defining long-term illness primarily as a clinical entity limits intervention, treatment, and rehabilitation to the amelioration of intrinsic residuals, or the disease process itself. Thus, treatment plans include medication, diet, or surgical intervention only, and other dimensions of a therapeutic regimen may be omitted.

Although few people have an entirely clinical perspective on long-term illness, there are instances in which this perspective predominates. Frequently, for legal purposes, illness must be defined in these terms in order for a client to receive economic compensation. This is true in the case of Workman's Compensation and to some extent all medical insurance, whether private or publicly funded.

Personal definitions. The meaning of a chronic illness to an individual and the way in which that individual comes to define himself once a long-term illness strikes are key elements in the individual's management of his illness. Several factors influence self-definitions in chronic illness, many of which are related to age, sex, and cultural and social expectations. Other factors, such as perceived loss of functional capacity and changes in life style, activity, and roles have an impact on the meaning attached to the illness.

Several typologies are useful for predicting or understanding the way in which chronic illness affects an individual (Melvin & Nagi, 1970; Safilios-Rothschild, 1970). Factors influencing meaning and behavior that are commonly included in these typologies are the point in the life cycle at which onset occurs; the nature and extent of the limitations; the degree of visibility of the condition and stigma attached; the nature of the onset (sudden or gradual); and the course, prognosis, symptoms, and treatment involved. Each of these characteristics is considered more fully later in the text and in the context of specific long-term illnesses.

Social definitions. Closely related to both clinical and personal definitions in long-term illness situations are definitions implicitly or explicitly made by others, including family, friends, employers, health care workers, employees of welfare/benefit offices, "people on the street," or society in general. These definitions are based on the expectations of behavior ingrained in individuals through the socialization processes that occur in all cultures and societies.

Social definitions become relevant whenever behavior deviates from normal. That is, whenever the behavioral expectations of age, sex, or roles differ from the observed behavior of an individual, there is likely to be a social comment. The influence of social definitions should not be underestimated. There is a rapidly accumulating body of literature which suggests that others' responses to an ill individual have a profound impact on the way in which the individual manages the situation (Reif, 1976).

The interactions of clinical, personal, and social definitional systems can be conceptualized as the major determining factors in the observed patterns of behavior (disability) of individuals with chronic illness (Fig. 1). The problem that arises with this or any con-

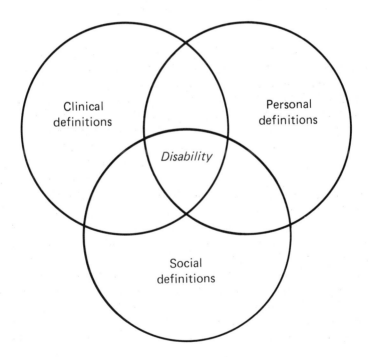

Figure 1. Disability as a function of the interaction of clinical, personal, and social definitions.

ceptualization is one of distinguishing between behavior that is the result of pathology (clinically defined chronic illness) and that which is a result of personally or socially defined chronic illness. The extent to which these distinctions can be made has important implications for the kind of care provided by health care professionals.

THEORETICAL PERSPECTIVES ON CHRONIC ILLNESS

Living with a chronic illness requires expertise in the management of the multiple dimensions of the condition. Some of these dimensions have been identified as preventing or managing medical crises, managing regimens that may require extensive changes in life style, reordering time, managing family relationships, and controlling symptoms (Strauss & Glaser, 1975). Other aspects of living with chronic illness may include managing a new identity, balancing the need for help or support from family and friends with the need for personal control and self-sufficiency or independence, and the need to reciprocate. Most of these dimensions have less to do with the disorder itself than with the consequences of the management of symptoms and/or the management of social relationships.

In this part of the chapter we analyze three theoretical perspectives that are useful for understanding the factors that influence client responses to chronic illness: the sick role, illness behavior, and the at-risk role. The purpose of this discussion will be to elaborate the limitations and promises of each of these in dealing with the issues of chronic illness. We incorporate into the discussion the components of response to chronic illness identified earlier as clinical, personal, and social.

The Sick Role in Chronic Illness

A discussion of the sick role in chronic illness must include the concept of role. In any situation in which an individual is interacting with others, all of whom have specified expectations of behavior, not all of which are compatible, there is likely to be tension and strain. Merton (1968) analyzes strain in terms of social structural variables; Goode (1960) describes role strain in terms of individual strategies; and Thomas (1966) discusses behavioral options that exist between disabled individuals and others when role conflict occurs. For the purposes of this discussion we refer only to the analyses of Goode (1960) and Thomas (1966). Those interested in the social structural components of role strain may wish to read more extensively in Merton (1968).

The concept of role strain (Goode, 1960) is relevant to any discussion of illness, whether acute or chronic. Goode (1960, pp. 484–486) notes that for most people the total set of role obligations is overdemanding. For an ill person the role of "sick" entails additional responsibilities and behavioral expectations. How does anyone sick or well manage the demands of several roles? What are the strategies for reducing role strain? Goode (1960, pp. 486–487) suggests five: compartmentalization, delegation, elimination of role relationships, extension, and barriers against intrusion.

Compartmentalization is the ability to set aside all competing demands on the self and attend only to the situation of the moment. In a study of strategies for managing maintenance hemodialysis, Dimond (1978) found that patients sometimes referred to "departmentalizing" their lives. By this they meant that in order to manage all the demands of "normal" daily life as well as four hours "on the machine" they simply had to attend to one thing at a time and learn to ignore everything else.

Delegation is the assignment of certain tasks, in one's arena of responsibility, to others. In a sense this is a practical way of compartmentalizing. The difficulty lies in deciding what may or may not be delegated to another.

Elimination of role relations involves reducing the number of relationships or frequency of interaction with selected others. This may increase the opportunity for continuing other relationships. In certain chronic illness situations in which fatique or time is a factor, the ability to alter or eliminate social relations may be a very useful strategy.

Extension involves expanding one's role obligations in order to cite additional commitments as a reason for not fulfilling other obligations. Although this option seems less likely to be effective in situations of chronic illness, there may be instances in which it is a relevant strategy.

Barriers against intrusion involve deliberate efforts to prevent the establishment of new relationships or the continuation of existing ones. In the latter case this strategy is akin to eliminating role relations. Both methods are directed at maintaining a manageable number of important role relationships and eliminating less important ones.

The work of Thomas (1966) is more specifically focused on the issues of role that are linked to disability-related behaviorial changes and to the association between disabled and nondisabled. Thomas (1966: pp. 3–6) describes five roles that may at one time or another be assumed by or imposed on disabled individuals.

1. *Disabled patient,* or classic sick role (Parsons, 1951): This is the role assumed by most individuals with a permanent disability. It includes the behavior expected of a hospitalized

person or of one under the continuous management of a physician.

2. *Handicapped performer:* A person in this role experiences a
    range of restrictions on his behavior (social, physical) that re-
    sult from the type and extent of his disability.
3. *Helped person:* This is the role of one who receives aid from
    others.
4. *Disability co-manager:* The chronically ill are co-managers,
    with physicians or families, of the consequences of disease.
5. *Public relations person:* The chronically ill are often asked to
    participate in media coverage of specific kinds of chronic ill-
    ness.

All or some of these roles have been experienced by many people
with long-term illness. A conflict may arise, however, when the "conceptions that disabled persons hold for themselves disagree with the
conceptions others hold for them in any or all of the above described
roles" (Thomas, 1966, p. 8). At the very least, such conflicts result in
confusion and asynchronous behaviors among individuals (Thomas,
1966, p. 8). They may also cause pronounced anxiety and stress depending on the frequency of occurrence and the situation (e.g., home or
work).

The behavioral responses of the chronically ill are determined in
part by the characteristics of the illness and by others' reactions to the
disability. Both sets of responses are influenced by the point in the life
span at which the chronic illness occurs. Benedict's (1938) concept of
role discontinuity is useful for analyzing an individual's management
of changes in performance capacity. The abrupt, unanticipated onset
of many chronic illnesses precludes a smooth transition from usual role
performance to changed capacities for performance. Role discontinuities may occur at several points depending on the number and complexity of roles affected by the illness.

Since most discussions of the role(s) of a sick person implicitly or
explicitly refer to or evolve from the classic description of the sick role
by Parsons (1951), it is important to have a working knowledge of the
Parsonian sick role. The reader is referred to Chapter 1 for a full discussion of the sick role. In the remainder of this section we examine sick
role as a framework for the study of chronic illness.

According to Parsons (1951), an individual who is sick (a) is not responsible for the condition (i.e., illness is involuntary), (b) is exempt
from normal social role obligations, (c) is obligated to get well (i.e., to
do what can be done to restore health), and (d) is obligated to seek and
accept professional care. This paradigm, although stated rather formally here, is the prevailing framework within which many health pro-

fessionals work. As a consequence of socialization (repeated interaction with sick people, observation of the behavior of peers with clients), we consciously or unconsciously expect sick people to seek professional help, to want to get well, and to comply with treatment. During the period of illness we expect that family and others will relieve the sick person of some of his responsibilities.

The basic drawback of this paradigm of sick role behavior is that it describes the ideal behavior of people with *acute* illnesses. It is not particularly relevant to people with *chronic* illnesses. Important distinctions can be made between behaviors that are expected when an illness is temporary and when it is permanent (Gordon, 1966; Kassebaum & Bauman, 1965; Twaddle, 1969). The most obvious is time. The sick role paradigm does not fit the case of chronic illness because of its indefinitely long or lifelong duration. "Exemption from normal social obligations cannot be justified [as suggested by Parsons, 1951] by the prospect of a return to productive function and social participation" (Gallagher, 1976, p. 209). Because the illness may be indeterminately long, the individual may resume part or all of his responsibilities. Thus, the exemption from usual role responsibilities found in acute illnesses may be selective rather than complete in chronic illness (Kasl, 1974). Exemptions are the most variable element in the sick role paradigm. Some conditions require none, some require only a few, and others require many. "Chronic or persistent incapacities . . . require changes in role relationships and activities which extend the capacities immediately affected. This may include a generalized reidentification of the disabled person in terms acceptable to other people, as well as to the disabled person's identification" (Haber & Smith, 1971, p. 84).

A second aspect of the sick role paradigm that does not fit chronic illness is the obligation to seek treatment. Treatment may involve pain, untoward drug effects, surgical mutilation, and changes in life style that impinge on personal freedom. When such stresses are prolonged, as they can be in chronic illness, the client cannot be obligated to put himself in that position (Gallagher, 1976, p. 209). The expectation that the individual will seek or accept treatment must be balanced by considerations of human dignity and quality of life. The cost (in social or psychological terms) of treatment in certain long-term illnesses far outweighs the benefits in terms of client values and life-style preferences.

A third aspect of the Parsonian sick role that has variable application in long-term illness situations is the obligation to cooperate with the plan of care. The expectation of compliance with the regimen proposed by competent professionals may support a dependency that is not productive for the chronically ill. "There is a substantial autonomous component to the role of the patient in the physician–patient relationship in long-term illness" (Gallagher, 1976, p. 210). The sick role paradigm does not account for a give-and-take relationship between patient and professional. The client with a chronic illness is to a large extent the manager of his care, making day-to-day decisions to modify the medical regimen to fit personal needs and preferences and to ameliorate symptoms as they arise. The client is not simply compliant but follows a therapeutic regimen *because it makes sense* (Gallagher, 1976, p. 210).

The management of chronic illness relies heavily on the support of family and lay people. Neither of these groups are included in the Parsonian framework of sick role, because both are largely outside the domain of health professionals. Adaptation to chronic illness depends on the individual's physical and social environment. Since occupational capabilities are so highly valued in American society, adaptation to chronic illness depends to some extent on flexible employment policies and practice. Households must often adjust to the special requirements of a chronically ill member, and families must generate methods for sustaining their commitment to this member.

From this discussion it is apparent that the classic conceptualization of sick role provides only a limited framework for studying chronic illness. In chronic illness, usual role performance may be only partially resumed after the acute stage of the illness; motivation to get well is an inappropriate expectation in the presence of irreversible pathology; considerations of quality of life may outweigh the obligation to seek treatment; and compliance with medical advice can be only a partial expectation when the client and the family are the major managers of the illness.

Alternatives to the Sick Role Paradigm

Given the inadequacy of the sick role paradigm, it is necessary to develop a conceptualization that is more appropriate for chronic illness. One way to accomplish this is to redefine role obligations in terms relevant to the individual's capacities and limitations. Haber and Smith (1971) propose a model of disability in which the normalization of exceptional behavior is provided within the framework of reciprocal role obligations as a means of facilitating role maintenance. Exceptional behavior is redefined as normal and acceptable in terms of new rules of interaction. Behavior that in other contexts might be considered deviant becomes normal. Haber and Smith (1971) refer to this process as "normative adaptation to incapacity" and suggest that it consists of three stages: recognition of inadequacy, attribution of responsibility, and legitimacy of performance behavior.

Recognition that an individual is unable to meet social or personal obligations, or that he is meeting his obligations only partially, or that he is placing unusual demands on others in the course of meeting role obligations is what Haber and Smith (1971) refer to as recognizing inadequacy. This recognition may come from others, the affected person, or from both. Once the inadequacy is identified, responsibility for the inadequacy must be determined. In the process of normalizing incapacity, responsibility is attributed to something beyond the control of the individual, e.g., illness or irreversible disease. The final phase of normalizing occurs when the incapacity is legitimated ("the accredited disabled") by someone recognized as capable of doing so, e.g., a physician. Once these three steps have been taken, an individual's social and personal role obligations can be redefined such that they are more in line with the individual's actual capabilities, and his performance can be evaluated against the redefined norms.

Haber and Smith's (1971) model has considerable appeal both theoretically and practically as an aid to understanding the behavior of the chronically ill. However, it does raise some problems. One of these is the potential for uneven distribution of legitimation. Individuals function in more than one group (organization or system). Less than normal performance may be sanctioned in some of these groups and not in others, causing confusion and uncertainty for the individual. Furthermore, the behavior of one individual may be recognized as disabled whereas that of another person with the same condition may not. Some of the variables that account for this discrimination are age, sex, development stage, socioeconomic status, and cultural beliefs and value systems. Thus, the expectations about the behavior of individuals with chronic illnesses are partly a function of the attributes of the illness and partly a function of attributes of the individual (Kassebaum & Bauman, 1965). "If the costs of adaptation [legitimation of incapacity] are too high for the individual, family, or community to tolerate, the incapable individual may be isolated or expelled" (Haber & Smith, 1971, p. 90). The extreme forms of isolation, e.g., institutionalization of the mentally ill, retarded, and aged, are well known. A less obvious form of isolation is created by the subtle discriminatory behavior of employing agencies; another form is the systematic exclusion of older persons from social interactive opportunities.

Besides uneven legitimation of incapacity and subtle forms of exclusion, there are other dilemmas of legitimation (or formal sanctions for exceptional behavior). One of these is stigmatization. Once incapacity is formally recognized, the potential for adverse consequences may increase. "Stigma is not a necessary condition of disability, although it must obviously be taken into account in considering the adjustments required for the utilization and maintenance of social interaction" (Davis, 1963, p. 132). Legitimation may also result in maladaptive behavior; i.e., the limitations imposed by legitimation may be greater than those imposed by the condition itself. This gives rise to the phenomenon of "invalidism" and other manifestations of inappropriate behavior that result from certain diagnostic labeling (Garrity, 1973; Hyman, 1971; Lewis, 1966; Reif, 1976).

In addition, a disabled person faces a specific set of problems relating to the synchronization of his behaviors with those of others (Thomas, 1964, p. 18). In essence this problem is one of validity. That is, an individual with a chronic illness behaves in a way that is either appropriate or inappropriate given the nature and extent of his handicap. Others also behave toward the handicapped person in ways that are either appropriate or inappropriate. To the extent that the interactive behaviors are in agreement or are not in agreement, they can be said to be synchronous or asynchronous respectively. Synchrony is not necessarily the goal, however. The behaviors of both parties must be commensurate with the true degree of the handicap. In analyzing the various possibilities of valid and invalid behaviors that might occur between the handicapped individual and others Thomas (1964, p. 35) identifies eight variations: true handicap, fictitious handicap, imposed handicap, autistic handicap, autistic normalcy, imposed normalcy, fictionalized normalcy, and true normalcy. Four of the situations are valid, and four are invalid. Validity is determined by the extent to which the behaviors of the individuals involved match the objective reality of the situation. Legitimation of the behavior of a chronically ill person thus can result in one of the following modes (Thomas, 1964, pp. 18–29):

1. *True handicap:* The behavior of the disabled, as well as the behaviors of others, are commensurate with the actual degree of the disabled person's handicap.
2. *Fictitious normalcy:* The disabled performs in a manner implying or indicating a lesser degree of handicap than truly exists; the behavior of others is also appropriate for the absence of handicap.
3. *Fictitious handicap:* The disabled and others jointly adopt invalid behavior in terms of the disabled person's true degree of handicap; the actual degree of handicap is exaggerated.
4. *Autistic handicap:* The disabled displays more handicapped behavior than the disability actually warrants; the behavior of others is commensurate with the true degree of handicap.
5. *Imposed handicap:* Others behave toward the disabled as if he were more handicapped than he actually is; the behavior of the disabled is valid.
6. *Imposed normalcy:* Others behave toward the disabled as if he were less handicapped than he actually is; the disabled maintains valid behavior.

7. *Autistic normalcy:* The disabled behaves as though he were not disabled; the behavior of others is commensurate with the true degree of handicap.
8. *True normalcy:* A nondisabled person behaves as normal (nondisabled); others relate to him on the assumption that he is normal.

Illness Behavior in Chronic Illness

Excusing an individual from responsibility for his condition, as noted by Haber and Smith (1971), does not relieve the individual of accountability for subsequent illness behavior. In many chronic illnesses the individual is not symptom free. Depending on the nature, frequency, and severity of symptoms, the task of controlling symptoms is more or less continuous. The basic problem of illness behavior is this: In the presence of symptoms, what will the individual do, and why (Kasl & Cobb, 1966)?

Illness behavior, defined by Mechanic (1962, p. 189) as "the ways in which given symptoms may be differentially perceived, evaluated and acted (or not acted) upon by different kinds of people," is a useful concept for the study of chronic illness (see Chapter 1 for an account of illness behavior). Much of the research dealing with the way in which symptoms are acted on has been done in the context of acute or limited illness; empirical data on illness behavior in chronic illness are minimal. However, the importance of this concept cannot be overlooked since the management of symptoms is a major challenge for those with chronic conditions. In chronic illness the problem is not so much one of eliminating symptoms as of keeping them from interfering with one's life activities.

Illness behavior is a function of several factors. Those that appear to be particularly important for determining response to symptoms in long-term illness are noted here. An individual's response to symptoms is a function of the nature of the symptoms (Kasl & Cobb, 1966)—not merely the objective nature of the symptoms, but the meaning that the symptoms have for the individual and others (Mechanic, 1978). Symptoms are differentially attended to on the basis of culture and ethnicity (Zborowski, 1952; Zola, 1966), on the basis of health beliefs and values (Kirscht, 1974), as a function of age and/or development stage (Kassebaum & Bauman, 1965); and as a function of affiliation with lay support groups (Suchman, 1965).

In considering the relevance to chronic illness of research findings on the illness behavior of the acutely ill or of those with self-limiting conditions, we must keep several things in mind. The nature and severity of the limitations imposed by chronic illness vary widely, and therefore the symptoms also have a wide range of variation. In some cases a person experiences continuous, sometimes frightening, and usually disturbing symptoms. The decision to report these depends on many factors, some of which include previous modes of dealing with the symptoms, the response of others to more or less continuous reporting of symptoms, and the knowledge based on experience that reporting symptoms will be beneficial. In some cases symptoms are produced by the performance of certain activities; knowing this, the individual refrains from these activities and therefore controls the symptoms.

The onset of a long-term illness has much to do with an individual's response to the symptoms of the illness. In general, the response to a sudden onset is overtly more stressed than the response to a slow, insidious progression of symptoms. Although not scientifically well founded, the reason for this may lie in the differences in anticipatory learning and practice in dealing with multiple and/or variable symptoms (Safilios-Rothschild, 1970).

Response to symptoms (illness behavior) may also be determined by the prognosis, or expected course, of the illness. What an individual does about symptoms depends on the extent to which he believes that taking some action will be beneficial. The expected course of the illness is a major predictor of the usefulness of seeking help for symptoms. Whether a chronic condition is stable, progressive, or intermittent influences an individual's response to symptoms (Safilios-Rothschild, 1970). A stable chronic condition requires no further medical care or life-style changes. Some chronic conditions are stable only when therapeutic regimens are followed. In this situation, the individual may respond to symptoms by returning to or more carefully adhering to the treatment regimen. Some chronic illnesses are marked by a slow, progressive deterioration of function. The individual is likely to attend symptoms in this case because he believes (or hopes) that, by doing something, he will slow the progress of the disease. Intermittent conditions are characterized by unpredictable remissions and exacerbations. Again, the appearance of symptoms is likely to generate concern and help-seeking behavior in an attempt to prolong remission and avoid exacerbation.

Many writers emphasize the importance of the meaning of symptoms to the individual in determining the action he will take in response to them. Melvin and Nagi (1970) discuss nine characteristics of long-term illness that are expected to influence the response of clients and care providers to symptoms:

1. The point in the life cycle at which the onset occurs
2. The nature of the limitations imposed by the illness
3. The degree of limitation imposed by the illness

4. The degree of visibility of impairments and the disfigurement associated with them
5. The stigma attached to the impairment
6. The predictability of the behavior associated with impairments
7. The type of underlying pathology
8. The relationship between the impairment and functioning in social roles
9. Pain and fear

Clearly, the factors that determine illness behavior in chronic illness are highly complex. The way in which an individual responds to symptoms in chronic illness is a function not only of the factors enumerated by Kasl and Cobb (1966) in their model of illness behavior but also of the characteristics of the chronic illness itself.

The At-Risk Role in Chronic Illness

The above discussions of sick role and illness behavior serve to identify two major issues in chronic illness: health maintenance and risk reduction. For a person with a chronic illness the task is to maintain control of the symptoms of the illness in order to function at an acceptable level in the social arena. The behavior required for this is neither exclusively sick behavior nor exclusively illness behavior; rather, elements of both types of behavior are necessary. These include decisions to seek (or delay) help in response to the appearance of new symptoms or for the management of recurrent symptoms, to adhere to a treatment plan, and/or to change certain patterns or habits in order to reduce risks (Kasl, 1974, p. 433). Baric (1969) describes the requirements for managing a chronic illness as the "at-risk role" and points out the characteristics of this role that distinguish it from the sick role. (a) The at-risk role is not institutionalized. (b) It has only duties attached to it; there are no privileges such as the reduced social obligations of the sick role. (c) It has an indefinite time span. (d) It lacks continuous reinforcement from health professionals and the social environment. (e) It lacks feedback provided by changes in symptoms and treatment. This formulation identifies aspects of behavior (norms, expectations, sanctions) on the part of the clients, significant others, and health care providers in chronic illness that may be quite different from behaviors appropriate in acute illness.

The traditional physician–patient relationship does not capture the essence of behaviors required by the at-risk role. A chronically ill person must be a manager of his own care and therefore must be medically sophisticated. The physician, on the other hand, must be content to forego the curing component of his profession and participate, with the client, in managing the illness (Gerson, 1976). In many instances the physician must struggle with issues of quality of life and treatment selection, as well as the experience of repeated failures (Fox & Swazy, 1974). The concept of illness as politics and negotiation suggested by Gerson (1976) and implied by Waitzkin and Waterman (1974) may be particularly appropriate for understanding physician–patient relationship in chronic illness.

One of the most important behaviors required of sick people is compliance. For a chronically ill person this involves contradiction and sometimes conflict. For example, staying on treatment and complying with medication orders is sick role behavior. A chronically ill person may feel well and yet recognize that risk factors are present. Taking medications when one is feeling well, taking medications when no change in symptoms results, taking medications that have uncomfortable side effects, and complying with a medication regimen indefinitely require making decisions about the appropriate balance between the benefits of risk reduction and the cost of compliant behavior (Kasl, 1974). In addition to compliance with a medical regimen, a chronically ill person often must deal with changes in life style, e.g., smoking, diet, and physical activity. Although these changes may be recognized as important for risk reduction, they may be difficult to comply with, particularly if a habit is long standing. Furthermore, changes in life style that are less obviously medically related are often prescribed by a physician, whose authority in this case may be perceived by the client to be quite marginal (Kasl, 1974). The issue of compliance in chronic illness, which often involves making unusual and difficult decisions, is different from the issue of compliance in acute illness and draws attention to the inappropriate features of the sick role model for long-term illness.

The differences in behavior and expectations of clients and health care providers in chronic versus acute illness situations extend to the family and significant others as well. The question of whether (and to what extent) an individual with a chronic illness achieves an adequate measure of adaptation depends, of course, on the underlying pathology and the therapeutic regimen. However, adaptation to and management of a chronic illness also depend on the level of support provided by family and others (Dimond, 1979, Gallagher, 1976; Haber & Smith, 1971).

All of the issues that affect the client and physician also affect the family. For example, the need for medical sophistication, the ability to negotiate treatment plans, adherence to a therapeutic plan, satisfaction with management rather than cure, and the anxieties and concerns surrounding exacerbation and crisis are important areas for family members. Some member of the family is generally involved in recognizing or validating changes in symptoms, helping to decide what to do about symptoms, encouraging adherence to the treatment plan (or collaborating with the client to deviate from the plan), and sometimes participating in direct care of the client. In addition, family members may have an influence on areas outside the illness per se, e.g., decisions about employment of social activities for the client.

The sphere of influence of the family in chronic illness is much broader than that of health care providers and much more long-term than that of families in acute illness situations. Consequently, it is likely that a client's long-term outcomes will be at least as much or more a function of his social environment than the underlying pathology or the prescriptions of health care workers.

In summary, the at-risk role is a more appropriate framework for chronic illness than is the sick role. It takes account of the unique features of chronic illness, e.g., the time factor; the active role of the client in managing the illness; the issue of compliance with treatment in the absence of symptoms and/or in the presence of symptoms that remain despite compliance; the different focus of the physician; and the important role of the family.

Summary
In this chapter we provided a brief historical overview of chronic illness and considered several conceptualizations found on chronic illness in the literature. We discussed the utility of each term in understanding the dynamics of long-term illness. We found that some were more useful than others, although each was relevant to some aspect of chronic illness.

The next task was to outline three perspectives that help to account for the behavior patterns manifested in chronic illness. We suggested that the major sources of disability (patterns of behavior resulting from a given chronic illness) can be found in the interaction of three definitional systems: clinical, personal, and social. We further suggested that distinguishing between the function and interactive components of these systems is a challenge to health researchers and has implications for health care providers.

In the second part of this chapter we analyzed chronic illness in the framework of the sick role, illness behavior, and the at-risk role. We saw that the theoretical frameworks used to conceptualize acute, short-term illnesses require modification when applied to long-term illnesses.

REFERENCES

Baric, L. Recognition of the 'at-risk' role: A means to influence health behavior. *International Journal of Health Education*, 1969,12, 24–34.

Benedict, R. Continuities and discontinuities in cultural conditioning. *Psychiatry*, 1938, 1, 161–167.

Daitz, B. The challenge of disability. *American Journal of Public Health*, 1965, 55, 528–534.

Davis, F. Deviance disavowal: The management of strained interaction by the visibly handicapped. *Social Problems*, 1963, 9, 120–132.

Dimond, M. Social support and adaptation to long-term illness (Doctoral dissertation, University of Wisconsin, Madison, 1978). *Dissertation Abstracts International*, 1978). 39, No. 3, 1869-A. (University Microfilms No. 78-1717)

Dimond, M. Social support and adaptation to chronic illness: The case of maintenance hemodialysis. *Research in Nursing and Health*, 1979, 2, 101–108.

Fox, R & Swazy J. *The courage to fail.* Chicago: University of Chicago Press, 1974.

Gallagher, E. Lines of reconstruction and extension in the Parsonian sociology of illness. *Social Science and Medicine*, 1976, 10, 207–218.

Garrity, T. Vocational adjustment after first myocardial infarction. *Social Science and Medicine*, 1973, 7, 705–717.

Gerson, E. The social character of illness: Deviance or politics? *Social Science and Medicine*, 1976, 10, 219–224.

Goode, W. A Theory of role strain. *American Sociological Review*, 1960, 25, 483–496.

Gordon, G. *Role Theory and Illness.* New Haven, Conn.: College and University Press, 1966.

Haber, L. Smith, R.T. Disability and deviance: Normative adaptations of role ment of disability. *Social Security Bulletin*, 1967, 30, 17–20.

Haber, & Smith, R.T. Disability and deviance: Normative adaptations of role behavior. *American Sociological Review*, 1971, 36, (February), 87–97.

Hyman, M. Disability and patients' perceptions of preferential treatment. *Journal of Chronic Diseases*, 1971, 24, 329–342.

Kasl, & Cobb, S. Health behavior, illness behavior, and sick role behavior. *Archives of Environmental Health*, 1966, 12, 246–266; 531–540.

Kasl, S. The health belief model and behavior related to chronic illness. M. H. Becker (ed.), *Health Education Monographs*. 2, 1974, 433–453.

Kassebaum, G., & Bauman, B. Dimensions of the sick role in chronic illness. *Journal of Health and Social Behavior*, 1965, 6 (Spring) 16–27.

Kirscht, J. The health belief model and illness behavior. *Health Education Monographs*, 1974, 2, 387–407.

Lewis, C. Factors influencing the return to work of men with congestive heart failure. *Journal of Chronic Diseases*, 1966, 19, 1193–1209.

Mayo, L. (ed.) Guides to action on chronic illness. *Commission on Chronic Illness.* New York: National Health Council, 1956.

Mechanic, D. The concept of illness behavior. *Journal of Chronic Diseases*, 1962, **15**, 189–194.

Mechanic, D. *Medical sociology* (2nd ed.). New York: Free Press, 1978.

Melvin, J., & Nagi, S. Factors in behavioral responses to impairments. *Archives of Physical Medicine and Rehabilitation*, 1970, **51**, 552–557.

Merton, R. *Social theory and social structure* (2nd ed.). New York: Free Press, 1968.

Nagi, S. Some conceptual issues in disability and rehabilitation. In M. Sussman (Ed.), *Sociology and rehabilitation.* Washington, D. C.: U.S. Department of Health, Education, and Welfare, 1966.

Parsons, T. *The social system.* New York: Free Press, 1951.

Reif, L. Cardiacs and normals: The social construction of a disability (Doctoral dissertation, University of California, San Francisco, 1975). *Dissertation Abstracts International*, 1976, **36**, 7003A. (University Microfilms No. 76-8246)

Ruesch, J., & Bradsky, C. The concept of social disability. *Archives of General Psychiatry*, 1968, **19**, 394–403.

Safilios-Rothschild, C. *The sociology and social psychology of disability and rehabilitation.* New York: Random House, 1970.

Strauss, A., & Glaser, B. *Chronic illness and the quality of life.* Saint Louis: Mosby, 1975.

Suchman, E. A. Social patterns of illness and medical care. *Journal of Health and Human Behavior*, 1965, **6**, 2–16.

Thomas, E. Problems of disability from the perspective of role theory. *Journal of Health and Social Behavior*, 1966, **7**, 2–13.

Twaddle, A. C. Health decisions and sick role variations. *Journal of Health and Social Behavior,* 1969, **10**, 105–115.

Waitzkin, H., & Waterman, B. *The exploitation of illness in capitalist society.* New York: Bobbs-Merrill, 1974.

Wright, B. *Physical disability: A psychological approach.* New York: Harper, 1960.

Zborowski, M. Cultural components in responses to pain. *Journal of Social Issues*, 1952, **8**, 16–30.

Zola, I. Culture and Symptoms. *American Sociological Review*, 1966, **31**, 615–630.

Chapter 3

Overview of Human Development

Chronic illness occurs at all ages and stages of development. The impact of long-term illness and the response to it differ according to the development stage of the individual and family. In this chapter we review and critique several major developmental perspectives from infancy through advanced age.

To review the major theories of aging is to embark on a nearly impossible task. First, most of what passes as developmental theory is incomplete and more properly described as beginning theoretical perspectives. Second, most of these perspectives are specific to particular age groups, e.g., childhood or adolescence, rather than comprehensive and unitary. To paraphrase Baltes and Willis (1977), developmental theories do not stand serene, complete, and unchallenged at some high level of abstraction. They are part of a dynamic and pluralistic exchange between scientists and their efforts to understand and explain complex phenomena.

Several approaches can be taken in reviewing and summarizing the state of the art in developmental theory. One can describe the various strata, phases, stages, or components of development, in which case one considers the biological, psychological, cognitive–intellectual, and sociocultural components. It is also possible to think of development in terms of major tasks to be accomplished at various life stages.

Erikson (1963) is perhaps best known for pursuing development in terms of major tasks, but others have also taken this approach (Havighurst, 1953; Keniston, 1975; Kimmel, 1980; Levinson, 1978; Peck, 1968; Stevenson, 1977).

A third approach, which is much less bound by age and stages of development, is suggested by Peters and Willis (1978). This framework includes four major concepts: variability, process, context, and interrelatedness. *Variability* refers to the fact that, although there are normative developmental processes at all stages of development, individual differences are always apparent. Thus, the "study of human development is a blend of the norm and the exception or variation from the norm" (Peters & Willis, 1978, p. 2). This concept becomes particularly relevant when one attempts to understand the behavior of a single individual. It is rarely possible or appropriate to think in terms of homogeneity at any stage of development. Individual differences are generally the rule, not the exception.

Process refers to the evolution of human development, which is almost always changing, rarely static. Change is a key factor in development and can occur at any stage as a result of maturation (biological change), learning (socialization or acculturation), or organismic alterations (changes caused by accident or disease) (Peters & Willis, 1978, p. 4). *Context* implies that development occurs within the environmental parameters of things (physical environment) or people (social environment). *Interrelatedness* indicates that the appropriate focus of attention in the study of development is the whole person rather than simply the biological, emotional, or cognitive processes.

Although it is possible to conceptualize the whole person in the sense suggested by Peters and Willis (1978), it is difficult from a practical standpoint to discuss or describe the whole person without referring to specific aspects of the process of human development. In this chapter we review most of the commonly recognized stages of development (infancy, childhood, adolescence, and young, middle, and late adulthood) using an arbitrary organizational system that covers the major theories of biological, cognitive, social, and emotional development for each of these stages. Throughout this discussion we incorporate the concepts of variability, process, context, and interrelatedness.

INFANCY

The recognition of infancy as a separate stage of human development with characteristic physical, cognitive, emotional, and social processes is a recent occurrence in the study of child development. The theories of infant development have evolved through their own stages, often separately from theories of later childhood maturation, from a descriptive recording of physical changes that occur in the first years of life to theories of information exchange between the infant and caregiver. By following the evolving theories, one can derive a composite, albeit incomplete, picture of the first stage of life.

Autogenic Theories

Until the 1950s, infancy was seen much as a prestage during which physical maturation of the neurological mechanisms for later cognitive and emotional processes occurred. The major mechanisms were those concerned with speech and mobility, for it was the onset of speech that marked the period in childhood during which cognitive processes were believed to begin (Stone & Church, 1979).[1]

The development of these mechanisms and physical maturation in general follow a cephalocaudal orientation corresponding to the behavioral sequences that begin in the first year. The infant begins to show head and neck control several weeks after birth and progresses to five motor movements of the fingers by the end of 14 to 16 months. The reflexive symmetrical and undifferentiated movements at birth are replaced by voluntary and specific actions involved in reaching, walking, and hand-to-mouth activities by 1 year. The extent of physical and behavioral change concentrated in so short a period of time makes the first year of life seem the most predetermined and unalterable stage of development. Landmarks of change are measured in weeks or months; for example, for a normal infant it can be reliably predicted that rolling over will occur around 3 months, sitting around 6 months, and walking between 12 and 14 months. In early theories of child development, this uniformity of change was cited as evidence that infancy was a period of physical maturation and that behavior was an *autogenic* response to the physical growth: what the infant did simply reflected some neurological change. Behavior was determined by the unfolding of the genetically determined neural network. An implication of this position was that the environment, as long as it was not lethal to the infant's physiology, played no significant role in enhancing or retarding development (Bayley, 1969; Gesell, 1925; Griffiths, 1954).

---

[1]The word "infant" is derived from the Latin *infans*, "not speaking." It is probably the nonverbal characteristic of the child from birth through 1 to 2 years of age that was the most salient determinant of the early studies of the infant. Speech is the main source of information of cognitive and emotional processes. Without speech as a measurement tool, how could one determine what an infant were thinking or even if an infant thought at all?

In the late 1950s, several divergent sources of evidence contra-
dicted the autogenic theory of infant behavior. First cross-cultural
studies showed that different child-rearing customs were associated
with different patterns of behavioral development, even though neurological maturation in the different cultures was the same. Infants in
non-Western cultures were found to wean, show bladder and bowel
control, and walk earlier or later than Western infants depending on
the patterns of child rearing. This empirical evidence brought into
question the one-to-one correspondence between physical maturation
and behavior.

A more theoretical criticism of the autogenic explanation of behavior came from Bowlby (1969) and Provence (1962), who emphasized the
role of maternal care in infant development. Their proposition, the
basis for a later theory of attachment, identified a set of "social" needs
during infancy that, although independent of biological requirements,
were necessary for normal development. Bowlby studied the effects of
maternal deprivation on neurologically normal infants and found lags
that were inconsistent with changes in physical development. Provence (1962) studied the development of infants institutionalized as or-
phans or abandoned children. Although the children received adequate
physical care and proper nutrition, they had no consistent caregiver
over time. They showed normal physical development but specific lags
in motor, speech, and social behaviors, leading to the conclusion that
at least a part of infant development was directly affected by the care-
giving environment and was not due to physical maturation alone.

The work of Bowlby and Provence served as the foundation for
two different approaches to the study of infants. The maternal-de-
privation studies had shown that infant development was affected by
environment in general and by what seemed to be a very specific relationship with the caregiver. The work raised important questions
about how an infant received information from the environment—what
were the characteristics of infant perception?—and about the formation and nature of the maternal–infant relationship. Through these
lines of study came the theories of infant learning, the basis of cognitive development, and infant attachment, the basis of social development.

Cognitive Development
The basis for what later became the study of cognitive development in
infants began with an exploration of how the infant's perception of
stimuli to different sensory organs developed. An infant's awareness
of the environment (here "awareness" is defined as perception and dis-

crimination) is surprisingly extensive in the first months of life,[2] but if one were to stop here with the description of sensory discriminations, the result would be an extension of the autogenic explanation of behavior. The question confronting cognitive developmentalists is, What is the infant able to do with the incoming information? The demonstration of infant learning did not begin until the 1960s. Bruner (1968) conducted a series of studies in which the infant was "taught" to use behaviors under its control to attain stimuli of preference. For example, infants under four months of age could learn to suck at various speeds to bring a blurred picture into focus. Infants were also taught to use various rates of nonnutritive sucking to increase "enface" contact with human beings and to increase verbal stimulation from an auditory recording. These laboratory studies yielded evidence from natural phenomena in infant behavior: Evidence for association learning in infants came from the case of the hungry infant being comforted by the sound of an opening refrigerator door or the sleeping infant awakening as the rocking chair comes to a stop. These phenomena were now viewed as being the result of associations, formed by the infant, between salient elements of the environment.

These isolated empirical studies of the perceptual and learning capacities of infants were integrated into a theory of infant cognition by Piaget (1968). He called the infant's experience of the environment a state of *egocentrism*. He claimed that the infant's awareness does not include self-awareness and is limited to that which is directly accessible to sensory perception. In the same way, an infant can learn to manipulate only that with which there is a sensory contact. That is, an infant under eight months will not look for a previously handled object that is removed from sight. (We have already cited the study which demonstrated that infants can learn to vary their rate of sucking to bring a picture into focus; they cannot, however, learn to produce the picture from a blank screen.) This "out of sight–out of mind" characteristic of the egocentric stage of development has been described as a

---

[2] Apart from the individual differences among infants, the following perceptive responses occur during the first quarter of the first year: (a) visual orientation to sound in the first week of life (Turkewitz, Birch, Moreau, Levy & Cornwall, 1966; Wertheimer, 1961); (b) visual preference to patterns and human faces, measured by length of time of gaze in infants several days of age (Carpenter, Terce, Stechler, & Friedman, 1970; Friedman, Carpenter, & Nagy, 1970); (c) visual tracking of moving objects within a week of birth; (d) "looming response" (a startle and avoidance response when a large shadow moves in a collision course with the infant) at two weeks of age (Ball & Tronick, 1971; Bower, Broughton, & Moore, 1970).

lack of object permanence. During the second half of the first year, object permanence begins to develop, and there are corresponding manifestations of separation and stranger anxiety. The infant holds an internal representation of the external world, both of social (mother versus stranger) and physical objects. At this stage, the infant will look for a lost toy and seek mother. There is speculation that memory has the physical capacity to wander from mother and explore the environment, and the cognitive capacity to hold a mental representation of her may provide the motive for returning.

Social and Personality Development

Cognitive development, as well as physical development, has been studied in infants who are reared in a dyadic relationship: the maternal–infant relationship. As Bowlby and Provence showed, this relationship has a fundamental influence on the development of the infant that is independent of gratification of physical needs. The understanding of the formation of this relationship and its characteristics has provided the foundation for theories of social and personality development and subsequently for a more recent interactional theory of infant development.

The first theories of social development in infants were theories of attachment and bonding. The early ideas about maternal–infant bonding came from animal studies of imprinting in infrahuman species, which showed that during periods shortly after birth animal infants "attached" to whatever object displayed the critical feature for that species. For example, infant ducklings "attach" to any object that moves within their field of vision (Hess, 1964; Lorenz, 1952).[3] Studies of human infants who experienced unfortunate disruptions in maternal–infant attachment gave evidence of the importance of social

---

[3]For higher animals, mammals, the attachment process is more complex. Harlow (Harlow & Harlow, 1962; Sackett, 1965) studied rhesus monkeys separated from their mothers at birth and reared in cages with either a monkey-sized wire-mesh "surrogate mother" or a monkey-sized terry-cloth "surrogate mother." The monkeys showed affection bonding to the terry-cloth surrogate, even when they were fed from some other spot in the cage. These monkeys also showed explorative behaviors normal for rhesus monkeys and separation anxiety when they were removed from the cage. Those monkeys raised with the wire-mesh surrogate showed retarded social and explorative development and no attachment except during exposure to fearful stimuli. However, the absence of a real mother had some important long-term effects. Athough the monkeys raised with the terry-cloth mother developed normal peer relations as adults, they were sexually ineffective and never showed mating responses.

relationship in development. We have already cited the work of Provence. Another 30-year longitudinal study by Skeels (1966) followed the development of 25 infants who were placed in an orphanage just after birth and later assessed as mentally retarded. Before 1 year of age, 13 of the infants were transferred to a school for retarded children, where each was cared for by a specific inmate of the school (in a sense adopted). These infants later had normal adult lives; only four of the infants left in the orphanage, however, became normal adults.

Other situations produce less drastic interruptions of the maternal–infant bond. One of these is the brief separation of a mother and infant shortly after birth because of illness. Maternal–infant separations that occur routinely in conventional maternity care practices have been criticized as disruptions of a critical bonding period that occurs just after birth. Studies of the development of premature infants after a long period of separation have produced changes in policy in critical care nurseries; a major change has been the inclusion of mothers and fathers in the infants' care. (Actually, these studies have shown that separation produces maternal distress more than it directly affects infant development.)

Although the studies of these short-term separations indirectly support the impact of attachment on general infant development, there is a laboratory method of assessing an infant's reaction to the absence of mother in terms of interaction with the environment. Ainsworth (Ainsworth, Bell, & Stayton, 1974; Ainsworth, Blehar, Waters, & Wall, 1978) uses the "strange-situation technique" to measure infant response to new people and objects in the presence and absence of mother. She has found that an infant explores the environment to a lesser extent when the mother is absent than when she is present. Ainsworth calls an infant's interaction with the environment "exploration from a secure base."

The strange-situation technique is being developed to test attachment behavior in blind and deaf infants and in infants who have suffered neglect or abuse. It is a powerful test for theory development because it measures that which can be described as the infant's sense of trust and security. When feeling secure, an infant is able to explore and move about in the environment. The material relationship provides the base from which an infant can test its developing perceptual and cognitive capacities to learn about the environment.

The development of a sense of trust during infancy is the basis for another set of theoretical perspectives of child development. These are the psychodynamic theories of Freud, Erikson, and Sullivan. In the Freudian theory of child development infancy is the oral phase of psychosexual development because the infant's major source of gratification is sucking and oral ingestion. Freud considered sucking and the subsequent feeling of satiation to be a source of erotic satisfaction. To the extent that its oral needs are not met, an infant will experience a feeling of frustration that will serve as the basis for neurotic tendencies during adulthood. Maternal care not only gives the infant satisfaction, but sets limitations on the immediate gratification of needs. Through the resolution of the tension created by the feelings of want and gratification (the id), on one hand, and the limitations placed on these (the superego), on the other, the infant begins to develop a sense of self (the ego).

Erikson (1963) modified Freud's theory of psychosexual development and described developmental stages in terms of conflicts that arise because of changes in biological capacities that take place through the individual's contact with the environment. Infancy is the incorporate stage, the period of taking in from the environment, during which a sense of basic trust versus mistrust develops. The infant develops a sense of trust if the environment is safe, consistent, and dependable in meeting the infant's needs. Each sensory modality has the capacity to satisfy the need for stimulation; hence, the infant learns to trust or mistrust through the taste of milk, the feeling of being held and rocked, and the sensation of being sung to or gazed at. If the intake needs are not met or if the infant experiences more pain than pleasure, the infant derives a representation of the world that is harsh and untrustworthy. In Eriksonian theory, the resolution of trust versus mistrust during infancy lays the groundwork for the resolution of tasks in the next stages of development.

Harry Stack Sullivan (1953) proposed a psychodynamic theory of personality development very similar to Erikson's; however, Sullivan's theory maintains that the way in which the infant experiences events in the environment influences his definition of self as well as of the world. The infant learns about the "bad" self—the self that hurts and hungers and cries—and about the "good" self—the one that feels warm and full and safe. Slowly, as the child grows, these separate concepts of bad and good self merge. To the extent that the good self overwhelms the bad, that is, the infant experiences more periods of gratification than of frustration, the child develops a sense of security, confidence, and self-love or self-esteem. To the extent that the bad, frustrating experiences overwhelm the good, the concept of self is one of inferiority and insecurity.

The content and approach of the psychodynamic theories differ from the perceptual and laboratory approaches cited earlier, the former use abstract entities that are definable in nonoperationalized terms. In spite of the differences, however, the theoretical approaches have an important element in common: each theory proposes that the infant learns about the environment through a collection of experiences. Learning theory calls this collection a set of contingencies; attachment theory calls it maternal–child interactions; and psychodynamnic theories, a need–gratification sequence. Each theory considers the infant to have a limited but developing set of information collectors, the senses, through which it learns. The infant learns cognitively through connections between actions and outcomes; socially, through connections between self and others; and emotionally, through connections between the outside world and internal feelings. The accumulation of these connections is developed.

Interactive Theory of Development

These theories of development have yet another element in common, and that is the role of the infant in development. In each theory is the assumption that the infant is a passive observer and receiver of the environment. Freud, Erikson, and Sullivan describe infancy as the oral taking-in phase. Attachment theories describe the effect of maternal–infant interactions on infant development. Until recently, infant development was seen to be the result of external forces on a physical and genetic response system. The role of infant characteristics, such as temperament, sex, and size, in determining developmental outcome was ignored. Patterns of mothering were studied as though every infant were the same, and it was assumed that results differed solely because of differing maternal interaction with the infant. In the 1960s a new theoretical approach to the study of infant development was taken in cognitive and social psychology. The role of the infant in maternal–child interaction was described as an active one that influenced maternal response and later child development. Lewis and Rosenblum (1974, pp xv–xvi), in the introduction to their book, *The Effect of the Infant on Its Caregiver,* discussed the new theoretical approach.

> Historically, it is true that most emphasis has been placed on the effect of the social and physical environment on the development of the infant and child. For example, the literature is replete with examples of how certain maternal behaviors affect specific infant functions. This emphasis needs to be corrected, lest we conclude that the infant is a passive organism constantly being affected but having no effect, constantly being altered but producing no change itself. Such a model of the developing child in fact is not only false but is on its face illogical. Even the mere size of a child in terms of its height and weight immediately, and with no other information, acts upon an approaching adult set upon engaging in social interaction.

Thus our task is not so much to convince the community that the organism affects and alters its caregivers, but rather to determine what might be the manner of this effect and how it might be measured.

One of the leading theorists of the interaction theory of development is Brazelton, who has studied maternal–child interaction in terms of a pattern of reciprocity. The cyclical pattern of attention and withdrawal occurs between a mother and infant shortly after birth. This pattern, including its sequencing and timing, is very much under the control of the infant. The infant uses gaze aversion, body movement, and head movement to control the amount of stimulation it allows to enter its system. Brazelton has shown that when mothers and infants are in synchrony, that is, when the mother responds to the infant's attending and withdrawal with reciprocal stimulation and withdrawal, the infant's attention span lengthens, and cognitive and social development (e.g., smiling, babbling, tracking of objects) occurs at a faster rate. The reciprocal pattern of interaction has also been shown in gaze and vocalization activities between mothers and infants (Brazelton, Koslowski, & Main, 1974).

These interactional coactions could be considered the precursors of the contingency responses that begin to increase during the infant's third and fourth months. Watson (1972) describes one of these contingency situations as a "game" in which the infant appears to expect certain responses by the caregiver as a result of its own behavior. The infant is in a sense becoming aware of the effects it has on its environment.

Another element of the interactional theory of development, which is based on a signal-detection model of information exchange, is the dependence of normal infant on the infant's and mother's capacities for stimulus recognition and response (Brazelton et al., 1974; Korner, 1974). The stimulus recognition and response in the infant and the mother is an informational exchange between them through which the infant develops contingency recognition, emotions, and attachment. In signal theory terms, the behaviors of an infant that reflect the infant's internal state are detected and interpreted by the mother, leading to a response by the mother that alters the infant's internal state and sets up another signaling sequence. The extent to which the signals given off by the infant are detected, decoded, and responded to depends on the sending and receiving capacities of both the infant and the mother. Thus, in interactional theory, social development is not a passive unfolding of predetermined behaviors or perceptual processes but rather is influenced by anything that affects the stimulus detection or response capabilities of either the mother or the infant. Anything that interferes with the informational exchange will interfere with the course of normal development. The impact on development will depend on the degree of disruption of, or interference, the information exchange and the compensations that the dyadic relationship can make to overcome the deficits.

The interactional theory of development offers an important framework for studying the effects of chronic illness or congenital impairment on infant development and for planning intervention strategies. The characteristics of a defect or illness can be analyzed according to the disruptive effect it will have on information exchange in the dyadic relationship. Fraiberg (1974) reported the effects of blindness in infants according to this framework. For a blind infant, there is no visual exchange of information: not only does the infant receive no visual information about the environment but, equally important, the infant cannot send cues to the caregiver through the visual system.[4] Other sensory modalities, such as tactile, auditory, and kinesthetic systems, must provide the signal cues.

The interactional theory of infant development is perhaps the most useful one for health care practitioners because it provides a basis for identifying developmental vulnerabilities based on the characteristics of the infant and parent as well as those of the disease. It also provides the basis for identifying compensatory interventions to overcome the disruptions caused by the illness.

The interactional theory of infant development provides an example of Peters and Willis's (1978) concepts of context and interrelatedness. For the infant the exchange of information with the environment through sensorimotor capacities results in changes in the cognitive, emotional, and social processes. The interactional theory adds the additional concept of exchange and feedback between the infant and its world. In normal development the infant enters into a harmonic exchange with its caregivers and its environment.

---

[4]The mother of a blind infant cannot depend on her infant's gaze to determine when the baby is attending or avoiding. Gaze aversion, both as a means for the infant of reducing stimuli and as a signal for the mother to disengage, must be replaced by some other attention-modulating response. The eye language in sighted infants that reliably elicits behaviors such as smiling and cooing as the child approaches the third and fourth months is disrupted in the blind. For the blind infant, the mother's voice becomes a less reliable ellicitor of a smile after the infant is one month of age. Tactile and kinesthetic stimuli are more powerful in producing smiling or babbling responses.

CHILDHOOD

Development during childhood is described in considerably less detail in the literature than is infant development. This is perhaps due to the fact that developmental changes are much less dramatic in childhood than in infancy.

Physical Development

In the first four years of life, physical (or biological) growth is a major component of development. It becomes less dramatic in later childhood. Because the body's regulatory mechanisms impose order in the process of physical development, we can describe certain normative patterns. However, these regulatory mechanisms are not immutable, and in the presence of environmental variations or genetic programming aberrations there can be considerable variation in physical development (Peters & Willis, 1978, p. 10).

The major physical changes that occur in early childhood are very rapid height and weight gains, an increase in ossification, replacement of baby teeth toward the end of early childhood, and changes in body proportions. With rapid changes in height the child becomes slimmer. Variations in physical development may be caused by a variety of factors, some of them normal and others not. Growth rate is noticeably related to sex in early childhood and preadolescence. Generally, girls are more advanced than boys in physical development and motor skills, but this is reversed in adolescence. Illness and environmental deficiencies, including nutritional and affectional deficits, can retard physical growth.

Physical development in childhood, although it may not be as dramatic as that in infancy, is enormously complex and rapid. A basic understanding of normal growth and development is critical for understanding the impact of long-term illness at this stage of life. The child's physiology is marked by a much wider range of fluctuations than the adult's. The plasticity of both anatomical development and physiological homeostatic mechanisms makes the child more vulnerable to rapid and severe shifts in the internal environment. The reader unfamiliar with this aspect of childhood is urged to consult a basic text on childhood physiology.

Cognitive Development

Perhaps the most well known cognitive theorist for this developmental stage is Piaget. Piaget's theory (Piaget, 1968; Piaget & Inhelder, 1969) is based on the assumption that all people, children included, try to make sense of their world. The way in which they achieve this changes with time but proceeds through an unvarying sequence of stages. Each stage has unique characteristics, yet is dependent on successful mastery of the preceding stages. Piaget (1968) identified four stages of cognitive development: sensorimotor, preoperational, concrete operational, and formal operational. Progress through each of these stages is summarized by P. Minuchin (1977, p. 7):

> The very young child makes sense of the world through the direct experience of his or her senses, and through the reactions of the environment to motor explorations (the "sensorimotor stage"). Through the early years the child grows in experience, knowledge, and symbolic mastery, but continues to reason in a fragmented way, liberally sprinkled with fantasy and contradiction. The child is then in the "preoperational, intuitive stage," still unable to integrate knowledge into a logical system. The early middle years are a period of transition into the "concrete-operational stage," during which the child becomes capable of systematic logical thought, at least in concrete, experiental and well-defined matters. Only at the upper reaches of this age range, however, do some children begin the transition to "formal-operational thought." Once that transition is accomplished, the child is able to deal with hypothetical situations in logical fashion. Piaget considers formal-operational thought to be the culmination of man's logical potential, which generally reaches full development in adolescence.

Children in the preoperational stage are likely to demonstrate thought processes referred to by Piaget (1968) as centered, egocentric, and lacking reversibility. In centered thought the youngster concentrates on one characteristic of an object and is unable to consider several characteristics (e.g., size, shape, and color) simultaneously. "Egocentrism" refers to the inability of the young child to take the viewpoint of another person. Thus, children assume that everyone thinks and feels about a situation the way they do. Preoperational children are unable to reverse their thinking, that is; they cannot consider a series of events simultaneously and understand the final event in relation to the earlier events (Peters & Willis, 1978, p. 28).

Whereas concrete-operational children are able to categorize, classify, and understand relationships only in concrete situations, formal-operational children can deal with reality in the abstract. Rules of logic dominate this stage of cognitive development. According to Piaget, the acquisition of formal-operational thought marks the end of cognitive development. The child is prepared for and capable of dealing with any problems that may arise in adulthood.

Cognitive development is a major emphasis in much of the writing on childhood development. This emphasis does not appear again until the literature on the older adult. At this stage the focus is on the extent to which (if at all) cognitive abilities deteriorate with advanced age.

Psychosocial Development

The most relevant theories of psychosocial growth and development in childhood (both early and middle) are those of Erikson and Sullivan. Other important perspectives are learning theory (Bijou & Baer, 1961) and ecological theory (Barker & Wright, 1955; Gump, 1975; S. Minuchin, 1974). Our review of psychosocial development in childhood will draw on aspects of each of these theoretical frameworks.

As noted earlier, Erikson (1963) modified and greatly expanded the psychodynamic tradition begun by Freud. Erikson's eight developmental stages and accompanying issues and tasks are useful for assessing psychological growth. The theme of Erikson's theory of development is that the individual moves through a series of stages, each with a critical psychological task to be mastered. These tasks offer the opportunity for growth and the development of an increasingly stable and mature personality. They also present the risk of failure, loss of self-confidence, and plateauing or retardation of psychosocial growth.

The major developmental task in early childhood is autonomy. The child is learning to control and independently manage many aspects of daily living. Erikson contends that when the child is unable to achieve a sense of mastery, shame and doubt result. Shame is characterized by embarrassment, impotence, anger, and rage against oneself. Doubt is the perception that nothing one does will determine the outcome; things and people external to the self control one's destiny.

The major developmental task for the preschooler is initiative (Erikson, 1963). Initiative subsumes many concepts, including assertiveness, learning, becoming dependable in relating to other people, and acquiring the capacity to plan for future activities. Failure to achieve initiative results in guilt, which includes a sense of defeatism, anger, fear of and reluctance to undertake future activities that require initiative, and a sense of deserving punishment.

Erikson describes the psychological task in later childhood, referred to as school age (sometimes as the latent period), as a sense of industry, that is, a sense that one is, or can learn to be, capable in the performance of necessary tasks within and outside the family sphere. The school-age child has become somewhat skilled in functioning within the comfortable circle of family and close family friends. Now the task is to apply these skills and knowledge to another world outside the family. The risk is that the child will develop a sense of failure, defeat, and inferiority.

In Erikson's framework, the successful completion or mastery at each stage is highly dependent on the environment. The child requires sufficiently challenging opportunities for growth, tempered with the appropriate support of other people, who may allow small failures but who will prevent continuous failure. Erikson's theory implies that successful mastery of one stage is necessary for growth and success at the next stage. Alternately, failure at any stage jeopardizes future development and growth.

Learning theorists do not conceive of development in terms of stages, and their theories therefore, are not specific to ages or periods of the life span. "Learning and growth are essentially cumulative processes, consisting of the accretion of new responses through reinforcement and modeling as the child grows" (P. Minuchin, 1977, p. 9). An individual's behavior can be reinforced in three ways: direct reinforcement by other persons or events, vicarious reinforcement through observation of the consequences of others' behavior, and self-reinforcement (Peters & Willis, 1978 p. 69).

A much less well defined approach to childhood development is described by P. Minuchin (1977) as an ecological theory, which is very similar to systems theory. A child develops within a particular kind of interactional context, the emphasis in ecological theory is on the *social* context, the primary actors being parents, siblings, and peers. Within this context the child influences and is influenced through continuous and cyclic interaction, feedback, and change. The ecological approach to childhood development has not yet been well tested, but several studies have demonstrated its relevance (Barker & Wright, 1955; Gump, 1975; S. Minuchin, 1974).

The Self
The development of beliefs and values about the self, including body image, social and sexual role identity, and self-esteem, takes place at all ages. Since these concepts are particularly important in chronic illness situations, we consider them specifically in this chapter.

Intrapersonal development can be defined as the growth of awareness of the self. Hess and Croft (1975) describe three aspects of awareness: self-concept, identity or self in a social context, and self-esteem. "Self-concept" refers to the ability to differentiate self from others. Thus, a small child begins to notice features such as hair color, sex, height, and facial features that distinguish him from other small children. The child also begins to classify himself as a member of certain groups, e.g. boys or girls. This is the beginning of identification of the self within a social context. The evaluation of self, or self-esteem, occurs with continuous and repeated interaction with others.

The development of the self is, in large part, a function of social interactional experiences. Many social–psychological theories include the important role of significant other people in the development of the self. The reflected appraisals of significant others, particularly the mother, are central to Sullivan's (1953) theory of self growth. The "good me," "bad me," "not me" personifications described by Sullivan are considered to be the outcomes of specific, intense, and repeated interactions between the mother (or mother figure) and the infant.

Similarly, although with some distinctions, the symbolic interaction theory of self ascribes a central role to significant others. In one of the earliest writings on the self, James (1910) described the self as known and knower, as object and subject, as "Me," and as "I." According to James the self has three aspects: material (body, clothes, family, home), social (recognition from others), and spiritual (totality of consciousness). James asserted that a person has as many social selves as there are individuals who recognize him and carry an image of him in their minds.

Cooley (1902) described the social self as an individual's imagining of how others perceive him and termed it the "looking-glass self." The self, according to Cooley, has three principal elements: Our imagining of how we appear to another person, our imagining of his judgment of that appearance, and self-feeling. Thus, "the thing that moves us to pride or shame is not the mere mechanical reflection of ourselves, but an imputed sentiment, the imagined effect of this reflection upon another's mind" (Cooley, 1902, p. 155).

Similarly, George Herbert Mead (1934) emphasized that a person will come to see himself in much the same way that he believes significant others see him; furthermore, he will act in accordance with the imputed expectations of others as to how he should act. Some of Mead's ideas about the way in which others affect the perception and evaluation of self were later incorporated into labeling theory. We refer to this theory later in the chapter with reference to self-esteem in late childhood.

The growth of self-esteem in childhood, as in all ages, is uneven. At certain times and in certain places, a child may feel secure and comfortable with his acknowledged limitations and capabilities. At other times he may be somewhat uncertain and self-critical. Self-esteem is rarely static. A child brings to each new situation self-evaluations formed in the family context. However, new experiences with peers, teachers, and others provide additional data for continuing self-appraisal. Environmental factors, especially other people, affect the growth of self-knowledge and self-esteem in a variety of ways: through the breadth of experiences provided for exploring capacities and feeling effective, by the quality of available models whom a child can emulate, and by the nature of response to a child's expressed feelings and self-invested efforts (P. Minuchin, 1977, pp. 88–89).

ADOLESCENCE

The term "adolescence" conjures up images of turmoil and tension, re-
bellion and restlessness, exploration, opportunity, and anxiety. Much
has been written about this stage of development, suggesting incred-
ible variations among young people on their way toward adulthood.
Extremes of physical, social, and emotional development occur during
adolescence. What exactly is unique about adolescence? What makes
it so wonderful or so worrisome?

There are three perspectives on adolescence in the literature: biological, psychoanalytical, and sociocultural. At the turn of the century
Hall (1904) wrote that the difficulties of adolescence were the result of
the biological maturation process and were thus inevitable. Thornburg
(1971, p. 3) notes that "although we no longer accept Hall's (1904)
storm and stress . . . theory that adolescence is an inevitable period of
emotional conflict, we cannot deny that today's youth are highly conflict oriented."

Classic Freudian thought influenced other writers, who acknowledged the psychological changes in adolescence as important determinants of behavior (Blos, 1962; A. Freud, 1946; Jersild, 1957). Writers
in the psychoanlytical tradition define adolescence as the "processes
of adaptation to the condition of pubescence, the physical manifestation of sexual maturation. . . . Typical adolescent behavior patterns,
often including irrational, impulsive and self-centered behavior, are
viewed as reactions to the sudden spurt in physical change, such as
rapid growth in physique, development of secondary sexual characteristics, and hormonal imbalance, in conjunction with the residue of
early unresolved psychological development" (Sze, 1975, p. 217). In
both the biological and psychoanalytical/psychological approaches,
adolescence is considered a universal phenomenon, implicit in both is
the passivity of the adolescent, who is molded by forces beyond his
control.

In the sociocultural approach, the notions of universality and passivity are rejected. Adolescent behavior is considered to be the result
of the interaction between the personal world of the adolescent and the
demands of society (Benedict, 1964; Bernard, 1962; M. Mead, 1935).
There is considerable agreement (M. Mead, 1974; Piaget, 1968) that
"adolescence is a prolonged, not necessarily smooth, transitional
period that makes possible a literate and technologically advanced
society" (White & Speisman, 1977, p. 7). Although the sociocultural
approach has been well stated and documented, the traditional bio-
psychological definition of adolescence has predominated.

Piaget and Erikson are prominent theorists not only of child development, but of adolescent development as well. It is useful to think of
Piaget's theory as a biological perspective on intelligence and

Erikson's as a psychosocial view of personality development. According to Piaget, "intelligence is understood best as an evolutionary, biological achievement that allows the individual to interact effectively
with the environment. Intellectual development, like other biological
achievements, is characterized by progressive changes in a process of
active adaptation" (White & Speisman, 1977, p 11). Erikson, in contrast, "views human growth in terms of conflicts. Each individual
must weather successive psychosocial crises, which represent conflicts
between the demands of social environment and biological or psychological needs and drives. . . . The developing individual progressively
gains active mastery of the environment, personality integration and
accurate perception of self and world" (White & Speisman, 1977, p.
10). Nonetheless, there are several aspects of development on which
Piaget and Erikson agree (White & Speisman, 1977, p. 19):

> Piaget and Erikson both examine the intellectual and emo-
> tional achievements of adolescence that lead to adult responsibili-
> ties. Both are interested in the broadening of a time perspective
> and the role of peer interactions in contributing to the adolescent's
> progress. Both pinpoint preparation for adult social and occupa-
> tional roles as the tasks to which adolescence is committed.
> Finally, both are interested in the ways in which particular en-
> vironments either foster support, or inhibit and deny, adolescent
> potential.

Physical Development
The biological dimensions of adolescent development are given prom-
inence in many texts on development. Adolescence represents much
more than the attainment of puberty, although this is often the dominant concern of writers, teachers, parents, health care workers, and
adolescents. Sexual maturation may contribute to the emotional tone
of adolescence. However, in accounting for the development of adolescence, pubertal changes seem secondary to changes in thought and
emotion (Piaget, 1969, p. 60). Furthermore, although psychoanalysis
emphasizes genitality as a prerequisite for full maturity, a truly loving
and intimate sexual relationship depends on the establishment of a
firm identity during adolescence (Erikson, 1968, pp. 136–137).

A spurt of physical growth is common for both male and female
adolescents but often is more noticeable in male adolescents. In all
adolescents the extent and timing of physical growth are highly variable. "From eleven through sixteen or seventeen years the range of
individual differences in physical structure and physiological function
at any given chronological age is greater than at any other time in the
human life span" (*Youth,* 1974).

Cognitive Development

As indicated earlier in this chapter, childen at progressive stages are capable of thinking about objects, characteristics of objects, and classes or categories. Adolescents can reflect on their own thoughts, construct whole systems, think in the purely hypothetical case, and think abstractly. According to Piaget the transition is from concrete, preoperational thinking to "formal operations" or to "hypothetical-deductive thinking" (Piaget, 1968). The adolescent is also able to think about time beyond the present, and this, Inhelder and Piaget (1958) suggest, is a major difference in the cognitive capacities of children and adolescents. It is this capacity to project thought into the future that allows an adolescent to plan future life goals. The adolescent is moving beyond the egocentricity of earlier thought processes toward what Piaget refers to as *decentering*. Decentering occurs not only in the mind, but also in social relations. The adolescent's ability to discuss life and life plans with peers is the key to this process (White & Speisman, 1977, p. 22). Piaget (1968) also relates the romantic experiences that begin in adolescence to the cognitive capacities of the individual. That is, the common experience of incongruence between the ideal and the real is a function of the cognitive development of adolescents. Active, sometimes unrealistic, imaginary adventures end for most adolescents when they begin to assume responsibility for gainful employment or college education (White & Speisman, 1977).

Psychosocial Development

The development crisis of adolescence is that of identity formation versus identity diffusion (Erikson, 1968). The capacity to abstract, to think in hypothetical terms, to think about one's own thoughts, and to consider one's life in some historical perspective is the cognitive requisite or antecedent to the development of a sense of identity. Identity diffusion results if an adolescent fails to achieve this sense of stability, uniqueness, and continuity of self. Erikson suggests that the expectations and developmental accomplishments that converge on an adolescent necessitate a "psychosocial moratorium," a time for quiet reflection and dreaming. The adolescent requires this "time-out period" in order to achieve an integrated personality. Analogously, Piaget suggests that the passions and dreams, emotionality, and idealism of adolescents are the foundations of personal creativity (White & Speisman, 1977, p. 23).

The concept of identity is central to the developmental stage of adolescence. White and Speisman (1977, pp. 40–41) delineate four elements of Erikson's "identity" that distinguish it from such related concepts as self-concept, self-esteem, and role. (a) Identity is a process the core of which is continuity of past and future. (b) Identity is an attribute of society as well as of the individual, identity crises are centered on the acceptance by society and by the adolescent of the choices made by the adolescent. Individuals are usually not conscious of their identity development. (d) The criterion for successful resolution of identity crisis is the achievement of an ethical capacity that allows the individual to take responsibility for the next generation. Individual identity reflects the interaction of biological, cognitive, social–psychological, and cultural processes (Erikson, 1968).

Youth

Keniston suggests that youth is a distinct stage of development that occurs between adolescence and adulthood. He identifies four major themes of this period (Keniston, 1975, pp. 335-339):

1. *Tension between self and society:* This tension differs from that experienced by adolescents. Adolescents struggle with identity; youths sense who they are and the potential for conflict between this self and the social order.
2. *Pervasive ambivalence toward self and society:* Young people experience major conflicts between the maintenance of personal integrity and the achievement of effectiveness in society.
3. *Estrangement and omnipotentiality:* Estrangement is characterized by a sense of isolation, unreality, and absurdity of life. Omnipotentiality is belief in absolute freedom, pure possibility, and the ability to achieve anything.
4. *Great value on change and concomitant fear of stasis.*

Keniston (1975) also describes the transformations that occur in the psychological and interpersonal development of youth as they progress toward adulthood. Following the lead of Erikson, he identifies the major developmental task or issue of youth as individuation versus alienation. Individuation is the resolution of tension between self and society, the balance between emphasis on the internal self and emphasis on the external. Failure to achieve this balance results in alienation. Alienation from self is submission to society ("joining the rat race"); alienation from society is total self-absorption.

Psychological growth in youth is inextricably related to interpersonal styles from identicality to mutuality. Identicality is characterized by the dichotomous perspective of "me and those who are identical to me (soul mates)" versus all others. The interactional preference of youth is based on parity (similarity). In contrast, mutuality, or complementarity, is the recognition and appreciation of "those who are different from me." Keniston states that the achievement of mutuality results in changed relationships with elders and parents. Relationships that were once characterized by worship or hatred are now based on reality and appreciation.

Keniston's analysis of youth was popularized in the 1960s when many young people were confused and angry over U.S. involvement in Vietnam. The validity of Keniston's thesis that youth represents a distinct stage of development is debatable. However, he does present some interesting and provocative ideas that should not be overlooked in a review of human development throughout the life span.

To summarize our discussion of adolescence and youth, the remarks of the President's Panel on Youth (*Youth*, 1974, p. 111) are appropriate. Youth is a time of:

1. Great variation in the rate of physical, intellectual and social development. Cognitive and physical abilities approximate those of mid-life adults;
2. Increasing differentiation of interests and abilities;
3. Changing patterns of preferred peer groups; growing heterosexual interests and emancipation from parents;
4. Increasing desires for independence, autonomy and identity—often expressed in gainful employment.

EARLY AND MIDDLE ADULTHOOD

The period of early and middle adulthood is longer than that of childhood and adolescence combined. The ages of individuals in this stage of life range from approximately 21 to 65. Considerable variation and change can occur over a 40-year period. "It is a complex period, a period in which an individual's past endowments and deficits, present opportunities and restraints all come into play, with consequences that determine future life prospects" (Sze, 1975, p. 371). Sarnoff (1962, pp. 402–403) notes that "as the adult lives out his existence, his behavior will reflect (a) old elements of personality, derivatives of childhood and adolescence, and (b) new elements—new motives, attitudes, interests—that he acquires in the course of his adult years."

Theoretical perspectives on early and middle adulthood are relatively scarce. More has been written about older adulthood, and certainly more has been written about infancy, childhood, and adolescence. Even Erikson's (1963) eight-stage theory of human development breaks down at the seventh stage (adulthood). There are some possible reasons for the paucity of organized theoretical approaches to early and middle adulthood. One of the major ones may be that changes and growth occur over a longer period of time and are not as readily identified as biological or physical as they are in childhood and adolescence (Kennedy, 1978, p. 6). In fact, some writers argue that biological changes are generally of little importance at this stage of development (Neugarten, 1968). Another reason is that social and environmental factors are much more varied and complex; there is a slow oscillation between continuity and change, and whatever change occurs is built into individual life histories, which by early and middle age are extremely varied. Troll (1979, p. 7), commenting on women at midlife, remarks: "Chronological age . . . is a misleading and ineffective gauge of people's changes over their life-span. Variation increases year by year. By mid-life people of the same age may have so little in common that age-related descriptions, let alone explanations, are of little meaning."

Keeping in mind the caveat expressed by Stevenson (1977, p. 15), that developmental tasks are useful as guides but are not meant to be absolute standards, we shall review some of the common concerns, issues, and tasks of early and middle adulthood. Erikson (1963) postulates three critical periods of personality development beyond adolescence: achieving intimacy versus isolation (alienation, loneliness), achieving productivity (generativity) versus stagnation, and achieving ego integrity versus despair. The first two are generally relevant to early and middle adulthood, and the latter to late adulthood. Success in any or each of these tasks makes it easier to achieve the next task. Erikson's model allows for positive development throughout the adult period of life.

Another approach to adulthood has been suggested by Havighurst (1953), who postulates that one *must* complete certain tasks in early adulthood in order to complete the tasks of middle adulthood. Among the tasks of early adulthood are selecting a mate, getting married, beginning a family, and starting a life occupation. The tasks of middle adulthood include accepting civic and social responsibility, guiding teenage children, and adjusting to aging parents.

Havighurst's description of the tasks of adulthood in general, and early adulthood in particular, reflects the societal attitudes and values of the early 1950s. Keniston's (1962, 1975) description of youth, introduced in the preceding section, is radically different form Havighurst's model. Considerably less radical than Keniston's analysis but more current than Havighurst's are the developmental tasks of early adulthood suggested by Stevenson (1977). The major objective of this stage is "to achieve relative independence from parental figures and a sense of responsibility for one's own life" (Stevenson, 1977, p. 15). One accomplishes this objective by developing an appropriate and satisfying style of life in the home, at work, and in society at large.

The 1970s might be called the "age of middle age." During the later years of his decade many books appeared that described various dimensions of middle age. The ones we consider to be most useful are those of Neugarten (1968), Peck (1968), Gould (1972, 1978), Sheehy (1976), Stevenson (1977), Levinson (1978), and Vaillant (1977). Each of these authors uniquely describes developmental tasks and issues that occur in middle age. Most of the studies focus on social and/or psychobiological factors; some are empirical, and some are entirely theoretical.

Expanding the seventh and eighth states of Erikson (1963), Peck (1968, pp. 88–90) suggests four major tasks of middle age: (a) valuing wisdom versus physical powers, (b) socializing versus sexualizing, (c) cathectic flexibility versus cathectic impoverishment, and (d) mental flexibility versus mental rigidity. Peck's description of middle age is in the psychoanalytical tradition and, although useful, is contrary to many of the current analyses of middle age. Neugarten (1968, pp. 382–383) describes what she considers to be six salient issues of middle age: (a) sensitivity to the self as a means of achieving goals, (b) body monitoring, a new sense of physical vulnerability, (c) change in time perspective from time since birth to time left to life, (d) heightened self-understanding, (e) sense of expertise, and (f) sense that accomplishments are not only appropriate, but expected at this stage of life. Neugarten's analysis is based on interviews with highly articulate and successful men and women between 45 and 55 years of age. She summarizes this stage as one of introspection, reflection, mastery, competence, and control of the environment (Neugarten, 1968, p. 384).

The difficulty with some of the early analyses of middle age is that they are based on what might currently be considered to be late middle age; the period from adolescence through about age 40 is frequently omitted. Levinson (1978) and Stevenson (1977), however, include this earlier period of life in their analyses. Stevenson (1977) divides the period of middle age into the Core of the Middle Years (ages 30 to 50, Middlescence I) and the New Middle Years (ages 50 to 70, Middlescence II). Middlescence is defined as "the stage in life when the adult life-style, the occupational mode, and the family life (or single life) pattern have been chosen and the individuals . . . settle down to implementing their choices (Stevenson, 1977, pp. 17–18). Stevenson summarizes the tasks of Middlescence I as assuming "responsibility for growth and development of self and of organizational enterprises; providing help to younger and older generations without trying to control them" (Stevenson, 1977, p. 18). The major objective of Middlescence II is "to assume primary responsibility for the continued survival and enhancement of the nation" (Stevenson, 1977, p. 25). It is apparent from the many writings of the past decade that the period we call middle age is a time of enormous growth and diversity of achievement. Given the fact of increased life expectancy, the period of late adulthood holds similar opportunities.

LATE ADULTHOOD

The later years are an integral part of the continuum of human development. Older adults, like people in any age group, share certain experiences and attitudes with each other. At the same time, their experiences and responses are immensely variable. Age in itself is not an explanation of behavior patterns over time. Behavior is the product of a personal history of adapting or responding to what Bengtson (1973, p. 9) refers to as developmental events: "occurrences which are experienced by individuals during the course of life and which have some systematic influence on the ordering of human behavior." As with earlier developmental stages, understanding late adulthood requires a perspective that includes the concepts of variability, process (growth and change), personal and historical context, and the interrelatedness of all aspects of development. The conceptual framework may be more crucial for examining late adulthood than earlier stages because the stage of late adulthood is often viewed in a very stereotypical way.

In this section we provide an overview of major theories of aging (biological, cognitive, social–psychological). Because of the field of gerontology is relatively new, considerable controversy surrounds most of these theories. However, it is important that nurses and other health care providers be familiar with current thinking in the field so that they can make appropriate use of it in practice.

Physical Development

According to a noted physiologist, aging is "a decline in physiologic competence that inevitably increases the incidence and intensifies the effects of accidents, disease, and other forms of environmental stress" (Timiras, 1972, p. 465). There are several major perspectives on biological aging. The first, which can be simply stated and then forgotten, is nonspecific "wear and tear" notion. This is the common-sense and popular idea that the body simply wears out over time. A second theory bases aging on homeostatic imbalance, or an inefficiency of crucial homeostatic mechanisms that maintain physiological balance in the human body. As Comfort (1964, p. 178) notes, "Aging is characteristically an increase in homeostatic faults." There appears to be no difference in the mechanisms for regulating equilibrium in the body between young and older people under resting conditions. Instead, it is the time frame in which the mechanisms occur that seems to change. Self-regulating feedback decreases in efficiency with age (Shock, 1977). Strains on the homeostatic mechanisms that were once easily tolerated may threaten the survival of older people (Kimmel, 1980). According to Eisdorfer and Wilkie (1977), the theory that the diminished efficiency of the physiological response to stress is responsible for aging is perhaps the most general and provides the clearest link between physiological, social, and psychological aspects of aging.

A third biological theory attributes aging to an accumulation of harmful insoluble particles in the cells with age, which interferes with normal metabolism and ultimately results in death (Carpenter, 1970). The accumulation theory of aging is promising, but, as Shock (1977) notes, if it is to receive continued attention the toxic substance presumed to accumulate in old cells must be isolated and identified.

The cross-linkage theories represent a fourth perspective on aging (Bjorksten, 1968). The formation of cross-linkages changes the chemical and physical properties of molecules and interferes with normal functioning. An increase in cross-linkages with age has been demonstrated in extracellular proteins, particularly collagen, and in the latter case results in such characteristics changes as wrinkled skin and slow wound healing (Kimmel, 1980). The cross-linkage theories of aging hold considerable promise.

The auto-immune theory, another promising theoretical perspective, suggests that aging occurs because of the development of antibodies that act on normal cells of the body and destroy them (Blumenthal & Berns, 1964; Walford, 1969). The destruction of self tissues by auto-immune antibodies is apparently the mechanism in certain illnesses, such as rheumatoid arthritis, that occur more frequently among older people.

Finally, there is a cellular theory of aging. There is a common but mistaken notion that in older adults cells begin to die faster than they are reproduced and that eventually there is an insufficient number of cells to maintain life. The situation, as Kimmel (1980) notes, is hardly this simple! In fact, most cells continue to reproduce and, theoretically at least, would allow the organism to live indefinitely. It may be, however, that cells reproduce only a finite number of times (Hayflick, 1966, 1970, 1977), and this finite growth potential may be a mechanism of aging (Kimmel, 1980). It may also be that cells reproduce imperfectly because of age or a random accumulation of errors in replication (Medvedev, 1964).

Other biological theories of aging include the somatic mutation theory (Curtis, 1966) and the stochastic and composite theories (Busse & Pfeiffer, 1969). However, as Sze (1975, p. 569) notes, "Despite differences in theoretical stance, all who consider the phenomena of old age are confronted with the inescapable fact of the inevitable deterioration of the human organism."

Cognitive Development

A substantial amount of research has been undertaken on cognitive changes associated with old age. These studies cover such aspects of cognition as rote memory, serial and paired-associate learning, creativity, and decision-making. The problems of interpretation are considerable. For example, depending on one's interpretation, one can find support either for a diminution of cognitive capacities with age or for no change at all. Kalish (1975, p. 35) delineates three methodological problems related to research on cognition. (a) Many age-related factors cause a loss in certain types of capacity but not in others. These factors may be disease states or simply lack of experience or sophistication in behavioral research procedures. Older adults may become anxious, confused, and resistant in the unfamiliar laboratory settings sometimes used for behavioral research. (b) Cross-sectional research is severely limited when applied to the study of age difference in widely separated age cohorts. Longitudinal studies have shown minimal decline in cognitive powers, whereas cross-sectional studies have shown substantial age-related differences. (c) It is difficult to measure one cognitive process without inadvertently measuring others. For example, measurements of immediate memory are influenced by the speed with which information is presented; outcomes of learning simple tasks may be confounded by anxiety, perceptual or sensory limits, or reaction time. Furry and Baltes (1973) suggest that fatigue is a major factor in some studies and that age-related differences are related to the length of the study.

Keeping in mind the methodological problems that limit interpretation of studies on cognition, we shall examine some general research findings. Immediate memory studies show that there is minimal decrement in recall of information. However, if there is any kind of interference with the task of memorizing, there is some evidence of negative association with age (Bromley, 1966). There are no age-related changes in recall of events that occurred many years in the past (long-term memory).

There is less conditionability, in the classic sense, among older adults than among younger people (Schonfield, 1969). Instrumental or operant learning studies have not been done with older adults (Botwinick, 1970). Behavior modification, for which operant learning is the paradigm, has been shown to be clinically effective with older people, but no comparison studies of younger people have been carried out.

Cross-sectional studies show a considerable decrease in intelligence with age. Longitudinal studies indicate a much smaller loss of cognitive capacity (Eisdorfer, 1963; Jarvik, Kallman & Falek, 1962). Kalish (1975, p. 40) suggests that the common notion that intelligence declines with age may reflect observations made of the very old, modest decrements that many older people experience, prejudice and expectations of the perceiver, and terminal decline. The last term indicates that "individuals who show a notable change in any one of a variety of measures of cognitive performance are more likely to be dead within a few years than those who show no particular change" (Kalish, 1975, p. 41; Riegel & Reigel, 1972).

Creativity has been investigated by many, but most of the work has been done with young people. Although one study (Lehman, 1953) gives evidence that major contributions to the arts and sciences have been made by young people, methodological errors detract from the results. Dennis (1966) notes that, when one considers all of the contributions of famous people, it is more likely that the peak of creativity occurs in the 50s; furthermore, productivity continues into the 60s and 70s as well.

Although there is evidence of a decline in biological and cognitive function with age, there is little evidence to suggest that this is a major concern of older people. Kalish (1975, p. 45) provides the following helpful summary: "Behavior, performance, and life satisfaction of older people [are] less influenced by the measured decrements uncovered by our research than initial logic suggests. Anticipation is frequently more frightening than actuality, although declines and losses, when extensive, are objectively as well as subjectively important. In spite of very real problems, the aging individual does appear to cope amazingly effectively with these losses." Kalish (1975, pp. 45–46) also suggests some of the reasons for these adaptive responses to loss:

1. Decrements occur gradually; adaptation is gradual.
2. Others one's own age are showing the same signs.
3. Older people (and younger) can adjust to chronic problems and continue to enjoy life, even though the same problem might have appeared overwhelming when it was initially noticed.
4. Decrements and losses of a physical nature are only one aspect of life; if other parts of life are going well (social relations, active involvement in groups), the physical problems may be more easily endured.
5. Anticipation, rehearsal, planning may have occurred prior to the decrement.

Psychosocial Development
The developmental tasks of late adulthood are different from, but contingent on, the successful management of previous life stages. Kimmel (1980, p. 403) characterizes development in young adulthood

as a centrifugal tendency propelling the individual away from self and out into the external world. The middle years are less explosive and more integrated in terms of self and society. In the later years there is a centripetal tendency, a turning inward with less emphasis on external affairs and more concern with internal processes. Some of the most well known perspectives on development in the later years are illustrative of Kimmel's characterization.

Erikson's (1963) delineation of the eighth developmental stage emphasizes internality: ego integrity versus despair. Elaborating on Erikson, Peck (1968) describes three developmental tasks of late adulthood: ego differentiation versus work role preoccupation, body transcendence versus body preoccupation, and ego transcendence versus ego preoccupation. This perspective suggests a general shift in emphasis from the work role to a broader range of role activities, a shift from preoccupation with physical wellness to satisfying human relationships, and valuing the knowledge that one's contributions to children, friends, and society will remain long after one's death.

Although labeled developmental, tasks attributed to late adulthood have often implied stasis. That is, the interpretation of the later stages of life has had an almost exclusively cognitive dimension: the older person coming to grips with what has been, not planning for what will be. Stevenson (1977) has taken exception to this prevailing interpretation and has suggested a set of developmental tasks that assume a continuing, active assault on life but that recognize the importance of introspection and life review. The major tasks of late adulthood, according to Stevenson (1977, pp. 28–29), include the pursuit of a second or third career, learning new skills, sharing wisdom with others, evaluating and putting into perspective one's past achievements and failures, and coming to terms with grief and loss related to the death of one's friends, spouse, and, ultimately, oneself.

We have described the social and psychological dimensions of development, the concepts of self, self-esteem, socialization, and roles, as important, even critical, to the management of different life stages. Late adulthood is no exception. In fact, certain social–psychological theories of this period are based on these concepts. Four of these—disengagement theory, activity theory, social breakdown and reconstruction, and socioenvironmental theory—are briefly described below.

Disengagement theory (Cumming & Henry, 1961; Havighurst, Neugarten, & Tobin, 1968; Neugarten & Associates, 1964) states that there is a mutual and inevitable withdrawal or disengaging of the individual and society. The benefits of this withdrawal are a release of the pressures of active participation in society for the individual and the opportunity for younger people to take over responsible positions in society. The functionalist perspective here is obvious. Several assumptions underlie this theory: (a) as a result of biological changes, the older person must slow down; (b) giving up social roles is an intrinsic part of the aging process; and (c) because of the increasing preoccupation with self and decreasing investment in or concern for others, a well-adjusted older person benefits from the disengagement process (Sze, 1975).

Closely related to disengagement theory is a set of commonsense ideas that is loosely referred to as activity theory. The basic notion is that, if one remains active and involved in life, one will be more satisfied. This idea has been minimally tested and is based largely on assumption. Lemon, Bengtson, and Peterson (1972) put forth two central propositions of activity theory: There is a positive relationship between social activity and life satisfaction in old age, and salient role loss is inversely related to life satisfaction: However, neither of these propositions was supported by empirical evidence (Lemon et al., 1972).

The social reconstruction syndrome developed by Kuypers and Bengtson (1973) borrows heavily from the concept of a "social breakdown syndrome" (Zusman, 1966), a labeling theory the intellectual roots of which lie in symbolic interaction. As we have indicated throughout this chapter, a person's self-concept depends in part on the way in which others respond to him. The social breakdown orientation has been applied by Kuypers and Bengtson (1973, p. 47) to show that an older person's sense of self, ability to mediate between self and society, and orientation to competence are related to the kinds of social labeling in aging. Kuypers and Bengtson (1973) argue that older people in America are valued very little and that a malicious cycle of labeling by others and self-identification as incompetent is set into operation. However, with appropriate and positive inputs from society the cycle can be broken or reconstructed—hence the term "social reconstruction syndrome." Three major classes of societal inputs facilitate reconstruction: (a) liberation from the functionalistic ethic and alternative evaluative systems, which would decrease the suspectibility of the older person to negative labeling; (b) improved housing, health, nutrition, transportation, and other maintenance conditions, which would reduce the older person's dependence and increase his sense of competence; and (c) the encouragement of internal control and development of problem-solving skills, which would increase the older person's ability to cope. The final outcome of the social reconstruction perspective is an internalization of a view of oneself as effective, competent, and useful (Bengtson, 1973, p. 48). Although logically appealing, this model, has not been tested, and thus whether it is applicable in reality remains to be seen.

Finally, the socioenvironmental theory (Gubrium, 1973), which borrows from both the activity and disengagement theories of aging, as well as the symbolic interaction tradition, is a very complex approach to aging. In essence, it suggests that there is a reciprocal relationship between the individual context and the social context that together make up the total environment of an old person and determine his level of action and morale. Within the individual context are resources that limit or enhance activity: health, financial solvency, and social support. Within the social context are societal activity norms and behavior expectations for older people. The interaction of societal norms and individual resources determines an older person's level of activity and thus his morale. Although the socioenvironmental approach has been, and continues to be, developed from empirical evidence, there is as yet no movement within the discipline of gerontology to embrace this theory over others.

In fact, at present there is no dominant paradigm, as Kuhn (1970) would say, in social gerontology. In the absence of such a paradigm, the bases for high morale, life satisfaction, and successful aging can be partially accounted for by the following conditions (Clark & Anderson, 1967, pp. 232–233):

1. Sufficient autonomy to permit continued integrity of the self;
2. Agreeable relationships with other people, some of whom are willing to provide help when needed without losing respect for the older person;
3. A reasonable amount of personal comfort in body and mind in one's physical environment;
4. Stimulation of the mind and imagination in ways that do not overtax physical strength;
5. Sufficient mobility to permit variety in one's surroundings;
6. Some form of intense involvement with life, partly in order to escape preoccupation with death.

SUMMARY AND CONCLUSIONS

In this chapter we have reviewed the developmental stages of infancy, childhood, adolescence, and young, middle, and late adulthood in terms of their salient biological, cognitive, psychological, and social dimensions. In the course of this review it has become clear that there are a number of fundamentally different perspectives on human development, each of which is based on different assumptions, raises different questions, and addresses different issues. To conclude this chapter we shall point out several of these differences and suggest a perspective that may provide some integration within the field of human development.

The first issue that seems apparent is the lack of a perspective on human development that covers the entire life span. Erikson and Piaget dominate the periods from infancy through adolescence. Early adulthood is notably bereft of a spokesperson; middle and late adulthood have several, but Neugarten is perhaps most notable. It is true that Erikson's eight stages cover the life span, but his exposition of the final stages is noticeably weak [although some writers have attempted to develop these stages further (Clayton, 1975; Peck, 1968)]. Nor have Piaget's interpretations of cognitive development been successfully extended into adulthood, although some recent work indicates attempts in this direction (Flavell, 1970; Piaget, 1972).

A perspective on human development that covers the life span might at first seem unnecessary. It might be argued that a separate model for each major developmental period is sufficient and that making the transition from the perspectives of Piaget and Erikson to those of Neugarten and others is acceptable. However, the fundamental distinctions among these theorists require major shifts in thinking when one moves from one to the other. Several examples of these differences will make this clear.

Perun and Bielby (1979) compare the concept of crisis as it appears in the works of Erikson and Neugarten. Crisis, in development literature, refers specifically to the relationships between critical situations and growth or change over the course of one's life (Perun & Bielby, 1979, p. 277). In Erikson's (1963, 1968) developmental model, crisis is a "pivotal mechanism triggering the completion of the current stage and the commencement of its successor" (Perun & Bielby, 1979, p. 279). Crisis is both a necessary and sufficient cause of developmental growth and change. Neugarten (1968, 1969, 1970) advocates an entirely different mechanism for growth and change. Crisis is neither inherent in nor a normal component of development; in fact, it is an aberration. Growth and development are paced, not by crises, but by a sense of timing of events in the life course. (Neugarten, 1970, pp. 71-72).

> There exists a socially prescribed timetable for the ordering of major life events; a time in the life span when men and women are expected to marry, a time to raise children, a time to retire. This normative pattern is adhered to, more or less consistently, by most persons within a given social group.

On the basis of this timetable the individual develops a "set of anticipations of the normal, expectable life cycle . . . expectations of the consensually validated sequences of major life events—not only what these events should be, but when they should occur" (Neugarten, 1969, p. 125). According to this model, crisis is an anomaly, which occurs as a consequence of asynchrony (Perun & Bielby, 1979). It seems apparent, even on the basis of a brief discussion, that it is not a simple matter to use Erikson's model of development for early life stages and then shift to Neugarten's model for adulthood and aging. To make this transition would require a major reversal in basic tenets and assumptions about human development. A universal model or theory of human development across the life span would eliminate such reversals.

A second issue that addresses the usefulness of a unifying model of human development across the life span has to do with fundamental questions about the nature of human beings, the nature of the environment, and the nature of the relationship between the two. Is human development primarily inner-individual or outer-individual? Does it occur as a result of an individual being acted upon or as a result of an individual's own actions? Is human development linear and discrete or dialectical?

We cannot answer all of these questions, but one example will give us an idea of the importance of a theoretical perspective that can be applied to the entire life span. If we contrast the work of Piaget and Neugarten, it again becomes apparent that we must make a major philosophical leap in order to move across the life span with more than one theoretical approach. Piaget's research on cognitive development is individual-centered and based on a biological model. Both the process of accommodation (of the subject to the subject) and assimilation (of the subject by the subject) are initiated, carried out, and completed by the individual subject. This sharp distinction between the subject and the object is representative of an individualistic or personalistic orientation (Riegel, 1977). Very little attention is given to other subjects and almost none to the interaction between subjects.

At the other extreme, Neugarten's work emphasizes the dependence of individual development on the social environment. The symbolic interactionist framework, which is based on the work of G. Mead (1934) and in which the interaction of the individual with society is the sine qua non of human development, is the basis of Neugarten's approach to adult development. In order for a life span paradigm of development to be useful, the nearly exclusive emphasis on the individual or the social condition would have to be bridged.

The interactive (dialectical) approach to human development is most comprehensively described by Riegel (1973, 1975, 1976, 1977), who takes issue with the notion that the human organism passively develops through exposure to the social context as well as the notion that the human organism actively grows within a passive social context. Riegel (1977, p. 72) suggests a dialectic in which "man changes nature, and changing nature changes man." In Riegel's (1975, 1976) dialectical theory there are four levels of human organization, which interact simultaneously to produce change: inner-biological, individual-psychological, cultural-sociological, and outer-physical (wars, earthquakes, floods). Riegel's conception of human development is summarized in the following statement (Riegel, 1975, p. 101):

> A dialectical interpretation of human development always considers at least two concurrent temporal sequences . . . taken separately these sequences are mere abstractions. Development results from the synchronization of any two and indirectly of all these progressions. Developmental leaps are brought about by lack of coordination and represent major forms of reorganization . . . they provide the fundamental basis for the development of the individual and for the history of society.

Riegel (1977, p. 72) further states:

> The epistemological foundations for the social sciences should lie in the dialectical interactions between the changing individual and the changing world. The study of the human being must take account of both individual-developmental and cultural-historical changes; thus a dialectical approach is necessary.

Chiriboga (1979) has incorporated Riegel's concept of a dialectic into a framework for organizing the recent literature on life transitions that is based on Kuhn's (1970) concept of scientific revolution. According to Chiriboga, Kuhn's framework (with some modifications) could easily become a theory of human development. The key ideas in the literature on life transitions are the following (Chiriboga, 1979, p. 4):

1. Development proceeds in a dialectic between periods of stability, disequilibrium, and renewed stability (Riegel, 1977).
2. Periods of stability are associated with the consolidation and refinement of a world view that guides the individual's commerce with the world (Parkes, 1971).
3. Periods of stability end when paradigmatic expectations conflict with incoming data (see Caplan, 1961, or Golan, 1978, on crisis).
4. Certain critical or marker events signal a paradigm shift.

These four points are brought together in what Chiriboga (1979) describes as the "scenario of life transitions" or, in Kuhn's language, a "scientific revolution."

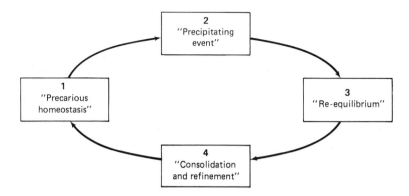

Figure 1. Events in the transition process from one life stage to another.

The circular model in Figure 1 shows the change and continuity that are characteristic of human development. The model can be entered at any point, but for descriptive purposes we enter at the point of precarious homeostasis (Williams & Wirths, 1965). At this point the individual's assumptive world is becoming increasingly disparate as a result of a continuing influx of new information. Tension builds as the individual attempts to cope using strategies that were previously effective but that may now be ineffective because of changes in the social or individual context. The next point is the onset of a precipitating event, which Neugarten (1977) and Levinson (1978) refer to as a marker event or signpost. It is important to note that in itself a marker event (e.g., menopause or retirement) may not be significant but in the context of other changes may initiate the "quest for a more satisfying paradigm" (Chiriboga, 1979). Such a paradigm would take into account the changes (biological, psychological, social, and historical) in the individual's life and include effective strategies for coping with these changes in a satisfying way. Reequilibration of the new developmental level is the next point in the model and includes a new world view, i.e., a new assumptive world. The process of and consolidation refining the new paradigm is the final point and continues until further changes threaten the assumptive world once again and create a precarious homeostasis.

Chiriboga's conceptualization of human development begins to consilidate the multiple perspectives reported in the literature into a single, although not simple, model. However, we are left with the problem of trying to describe and analyze the single dimensions of development (biological, cognitive, social–psychological) while preserving the notion of continuous and complex interconnectedness (dialectic) between each singular dimension and between each dimension and the environment. There may also be some concern that the concept of transitions and the "scenario" of development suggested by Chiriboga are applicable only to adult phases of development. Patricia Minuchin's (1977) writings on development in the middle years of childhood provide evidence that a dialectic approach to development is relevant and the concept of transitions is appropriate in childhood. Minuchin states that the middle-years child is in transition; that transitions are important, even critical, for individual children; that children explore, retreat, and go through periods of disequilibrium before growth is consolidated; that individual children vary in their capacity to cope with transitions; and that the cycle of disequilibrium → resolution → new unbalance must be central to any theory of development (Minuchin, 1977, pp. 3-4).

REFERENCES

Ainsworth, M. D. S., Bell, S. M. V., & Stayton, D. J. Individual differences in strange-situation behavior of one year olds. In H. R. Schaffer (Ed.), *The origins of human social relations*. London: Academic Press, 1974.

Ainsworth, M. D., Blehar, M. C., Waters, E., & Wall, S. *Patterns of attachment: A psychological study of the strange situation*. Hillsdale, N.J.: Lawrence Erlbaum Assoc., 1978.

Ball, W., & Tronick, E. Infant responses to impending collision: Optical and real. *Science*, 1971, 171, 818-820.

Baltes, P., & Willis, S. Toward psychological theories of aging and development. In J. E. Birren & K. W. Schaie (Eds.), *Handbook of the psychology of aging*. New York: Van Nostrand, 1977.

Barker, R., & Wright, H. *Midwest and its children: The psychological ecology of an american town*. New York: Harper, 1955.

Bayley, N. *Manual for the Bayley Scale of Infant Development*. New York; Psychological Corporation, 1969.

Benedict, R. *Patterns of culture*. Boston: Houghton Mifflin, 1964.

Bengtson, V. *The social psychology of aging*. New York: Bobbs-Merrill, 1973.

Bernard, H. W. *Human development in western culture*. Boston: Allyn & Bacon, 1962.

Bijou, S., & Baer, D. *Child development: A systematic and empirical theory*. New York: Appleton, 1961.

Bjorksten, J. The cross-linkage theory of aging. *Journal of the American Geriatric Society*, 1968, 16, 408-427.

Blos, P. *On adolescence*. New York: Free Press, 1962.

Blumenthal, H. T., & Berns A. W. Autoimmunity in aging. In B. L. Strehler (Ed.), *Advances in gerontological research* (Vol. 1) New York: Academic Press, 1964.

Botwinick, J. Geropsychology. In P. H. Mussen & M. R. Rosenzweig (Eds.), *Annual review of psychology*. Palo Alto, Calif.: Annual Review, 1970.

Bower, T. G. R., Broughton, J. M., & Moore, M. K. Infant responses to approaching objects. *Perception and Psychophysics*, 1970, 9, 193–196.

Bowlby, J. *Attachment and loss* (Vol. 1). New York: Basic Books, 1969.

Brazelton, T. B., Koslowski, B., & Main, M. The origins of reciprocity: The early mother–infant interaction. In Lewis, M. & Rosenblum, L. A. (Eds.), *The effect of the infant on its caregiver*. New York: Wiley, 1974.

Bromley, D. B. *The psychology of human aging*. Baltimore: Penguin, 1966.

Bruner, J. S. *Process of cognitive growth: Infancy*. Worcester, Mass.: Clark University Press, 1968.

Busse, E., & Pfeiffer, E. (Eds.). *Behavior and adaptation in late life*. Boston: Little, Brown, 1969.

Caplan, G. *An approach to community mental health*. New York: Grune & Stratton, 1961.

Carpenter, G. C., Terce, J. J., Stechler, G., & Friedman, S. Differential behavior to human and humanoid faces in early infancy. *Merrill–Palmer Quarterly*, 1970, 16, 91–108.

Chiriboga, D. Conceptualizing adult transitions: A new look at an old subject. *Generations*, 1979, 4, 4–6.

Clark, M., & Anderson, B. G. *Culture and aging*. Springfield, Ill.: Thomas, 1967.

Clayton, V. Erikson's theory of human development as it applies to the aged: Wisdom as contradictive cognition. *Human Development*, 1975, 18, 119–128.

Comfort, A. *Aging: The biology of senescence*. New York: Holt, Rinehart, 1964.

Cooley, C. H. *Human nature and the social order*. New York: Scribner's 1902.

Cumming, E., & Henry, W. *Growing old: The process of disengagement*. New York: Basic Books, 1961.

Curtis, H. J. *Biological mechanisms of aging*. Springfield, Ill.: Thomas, 1966.

Dennis, W. Creative productivity between the ages of 20 and 80 years. *Journal of Gerontology*, 1966, 21, 1–8.

Eisdorfer, C. The WAIS performance of the aged: A retest evaluation. *Journal of Gerontology*, 1963, 18, 169–172.

Erikson, E. *Childhood and Society* (2nd ed.). New York: Norton, 1963.

Erikson, E. *Identity: Youth and crisis*. New York: Norton, 1968.

Flavell, J. Cognitive changes in adulthood. In L. R. Goulet & P. B. Baltes (Eds.), *Life-span developmental psychology: Research and theory*. New York: Academic Press, 1970.

Fraiberg, S. Blind infants and their mothers: An examination of the sign system. In Lewis, M. & Rosenblum, L. A. (Eds.), *The effect of the infant on its caregiver*. New York: Wiley, 1974.

Freud, A. *The ego and the mechanisms of defense*. New York: International Universities Press, 1946.

Friedman, S., Carpenter, G. C., & Nagy, A. N. Decrement and recovery of response to visual stimuli in the newborn human. *Proceedings of the 78th Annual Convention of the American Psychological Association*, 1970, 5, 273–274.

Furry, C. A., & Baltes, P. B. The effect of age differences in ability: Extraneous performance variables in the assessment of intelligence in children, adults, and the elderly. *Journal of Gerontology*, 1973, 28, 73–80.

Gesell, A. L. *The mental growth of the preschool child: A psychological outline of normal development from birth to the sixth year, including a system of developmental diagnosis.* New York: Macmillan, 1925.

Golan, N. *Treatment in crisis situations.* New York: Free Press, 1978.

Gould, R. The phases of adult life: A study in developmental psychology. *American Journal of Psychiatry*, 1972, 129, 521–531.

Gould, R. *Transformations: Growth and change in adult life.* New York: Simon & Schuster, 1978.

Griffiths, R. *The ability of babies.* New York: McGraw-Hill, 1954.

Gubrium J. *The myth of the golden years: A socioenvironmental theory of aging.* Springfield, Ill.: Thomas, 1973.

Gump, P. Ecological psychology and children. In M. Hetherington (Ed.), *Review of child development research* (Vol. 5). Chicago: University of Chicago Press, 1975.

Hall, G. S. *Adolescence.* New York: Appleton, 1904.

Harlow, H. F., & Harlow, M. K. Social deprivation in monkeys. *Scientific American*, 1962, 207, 136–146.

Havighurst, R. *Human development and education.* New York: Longman, 1953.

Havighurst, R., Neugarten, B., & Tobin, S. Disengagement and patterns of aging. In B. Neugarten (Ed.), *Middle age and aging.* Chicago: University of Chicago Press, 1968.

Hayflick, L. Senescence in cultured cells. In N. Shock (Ed.), *Perspective in experimental gerontology.* Springfield, Ill.: Thomas, 1966.

Hayflick, L. Aging under glass. *Experimental Gerontology*, 1970, 5, 291–303.

Hayflick, L. The cellular basis for biological aging. In C. E. Finch & L. Hayflick (Eds.) *Handbook of the biology of aging.* New York: Van Nostrand, 1977.

Hess, E. H. *Imprinting in birds.* Science, 1964, 146, 1128–1139.

Hess, R. D., & Croft, D. *Teachers of young children.* New York: Houghton Mifflin, 1975.

Inhelder, B., & Piaget, J. *The growth of logical thinking from childhood to adolescence.* New York: Basic Books, 1958.

James, W. *Psychology: The briefer course.* New York: Holt, Rinehart, 1910.

Jarvik, L. F., Kallman, F. J., & Falek, A. Intellectual changes in aged twins. *Journal of Gerontology*, 1962, 17, 289–294.

Jersild, A. *The psychology of adolescence.* New York: Macmillan, 1957.

Kalish, R. *Late adulthood: Perspective on human development.* Monterey, Calif.: Brooks/Cole, 1975.

Keniston, K. Social change and youth in America. *Daedalus,* Winter 1962, pp. 145-171.

Keniston, K. Youth as a stage of life. In W. Sze (Ed.), *Human life cycle.* New York: Aronson, 1975.

Kennedy, C. E. *Human development: The adult years and aging.* New York: Macmillan, 1978.

Kimmel, D. *Adulthood and aging* (2nd Ed.). New York: Wiley, 1980.

Korner, A. F. The effect of the infant's state, level of arousal, sex, and ontogenetic stage on the caregiver. In Lewis M. & Rosenblum L. A. (Eds.), *The effect of the infant on its caregiver,* New York: Wiley, 1974.

Kuhn, T. S. *The structure of scientific revolutions* (2nd. ed.). Chicago: University of Chicago Press, 1970.

Kuypers, J. A., & Bengtson, V. L. Social breakdown and competence: A model of normal aging. *Human Development,* 1973, **16**, 181-201.

Lehman, H. C. *Age and achievement.* Princeton, N.J.: Princeton University Press, 1953.

Lemon, B. W., Bengtson, F. L., & Peterson, J. A. Activity types and life satisfaction in a retirement community. *Journal of Gerontology,* 1972, **27**, 511-523.

Levinson, D. *The seasons of a man's life.* New York: Knopf, 1978.

Lewis, M. & Rosenblum, L. A. *The effect of the infant on its caregiver.* New York: Wiley, 1974.

Lorenz, K. *King Solomon's ring.* New York: Crowell, 1952.

Mead, G. H. *Mind, self and society.* Chicago: University of Chicago Press, 1934.

Mead, M. *Sex and temperament in three primitive societies.* New York: Morrow, 1935.

Mead, M. Adolescence. In H. V. Kramer (Ed.), *Youth and culture: A human development approach.* Monterey, Calif.: Brooks/Cole, 1974.

Medredev, Z. A. The nucleic acids in development and aging. In B. L. Strehler (Ed.), *Advances in gerontological research* (Vol. 1). New York: Academic Press, 1964.

Minuchin, P. *The middle years of childhood.* Monterey, Calif.: Brooks/Cole, 1977.

Minuchin, S. *Families and family therapy.* Cambridge, Mass.: Harvard University Press, 1974.

Lewis, M. & Rosenblum, L. A. *The development of affect.* New York: Wiley, 1978.

Neugarten, B. (Ed.). *Middle age and aging.* Chicago: University of Chicago Press, 1968.

Neugarten, B. Continuities and discontinuities of psychological issues into adult life. *Human Development*, 1969, **12**, 121–130.

Neugarten, B. Dynamics of transition of middle age to old age. *Journal of Geriatric Psychiatry* 1970, 4, 71–87.

Neugarten, B. Personality and aging. In J. E. Birren & K. W. Schaie (Eds.), *Handbook of the psychology of aging*. Van Nostrand, 1977.

Neugarten, B. & Associates. *Personality in middle and late life*. New York: Atherton Press, 1964.

Parkes, C. M. Psychosocial transitions: A field for study. *Social Science and Medicine*, 1971, **5**, 101–115.

Peck, R. Psychological developments in the second half of life. In B. Neugarten, (Ed.), *Middle age and aging*. Chicago: University of Chicago Press, 1968.

Perun, P. & Bielby, D. Mid-life: A discussion of competing models. *Research on Aging*, 1979, **1**, 275–300.

Peters, D., & Willis, S. *Early childhood*. Monterey, Calif.: Brooks/Cole, 1978.

Piaget, J. *Six psychological studies*. New York: Vintage Books, 1968.

Piaget, J. The intellectual development of the adolescent. In G. Caplan & S. Lebovici (Eds.), *Adolescence: Psychosocial perspectives*. New York: Basic Books, 1969.

Piaget, J. Intellectual evolution from adolescence to adulthood. *Human Development*, 1972, **15**, 1–12.

Piaget, J. & Inhelder, B. *The psychology of the child*. New York: Basic Books, 1969.

Provence, S. Clinician's view of affect development in infancy. In Lewis M. & Rosenblum L. A. (Eds.), *Development of affect*. New York: Wiley, 1978.

Provence, S. & Lipton, R. *Infants in institutions*. New York: International Universities Press, 1962.

Riegel, K. On the history of psychological gerontology. In C. Eisdorfer & M. P. Lawton (Eds.), *The psychology of adult development and aging*. Washington, D.C.: American Psychological Association, 1973.

Riegel, K. Adult life crises: A dialectic interpretation of development. In N. Datan & L. Ginsberg (Eds.), *Life-span development psychology*. New York: Academic Press, 1975.

Riegel, K. The dialectics of human development. *American Psychologist*, 1976, **31**, 689–700.

Riegel, K. History of psychological gerontology. In J. E. Birren & K. W. Schaie (Eds.), *Handbook of the psychology of aging*. New York: Van Nostrand, 1977.

Riegel, K., & Riegel, R. Development, drop and death. *Developmental Psychology*, 1972, **6**, 306–319.

Sackett, G. P. Effect of hearing conditions upon the behavior of rhesus monkeys. *Child Development*, 1965, **36**, 855–868.

Sarnoff, I. *Personality dynamics and development.* New York: Wiley, 1962.

Schonfield, D. Learning and retension. In J. E. Birren (Ed.), *Contemporary gerontology: Concepts and issues.* Los Angeles: Andrus Gerontology Center, 1969.

Sheehy, G. *Passages: Predictable crisis of adult life.* New York: Dutton, 1976.

Shock, N. Biological theories of aging. In J. E. Birren & K. W. Schaie (Eds.), Handbook of the psychology of aging. New York: Van Nostrand, 1977.

Skeels, H. M. Adult status of children with contrasting early life experiences. *Monographs of the Society for Research in Child Development*, 1966, **31** (3).

Stevenson, J. *Issues and crises during middlescence.* New York: Appleton, 1977.

Stone, J. & Church, J. *Childhood and adolescence: a psychology of the growing person.* (4th ed.) New York: Random House, 1979.

Sullivan, H. *The interpersonal theory of psychiatry.* New York: Norton, 1953.

Sze, W. C. (Ed.). *Human life cycle.* New York: Aronson, 1975.

Thornburg, H. D. (Ed.). *Contemporary adolescence: Readings.* Monterey, Calif.: Brooks/Cole, 1971.

Timiras, P. S. *Developmental physiology and aging.* New York: Macmillan, 1972.

Troll, L. Women at mid-life: Conditions for transition. *Generations*, 1979, **4**, 7-9.

Turkewitz, G., Birch, H. G., Moreau, T., Levy, L., & Cornwall, A. C. Effect of intensity of auditory stimulation on directional eye movements in the human neonate. *Animal Behavior*, 1966, **14**, 93-101.

Vaillant, G. *Adaptation to life.* Boston: Little, Brown, 1977.

Walford, R. L. *The immunologic theory of aging.* Baltimore: Williams & Wilkins, 1969.

Watson, J. S. Smiling, cooing, and "the game." *Merrill–Palmer Quarterly*, 1972, **18**, 323-339.

Wertheimer, M. Psychomotor coordination of auditory and visual space at birth. *Science*, 1961, **134**, 1962.

White, K. & Speisman, J. *Adolescence.* Monterey, Calif.: Brooks/Cole, 1977.

Williams, R. H., & Wirths, C. G. *Lives through the years.* New York: Atherton Press, 1965.

Youth: Transition to adulthood (Report of the Panel on Youth of the President's Science Advisory Committee). Chicago: University of Chicago Press, 1974.

Zusman, J. Some explanations of the changing appearance of psychotic patients: Antecedents of the social breakdown syndrome concept." *Millbank Memorial Fund Quarterly*, 1966, **44**, 363-394.

Chapter 4

The Family in Health and Illness

Basic to the understanding of a patient with chronic illness is an understanding of the family context within which the patient lives. Because the family is the individual's most important social unit, it constitutes the most important social context within which illness occurs and is resolved. It thus serves as a primary unit in health and illness (Litman, 1974 (a), p. 495). The family is involved in promoting everyday health behaviors, defining when a family member is sick and thus validating the sick role, and initiating medical care for the ill person (Pratt, 1973).

It is in the area of mental health and illness that the role of the family has been most widely researched (Jones, 1980). It is well documented that family attitudes and actions affect the timing of the initial identification of mental illness, the therapeutic process, the type and length of hospitalization, and the patient's placement in the community. This important effect of the family on the mental health of a member has resulted in a new treatment approach: Family therapy was founded in the early 1950s in recognition of the family's role in the health and illness of a psychiatric patient (Guerin, 1976). The conceptual focus on the family system as a whole instead of one member is the key element of this approach. An individual's symptoms are viewed as by-products of relationship struggles, and interventions are thus geared toward understanding individual behavior patterns that arise out of and feed back into the complicated matrix of the family system (Jones, 1980).

Although, as mentioned above, it has been most extensively studied in relation to mental illness, the role of the family is fundamental to the study and treatment of every type of illness, particularly chronic illness. The interrelationship between health and illness and the family is a highly dynamic one in which each may have a dramatic effect on the other (Litman, 1974, (a) p. 495). How a family member plays out the sick role and how the family reacts to him may influence not only the treatment process and the patient's recovery, but also the health and general functioning of the family (McEwan, 1972). As will become evident in this chapter, the family's response to illness is influenced by several factors. For example, the family's role as an *etiological factor* in chronic illness may be associated with the family's level of stress (Hill, 1958), which in turn is associated with the precipitation or exacerbation of a chronic illness. How a family *responds* to a chronic illness may be affected by the allocation of roles within the family or the extent of emotional support available, as well as by structural factors such as the family's financial status, ethnicity, or race.

The purpose of this chapter is to give the reader a basic theoretical and empirical view of the modern American family and its role in the health and illness behaviors of a family member. It would be impossible to review in detail all of the theories of the family that have been developed over the past 30 years. We thus first present an overview of theoretical alternatives by which to view the family and then present in greater detail the theoretical model of Bert Adams (1980). In the third section of the chapter we discuss conceptual and empirical writings associating the family with various aspects of health, illness, and sick role behaviors of family members. In the final section, we outline a family assessment guide, based on the theoretical model of Bert Adams, which incorporates the research findings presented in the third section of the chapter. This guide is meant to assist the clinician in assessing a family's vulnerability to a chronic illness as well as predicting the family's reaction to that illness.

FAMILY THEORIES: AN OVERVIEW

Since the early 1950s, family theorists have increasingly attempted to organize the accumulated conceptual knowledge of the family. They have continually refined existing theoretical writings to explain particular aspects of family organization and behavior. No one family theory, at this point can be put forth as being right or wrong; rather, each theoretical approach is a way of looking at and rationally explaining phenomena related to the family. The advantage of a theoretical understanding of the family for a clinician is that it allows the clinician to study and analyze family behavior in an organized and logical manner, to see family interactions as patterned, consistent, and predictable under certain conditions (Eshleman, 1974).

In the past 30 years there have been a considerable number of changes in the formulation of theoretical approaches to the family. The first attempt to organize these approaches in a meaningful manner was that of Hill, Katz, and Simpson (1957). After reviewing the current state of the field, Hill and his associates concluded that seven theoretical approaches to the family were being developed: institutional-historical, interactional role analysis, structural-functional, situational-psychological habitat, learning theory-maturational, household economics–home management, and family development or life cycle. Three years later, after a more systematic review, Hill and Hansen (1960) concluded that there were actually five major approaches to study of the family: interactional, structural–functional, situational, institutional, and developmental.

These two initial attempts at organization stimulated the publication of a large number of articles and books providing overviews of theoretical approaches to the family. For example, the five theoretical approaches were examined in the *Handbook of Marriage and the Family,* edited by Christensen (1964), and further delineated and expanded in *Emerging Conceptual Frameworks in Family Analysis,* by Nye and Berardo (1966). By 1971 it was generally recognized that, of the five frameworks, only the following three were theoretically viable (Broderick, 1971): structural–functional, interactional, and developmental.

A more recent organizational attempt is represented by the two-volume set of theoretical essays on the family entitled *Contemporary Theories about the Family* (Burr, Hill, Nye, & Reiss, (1979). In Volume I the authors discuss empirical research related to the family and change, family interaction, and family problems and, on the basis of this research, inductively develop several theoretical approaches. In Volume II these approaches are integrated into more theories in an attempt to place the family subfield into the mainstream of sociological theory.

It is now generally recognized (Adams, 1980; Broderick, 1971; Eshelman, 1974; Rodgers, 1973) that, reduced to the bare minimum, theoretical writings about the family may be subsumed under three frameworks; we briefly present an overview of these three.

Structural-Functional

The structural–functional framework defines the family as a social system. Family analysis using this approach consists of examining the family's relationships with other major social structures (institutions) such as medicine, religion, education, government, and the economy and, thus determining the family's place in the overall structure of society. Emphasis is placed on the functions performed by the family. For example, a great deal of family analysis using this approach has consisted of defining the universal, basic functions of the family and defining which societal functions are no longer performed by the family in the United States as a result of industrialization.

The individuals in the family and family units receive less attention in the structural–functional approach than in others. Although the family is considered to be composed of individuals, they are studied from their status-role vantage point. Both the individuals' functions in maintaining the family system and the family system's functions in maintaining the general social system are analyzed. Behavior is studied in the context of its contribution to the multilayered maintenance of the social system. The goal of the family theorist or researcher may be either to understand the social system or family system by studying the components of the respective systems, or to understand one or more systems in *relation* to the overall social system (Adams, 1980; Hill & Hansen, 1960; Nye & Berardo, 1966).

Research studies that utilize this approach characteristically view the family as being open to outside influences and transactions; yet, at the same time, the family system tends to maintain its boundaries. Individual family members contribute to this boundary maintenance either by acting in response to the demands of the system or by acting under the constraints of the family structure. In any case, the individual family member is viewed more as a *reactive* person fulfilling a status and role than as an active, action-initiating person. Similarly, the family is seen to be a passively adapting element of the system rather than as an agent of change. The starting point is stability of the general social system. In short, this framework tends to emphasize the static elements of societal structure and to neglect change and structural dynamics (Sprey, 1969).

Interactional

The general term "interactional approach" may be applied to several theoretical frameworks within which family behavior is examined in terms of individual analysis. In the interactional approach the family is considered to be a unity of interacting personalities, each occupying a position within the family to which a number of roles are assigned (Hill & Hansen, 1960). Thus, each individual perceives norms of role expectations for his behavior. In each situation, an individual defines the role expectations from two vantage points: that of the source or reference group and that of his own self-conception. He then acts out the role. Family analysis consists of examining overt inter-acts, or the playing out of interacting roles within the family.

In contrast to the emphasis of the structural–functional approach on a large-scale systems analysis, the emphasis of the interactional approach is on small-scale individualized analysis. Also in contrast to structural–functional theorists, interactional family theorists consider the family to be a completely closed unit that has little relation to outside institutions. They emphasize the internal aspects of the family, somewhat to the neglect of the family as an entity in relation to the community or collateral associations (Hill & Hansen, 1960).

To a great extent, research utilizing this framework has focused on role analysis. Such issues as interstatus relations and how these relations become the basis for authority patterns and action taking have been explored. Other areas of study have included communication processes, conflict, problem solving, and decision making within the family. Because of the small-scale unit of analysis, propositions developed out of this framework have been limited to statements about individual families or specified groups within a family. Institutional or cultural patterns of family analysis have not been considered.

Developmental

The developmental approach is the most recent of the three theoretical family frameworks. It is in many ways a compilation of several frameworks since it attempts to incorporate many of the compatible aspects of other frameworks into a unified theme. Although several presentations of the approach have been put forth (Hill & Rodgers, 1964; Rodgers, 1963), it is still being formulated to some extent.

Like the interactional approach, the developmental frameworks sees the family as consisting of a series of interacting personalities, intricately organized internally into paired positions such as husband–father, or son–brother. Norms prescribe appropriate role behavior for each of the positions and specify the manner in which reciprocal relations are to be maintained. A unique aspect of this approach is that role behaviors are analyzed over time; that is, changes in role behaviors are analyzed with the changing ages of the occupants of the positions. The intimate, small group called the family has a predictable natural history, which is designated by stages, beginning with the simple husband–wife pair. The group becomes more complex with the addition of each new family member. The group again becomes simple and less complex, however, as the younger generation leaves home to work or get married, and the group once again shrinks to the husband–wife pair. As the age of the members and composition of the family change, so do the quality and type of interaction. At each family life-cycle stage, there are developmental needs of the family that must be met and tasks that must be performed. Analysis of behavior in relation to these needs and tasks constitutes one level of family analysis.

The developmental approach outlines a number of well-defined stages of family life. Each stage has its own peculiar source of family conflict and solidarity. In an attempt to transcend the structural–functional (large-scale analysis) and interactional (small-scale analysis) frameworks, the developmental approach analyzes family behaviors along three dimensions of increasing complexity: the changing developmental tasks and role expectations of the children; the changing developmental tasks and role expectations of parents; and the changing developmental tasks of the family as a unit, which arise from cultural imperatives at various stages in the family life cycle. Thus, the developmental approach attempts to integrate the small- and large-scale analyses of the previous two approaches while viewing the family as an open system in relation to other configurations in society.

BERT ADAMS: THE MODERN AMERICAN FAMILY

Clearly, no one framework at this point has won all the prizes. The developmental approach is still in a stage of conceptualizaton and refinement. Although the structural–functional approach allows for comparisons between the family and other societal institutions, it provides only partial explanations regarding specific families at specific times. The interactional approach yields a great deal more information about family differences that exist within the larger society but reveals much less about the larger, institutional aspects of the family.

To understand the role of the family in relation to health, illness, and sick role behaviors, it is necessary to combine elements of each of the above described theoretical approaches. The family must be viewed in relation to other societal institutions such as the economy and medicine (structural–functional framework). The internal dynamics of the family must be examined to understand each member's interpretation of an illness and the consequent actions taken (interactional framework). Finally, the life-cycle stage of the family must be taken into account to understand the changing familial developmental tasks and role expectations in relation to health and illness (developmental framework). In the following pages, we present the theoretical family framework of Bert Adams (1980) since it incorporates each of these aspects. The structural–functional approach is evident in Adams's concepts of institutional and personal embeddedness. The interactional approach is evident in his discussion of parental roles, marital roles, and husband–wife issues. Finally, a developmental orientation is present in his account of family tasks and expectations at different developmental stages.

Adams (1980) outlines a five-continuum model for examining theoretically the modern American family. The continua are type of family formation, type of socialization, marital role structure, degree of institutional embeddedness, and degree of personnel embeddedness. The logical extremes of each continuum are illustrated in Figure 1.

Family Formation

One logical extreme of the family formation continuum is a society in which marital arrangements are made by the parents, and strong exogamous and incestuous prohibitions leave the individual only one category of persons to marry. At the other extreme is a society in which there are random liaisons between individuals and no prevailing legal marriage system. An example of restricted choice is the situation that existed in colonial America, in which individuals chose their own

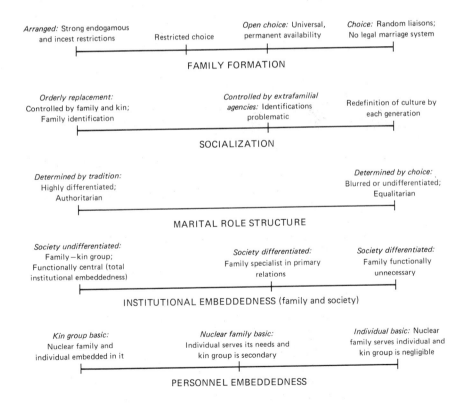

Figure 1. Five ideal, typical continua on which to locate family characteristics and changes. *Reprinted with permission from Adams (1980, p. 101)*

mates, but religious and racial status, residential immobility, or other restrictions severely limited the range of choice. Under conditions of open choice, or universal, permanent availability, anyone in society is potentially available to an individual for marriage. Permanent availability means that unsatisfactory relationships can be terminated and new ones begun at any time.

The position of the modern American family (Fig. 2) is midway between restricted choice and open choice (Adams, 1980; p. 247). The rationale here is that, although the formation of nuclear family units in the United States involves personal choice, romantic love, courtship, and the like, there remains a certain degree of restriction. Six important variables (Adams, 1980, p. 238) that limit mate selection in this country are social class, religious preference, age, education, race, and ethnicity. Depending on the *importance* of each variable to an individual, mate selection may be positively (encouraged) or negatively (discouraged) influenced. Figure 3 represents the various possibilities. Thus, if age and education are important variables to an individual and family, marriage to an individual of equal age and education is encouraged.

Socialization

The socialization continuum (Fig. 1) has, at one extreme, a society in which culture is redefined very little with each succeeding generation; there is, in other words, a high degee of socialization, or passing on of values and culture. The family controls the learning process so that the children's values are likely to be congruent with parental values. At the other extreme is a society in which each generation completely redefines the values; that is, socialization does not take place. A child may grow up to have health and illness values that are completely different from those of his parents. Somewhere in the middle is a society in which there is some definition of values but also some passing on of values to the next generation. The position of the modern

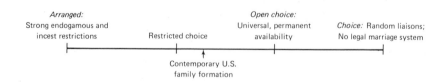

Figure 2. Mate selection or family formation in the contemporary United States in relation to the family formation continuum. *Reprinted with permission from Adams (1980, p. 247)*

Figure 3. Predictors of mate selection. *Adapted from Adams (1980, p.238)*

American family on the socialization continuum (Fig. 4) lies between orderly control by the family and extrafamilial agencies. For example, it is problematic, yet possible that a child will grow up to have health and illness values similar to those of his parents. To some extent, many socialization functions have been taken over by extrafamilial agencies such as schools and mass media (Adams, 1980, p. 199); yet these agencies are not so much in competition with the family as they are extensions of parental influence.

Marital Role Structure
The roles of individuals within the family may be determined by tradition so that a society includes only one definition of the role of wife or husband (Adams, 1980, p. 102). In this case an individual has no role definition options. In such a society the traditional definition of family roles includes a carefully worked out division of labor and an authoritarian (usually patriarchal) control of resources and decisions. At the opposite extreme is a society in which the definition of husband or wife is determined completely by choices. The choices are such that the members of the family unit may share equally in decision making and control of resources if they wish. Tradition dictates no predetermined division of labor. According to Adams (1980, p. 297), the modern American family has two positions along the continuum, depending on social class (Fig. 5). In working-class marriages, roles and division of labor are more likely to be determined by tradition whereas, in middle-class marriages, roles are more likely to be determined by choice. The

Figure 4. Approximate location of socialization in the contemporary United States on the socialization continuum. *Reprinted with permission from Adams (1980, p. 199)*

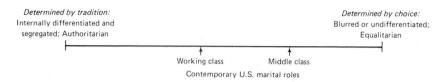

Figure 5. Marital roles in the contemporary United States in relation to the marital role continuum. *Adapted from Adams (1980, p. 297)*

increase in dual-career families in both the working and middle classes has stimulated a more equalitarian form of marital role relationships in some families. In these families, the husband and wife share equally in economic support of the family, in housework, and in making decisions, including those regarding the health and illness of themselves and their children.

Institutional Embeddedness

Institutional embeddedness describes the extent to which other institutions in a society are "embedded" in or undifferentiated from the kinship system—thus the extent to which political, religious, medical, and economic institutional activities are embedded within the family. The head of the family line may also be the political ruler, the performer of religious ritual, the primary educator, and the doctor. A second form of institutional embeddedness is present if a "nuclear unit" (a set of parents and their children) is the seat of multiple societal activities but is emancipated from the larger kin group.

At one extreme there is no differentiation between the family group and the other institutions of society, and at the other extreme family functioning and the functioning of other societal institutions are mutually independent. According to Adams (1980, p. 419) (Fig. 6), the modern American family falls midway between the two extremes. Other institutions have to a great extent become differentiated from the nuclear family and kinship group. However, the family still special-

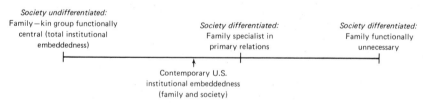

Figure 6. Tentative location of the contemporary United States family on the institutional embeddedness continuum. *Reprinted with permission from Adams (1980, p. 419)*

izes in primary relations, socialization, economic consumption, recreation, religion, and some aspects of medical care.

Personnel Embeddedness

There are two stages, or types, of personnel embeddedness. Each type has an interactional and value element (Adams, 1980, p. 103). Kin group embeddedness means that the kin group is the primary milieu for social interaction and is valued more highly than either the nuclear family or the individual. The nuclear family unit has little independence from its kin group; kin group solidarity is considered to be more important than nuclear family solidarity. Both the individual and his nuclear family function within and close to the overall kinship structure. In a second form of personnel embeddedness, the kin group as a whole is weak but the individual is still expected to function primarily within and serve the needs of the nuclear family. Thus, there is a closely knit nuclear family, which is seen as a unit rather than a group of individuals. At the pole opposite to personnel embeddedness is the situation in which the family is viewed as serving the needs of the individual. Concern is with each member's individual welfare, and both family and kin interactions are less important than activities outside the family; there is a high degree of individualism and independence. The major question raised by a high degree of personnel embeddedness is, "How can I be successful so as to bring honor to my family?" The major question raised by a low degree of personnel embeddedness, or individualism, is, "How can the family help the individual?"

It is generally acknowledged that contemporary U.S. culture is characterized by individual dominance rather than kin group dominance, as shown in Figure 7. Individual dominance in the United States is a result of the separation of several societal institutions from the family. For example, in a society in which there is no separate medical institution so that all medical care takes place within the family or kin group, all illness and sick role behavior will take place within the nuclear family or kin group structure. However, when medi-

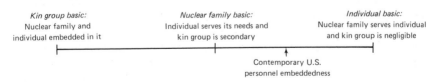

Figure 7. Tentative location of the contemporary United States family on the personnel embeddedness continuum. *Reprinted with permission from Adams (1980, p. 419)*

cine is separate from the family so that one goes to a physician for treatment, less responsibility is allotted to, and interactional time spent within, the family structure.

Mate choices in the United States are based primarily on personal desires but are somewhat restricted by values considered important by the family such as religion or race. Socialization is influenced by both the family and other societal institutions. However, the influence of the parents in passing on cultural values is substantial. There is a modified marital role choice in which certain options are available to both sexes. These options are restricted by tradition, however, so that the economic–family division of labor by sex is still quite operative in the working-class family and subtly operative in the middle-class family. Extrafamilial institutions have become highly differentiated from the kin group and nuclear family, so that the family is not very institutionally embedded within society. Nuclear family personnel embeddedness is also fairly low within society, so that individual dominance rather than kin group dominance prevails.

THE FAMILY'S ROLE IN HEALTH AND ILLNESS

In Chapter 1 we discussed the differences between the concepts of disease, illness, and sickness. Disease refers to a biological status, illness is the individual's perception of that biological status, and sickness refers to the social phenomenon of interpretation of the person's illness by other people. In Chapter 1 we also discussed the behaviors associated with health and illness. Health behaviors are those performed by a person believing himself to be healthy for the purpose of preventing disease (Kasl & Cobb, 1966, p. 246). Illness behaviors are those performed by a person who believes himself to be ill for the purpose of defining his state and finding a remedy. Sick role behaviors are those performed a person who consider himself ill for the purpose of getting well. In a variety of ways, the family is integrally involved in promoting health, illness, and sick role behaviors. In the following pages we present an overview of the interrelationship of family variables and the health, illness, and sick role behaviors of family members. Specifically, we discuss the family as a causative agent in a family member's illness, the family and illness behaviors, the family and sick role behaviors, and the impact of illness on the family as a unit.

The Family as a Causative Agent in Illness

The family unit may be considered an agent in producing illness in several ways. The family may transmit illness through a hereditary link or through the spread of infectious diseases (Litman, 1974 (a),

p. 499). In a less direct manner, the family is a causative agent when a family crisis precipitates an illness.

It is well documented (Litman, 1974 (a), p. 499) that the family is a vehicle for the direct transmission of hereditary diseases. In addition to being a genetic link, the family is a vehicle for the contracting of infectious diseases. The spread of infectious diseases occurs more easily within the family than within any other social group (Haggerty & Alpert, 1963). The family is also an indirect source of illness. For example, the physical or mental condition of one family member affects the health of other members (Jones, 1980). A common crisis, such as the death of a grandparent, a move, or the loss of a parent's job, can produce, for example, a streptococcal infection by lowering one's resistance to infection (Haggerty, 1968). Finally, as mentioned earlier, the role of the family is important in the mental health and mental illness of each family member (Jones, 1980; Litman, 1974 (b)).

The Family and Illness Behaviors

Throughout this text "illness" has denoted a person's *perception* of his health status; illness behaviors are geared to define the status and seek a remedy for the illness. The family is involved in illness behaviors in a variety of ways; it influences how a family member learns to define illness, decides when medical care should be sought and where or how, and takes part in the treatment of the disease. Thus, a major consideration in the treatment of an individual is the degree of congruence between the goals of treatment and the goals of the family. Research has shown that some families are uncooperative and the therapeutic regimen prescribed ineffective because treatment is incongruent with the family functions, values, and habits (Mabry, 1964).

It is within the family that a person learns to define health and illness and what to do about each condition (Mechanic, 1978). The most important figure in the development of these definitions is the wife-mother (Litman, 1974(a)). For example, it has been shown that the mother has the most powerful influence on the children's attitudes toward health and illness and food habits. Overall, whatever type of measure used, the wife-mother remains the central agent in defining illness and deciding the type of cure and care to be used in the family (Litman, 1971).

Closely linked to the family's role in defining illness is the family's role in deciding whether to seek professional care for the illness. Earlier we saw that the lay referral system is instrumental in the decision to seek out some form of professional assistance. Research has shown that this lay referral system consists largely of family members (Freidson, 1961). It is not surprising that the most important family member is the wife-mother (Litman, 1971). One study showed that the decision to seek professional help rested with the mother 64.7 percent of the time (Litman, 1971). If an ill person decides to seek professional care, he most often (88 percent of the time) discusses the symptoms with at least one other person, most often the spouse (45.7 percent) before he is examined by a professional practitioner (Miller, 1973). However, there are social class differences; upper- and middle-class family members, regardless of sex, are more likely to discuss symptoms with their spouse than are their working-class counterparts.

Research evidence increasingly supports the finding that the family plays an important role in determining the family's use of health care services (McKinlay, 1972). Such factors as family size, composition, income, age, and health beliefs may predispose some to use more health care services than others (Aday & Eichhorn, 1973; Anderson, 1968). Family size, in particular, has been shown to be a useful indicator of utilization (Anderson & Kasper, 1973). Most frequently it is found that the larger the family, the fewer services are used. Another important indicator is the stage in the family's development cycle (McEwan, 1972). Prechild families that are characterized by small size and young, healthy adult members use fewer services than families in their reproductive years. Later, as the size of the family begins to decline, there is a parallel reduction in the amount of professional services used.

In the previous section we emphasized that an important aspect of the family is the extent to which it is institutionally embedded in society, that is, the extent to which family functions are differentiated from societal functions. Although it is generally maintained that the family's role in the care of illness has become differentiated from that of the medical care system (Adams, 1980; Parsons & Fox, 1952), some aspects of care are not differentiated (Litman, 1974 (a), p. 504). For example, it appears that American families maintain a fairly large inventory of drugs and medications to use for home treatment (Roney & Nall, 1966). The number of such medications, furthermore, is greater for each succeeding generation in the case of allergy medications, cold pills, salves and ointments, pain relievers, tranquilizers, and sleeping pills. Only in the case of cardiovascular drugs has there been a decline in the use of home remedies.

The Family and Sick Role Behaviors

The concept of sickness involves an interactional phenomenon in which an ill person's status is interpreted by others. Sick role behaviors, on the other hand, are geared toward alleviation of the illness or getting well. As was apparent in Chapter 1, sick role performance not only is a function of the physical fact of disease, but is largely influenced by a person's perception of the disease (illness) and the support or lack of support received from the person's significant others (sickness). It is not surprising that the mother finds it difficult to accept the sick role (Mechanic, 1964). She also finds it difficult to fulfill her normal role obligations when one or more family members are ill (McNamara, 1967). It has been found consistently that mothers are more likely to seek medical care for their children than they are for themselves. The mother-wife also plays an important role in legitimizing the sick role for her husband (Mechanic, 1978). With the wife's support, the husband will more readily accept the sick role.

Other important variables that influence whether a family member will accept the sick role are family size and social class. It has been found (Petroni, 1969) that, although neither family size nor social class alone influences sick role performance, jointly the two have a definite effect. Thus, lower-class people from large families are less likely to consider themselves ill and to seek medical care than lower-class people from small families. Sick role behavior in middle-class families is not dependent on family size.

The manner in which the sick role is carried out in the modern American family is closely linked to the extent to which an individual is personally embedded within the family. The extent to which the modern American family is an isolated, nuclear unit (personnel embeddedness) with few children and physically and functionally isolated from kin has been a point of controversy for several years (Adams, 1980; Litwak, 1960). We saw earlier that the American family is isolated to a great extent (Adams, 1980); however, it is also well documented that the family structure frequently consists of bilateral kinship lines that might encompass several generations (Sussman, 1968). The implication of this personnel embeddedness in the study of sick role behaviors is that kin relations comprise the major form of help in times of sickness (Sussman, 1959, 1967, 1968). It was found, for example, that the major form of assistance during illness was provided by members of kin-related families. In 92 percent of the illnesses reported, there was some form of family member assistance.

The extent to which the family is institutionally embedded within the larger society also influences the manner in which the sick role is performed within the family. It was stated in a classic formulation some 30 years ago (Parsons & Fox, 1952) that the modern American family no longer carried out the sick role functions of the family. Rather, the family relied completely on the health care (extrafamilial) institutions within society. In support of this (Litman, 1971), nearly half (43.2 percent) of the families questioned in one comprehensive study indicated, regardless of generation, that they would find it difficult to care for a sick member at home for a prolonged period of time. Over half of the sample (58.6 percent) indicated a willingness to give up responsibility for the care of a sick member to the hospital, stating that the care would be better there. However, there was also some ambivalence about the family's responsibility in the care of a sick member. Thus, although there was a large extent of agreement (80.2 percent) that the sick member would convalesce better at home, almost one-third (31.8 percent) of the families said they would be unable to care for a sick person at home under any circumstances.

Other research shows that the modern American family has not completely given up the care of its sick members. For example, it was found (Peterson, 1972) that although, most families are willing to relinquish the care of a family member to the hospital, many families are willing to care for the sick member if he is not sick enough to be hospitalized. It is important to remember that such nonhospitalized care accounts for the major proportion of a sickness episode.

The Family as Dependent Variable:
The Case of Chronic Illness

To consider the family as a dependent variable is to determine the effect of an illness on the family as a unit. Hill (1958) suggested that, in a period of crisis such as that caused by an illness, the family's structure is modified as the family member's capacity to perform his usual role within the family is reduced. Thus, the family may enter a state of disequilibrium in which a readjustment of power and role relationships takes place while a new equilibrium is being established. The length of time needed to establish the new equilibrium depends on several variables such as the type of crisis, the member's definition of the crisis, and the resources available to the family for dealing with the crisis.

A family member's illness may affect the family in many ways. An increase in role tensions (Klein & Bogdonoff, 1968), as well as somatic symptoms among family members, has been reported. Mental retardation in a child resulted in a reduction of family prestige (Farber, 1959, 1960; Farber & Ryckman, 1965), and hemophilia in a child resulted in tensions related to less social mobility (Salk, Hilgartner, & Granich, 1972). The family adjusts to a child's chronic illness in the same manner in which it adjusts to other stresses (Cohen, 1962).

A second important variable is the nature of the illness itself. The more prolonged and complicated the illness, the more likely it is to upset family members' role relationships. A chronic illness, therefore, is more detrimental to family functioning than is a short-term, acute illness (Litman, 1971).

In any analysis of the family's role in chronic illness, an interactional view must be taken. That is, the illness has an impact on the family, which in turn affects the sick role behaviors of the chronically ill member. For example, the impact on family functioning will affect the ill member's role allocation within the family and the manner in which he is rehabilitated within the family. The patient's ability to reassume his preillness responsibilities within the family are a function of his "centrality" to the family unit (Litman, 1971). Important variables to consider here are the perceived disruption within the family, the availability of another person to assume the sick person's responsibilities, and the extra burdens placed on the family by the illness. If a high degree of role reversal is established and the ill person assumes no responsibilities for household tasks, he is less likely to rehabilitate successfully (Deutsch & Goldston, 1960).

Summary
In the first section of this chapter we examined four major approaches to family theory. The structural functional approach defines the family as a social system. Theorists using this framework are concerned with the family and its relation to other social structures such as educational, religious, or economic systems. Little attention is given to individuals within the family. The interactional theory approaches the family as a unit of interacting individuals, each with particular role responsibilities. The developmental approach also defines the family in terms of interacting persons. The developmental approach, however, focuses on the interactional changes between family members over time. Roles are assessed as the family evolves: the husband-wife pair; the addition of new family members; and the husband-wife pair as grown children leave home. The Bert Adams family framework, the fourth approach, is a synthesis of the structural functional, interactional, and developmental theories of family. The assessment guide, which follows, is organized around the five perspectives of the family developed by Adams.

In the latter part of this chapter, the family was analyzed in terms of its role in regard to health and illness. We considered the family as an agent in producing illness, illness behavior, and sick role behavior. Finally we considered the impact of illness, chronic illness in particular, on the family.

FAMILY ASSESSMENT GUIDE

  I. Family formation
    A. Family formation and composition
       1. At what stage in the family life cycle is the family?
       2. What is the family's composition?
       3. What is the family's social class, and how is this related to the family's health care status?

    4. What is the family's religious orientation? How actively involved is the family in organized religion?

    5. What is the family's ethnicity and cultural heritage? To what extent have ethnicity and cultural heritage been maintained? How does this relate to health status?

  B. Developmental history

    1. What is the developmental history of the family, and how is it related to family health and illness values?

    2. To what extent has the family been crisis-prone in the past?

    3. Have there been any recent crises? How have they affected the family?

    4. What current stresses is the family reacting to?

II. Socialization

  A. Role models

    1. To what extent are cultural values carried on to each succeeding generation?

    2. Who are the role models for each family member? To what extent are the role models appropriate?

  B. Family attitudes toward health and illness

    1. What are the family's definitions of health and illness?

      a. What are the family's own health care practices?

      b. What are the family's medically based preventive measures to retain a healthy status?

    2. For what kinds of illness does the family consider professional care necessary?

      a. Does the family have a family physician?

      b. Does the family perceive professional health care services to be valuable?

      c. Does the family comply with professional health care regimens?

    3. What are the family's drug habits? use of alcohol? dietary habits? hygiene and cleanliness? exercise? recreation values?

  C. What are the family's child-rearing practices?

    1. Who assumes responsibility for child care?

    2. How are the children regarded in the family?

    3. How is the children's health regarded in the family?

III. Marital and family role structure

  A. Family role structure

    1. To what extent are the husband–wife roles traditional or modern?

    2. What role does each family member fulfill, and how important is each role for family functioning?

      3. Are family roles congruent with overall family expectations?

      4. Are family roles competently carried out?

      5. How flexible are family roles?

      6. How are decisions made within the family?

      7. Who holds the power position within the family?

B. Economic structure

      1. Who is the economic provider in the family? How are decisions made regarding spending within the family?

      2. Does the family receive any supplementary income?

      3. What is the family's status regarding health care insurance?

C. Health and illness

      1. Who is the primary person in the making of health care decisions?

      2. Who takes on the therapeutic role in times of illness within the family?

      3. What is the wife-mother's role within the family in relation to health and illness?

      4. Have the family roles changed in the past because of family illness?

IV. Institutional embeddedness

A. Health care services

      1. How does the family view the health care system?

      2. To what extent does the family use health care services?

      3. How accessible are health care services to the family?

      4. Is the family aware of health care services relative to its needs?

      5. What health care services have the family received in the past?

      6. What is the family's opinion regarding health care services received in the past?

B. Home care of sick family members

      1. To what extent does the family consider it to be its responsibility to care for ill family members at home?

      2. What types of home remedies are used?

      3. Have sick family members been taken care of in the home in the past?

      4. What types of medications are taken by each family member? Which of these medications are prescribed by a physician and which are self-prescribed remedies?

C. Comunity resources

      1. How does the family view community resources?

      2. To what extent does the family use community resources?

    3. How accessible are community resources to the family?
    4. Is the family aware of community resources relative to its needs?
    5. What social support systems does the family have within the larger community?

V. Personnel embeddedness
  A. Individual versus kinship emphasis
    1. What is the emphasis in the family on individual versus overall family needs?
    2. Tow what extent do family members perceive the needs of other family members?
    3. Are each family member's needs respected by other family members?
  B. Closeness of family relationships
    1. How close are family ties between family members?
    2. To what extent do family members depend on each other for support in times of crisis?
    3. What are the communication patterns between family members?

REFERENCES

Adams, B. *The Family: A Sociological interpretation* (3rd ed.). Boston: Houghton Mifflin, 1980.

Aday, L, Eichhorn, R. C. *The utilization of health services: Indices and correlates—A research bibliography, 1972* [DHEW Publication No. (HSM) 73-3003]. Washington, D.C.: U.S. Government Printing Office, Washington, 1973.

Anderson, R. A. *A behavioral model of families' use of health services research* (Series No. 25). Chicago: University of Chicago Center for Health Administration Studies, 1968.

Anderson, R., Kasper, J. D. The structural influence of family size on children's use of physician services. *Journal of Comparative Family Studies* 1973, 4, 116–130.

Broderick, C. B. Beyond the five conceptual frameworks: A decade of development in family theory. *Journal of Marriage and the Family,* 1971, **33**, 139–159.

Burr, W. R., Hill, R., Nye, F., & Reiss, I. L. *Contemporary theories about the family* (2 vol.) New York: Free Press, 1979.

Christensen, H. (Ed.). *Handbook of marriage and the family.* Chicago: Rand McNally, 1964.

Cohen, P. C. The impact of the handicapped child on its family. *Social Casework,* 1962, 43, 137–142.

Deutsch, C. P., Goldston, J. A. Family factors in home adjustment of the severely disabled. *Marriage and Family Living*, 1960, 122, 312–316.

Eshleman, J. R. *The family: An introduction.* Boston: Allyn & Bacon, 1974.

Farber, B. Effects of a severely mentally retarded child on family integration. *Social Research and Child Development*, 1959, 24(2, Serial No. 71).

Farber, B. Family organization and crisis: Maintenance of integration in familes with a severely retarded child. *Social Research and Child Development*, 1960, 25(1, Serial No. 75).

Farber, B., & Ryckman, D. B. Effects of severely mentally retarded children on family relationships. *Mental Retardation Abstract*, 1965, 2, 1.

Freidson, E. *Patient's view of of medical practice.* New York: Russell Sage, 1961.

Guerin, P. *Family therapy.* New York: Gardner, 1976.

Haggerty, R. J. Family crises: The role of the family in health and illness. In R. J. Haggerty, & Green (Eds.), *Ambulatory pediatrics.* Philadephia: Saunders, 1968.

Haggerty, R. J., & Alpert, J. J. The child, his family and illness. *Postgraduate Medicine*, 1963, 34, 228–235.

Hill, R. Social stressses on the family. *Social Casework*, 1958, 39, 139–158.

Hill, R. & Hansen, D. The identification of conceptual frameworks utilized in family studies. *Marriage and Family Living*, 1960, 22, 299-311.

Hill, R., & Rodgers, R. The developmental approach. In H. T. Christensen (Ed.), *The handbook of marriage and the family.* Chicago: Rand McNally, 1964.

Hill, R., Katz, A. M., & Simpson, R. L. An inventory of research in marriage and family behavior: A statement of objectives and progress. *Marriage and Family Living*, 1957, 19, 89–92.

Jones, S. *Family therapy: A comparison of approaches.* Bowie, Md.: Brady, 1980.

Kasl, S., & Cobb, S. Health behavior, illness behavior, and sick role behavior. *Archives of Environmental Health*, 1966, 12, 246–266; 531–541.

Klein, R., Dean, A., & Bogdonoff, M. The impact of illness upon the spouse. *Journal of Chronic Disability*, 1968, 20, 241–250.

Litman, T. J. *Health care and the family: A three generational study* (an exploratory study conducted under Grant No. CH00167-02 from the Division of Community Health Services and Medical Care Administration, Bureau of Health Services, United States Public Health Service), 1971.

Litman, T. J. The family as a basic unit in health and medical care: A social-behavioral overview. *Social Science and Medicine*, 1974, 8, 495–519. (a)

Litman, T. J. *The sociology of medicine and health care—The first fifty years: A bibliography* (chaps. 6 & 7). San Francisco: Glendessary Press, 1974. (b)

Litwak, E. Geographical mobility and extended family cohension. *American Sociological Review*, 1960, 25, 385–395.

Mabry, J. H. Medicine and the family. *Journal of Marriage and the Family,* 1964, **26**, 161–165.

McEwan, P. *The social approach.* Working paper prepared for the World Health Organization Consultation on the Statistical Aspects of the Family as a Unit in Health Studies (DSI/72-6, App. 3). Geneva: World Health Organization, 1972.

McKinlay, J. B. Some approaches and problems in the study of the use of services: An overview. *Journal of Health and Social Behavior,* 1972, **13**, 115–152.

McNamara, M. Psycho-social problems in a renal unit. *British Journal of Psychiatry,* 1967, **131**, 1231–1238.

Mechanic, D. Influence of mothers on their children's health attitudes and behavior. *Pediatrics,* 1964, **33**, 445–453.

Mechanic, D. *Medical sociology* (2nd ed.). New York: Free Press, 1978.

Miller, M. H. Seeking advice for cancer symptoms. *American Journal of Public Health,* 1973, **63**, 956–965.

Nye, F. I., & Berardo, F. M. *Emerging conceptual frameworks in family analysis.* New York: Macmillan, 1966.

Parsons, T., & Fox, R. Illness, therapy and the modern ubran American family. *Journal of Social Issues,* 1952, **8**, 31–44.

Peterson, E. T. The impact of adolescent illness on parental relationships. *Journal of Health and Social Behavior,* 1972, **13**, 429–437.

Petroni, F. A. Social class, family size and the sick role. *Journal of Marriage and the Family,* 1969, **31**, 728–735.

Pratt, L. The significance of the family in medication. *Journal of Comparative Family Studies,* 1973, **4**, 13–35.

Rodgers, R. H. *Family interaction and transaction: The developmental approach.* Englewood Cliffs, N.J.: Prentice-Hall, 1973.

Roney, J. G., & Nall, M. O. *Medication practices in a community: An exploratory study.* Palo Alto, Calif.: Stanford Research Institute, 1966.

Salk, L., Hilgartner, M., & Granich, B. The psychosocial impact of hemophilia on the patient and his family. *Social Science and Medicine,* 1972, **6**, 491–505.

Sprey, J. The family as a system in conflict. *Journal of Marriage and the Family,* 1969, **31** 699–706.

Sussman, M. B. The isolated and nuclear family: Fact or fiction. *Social Problems,* 1959, **6**, 333–339.

Sussman, M. B. *Intergenerational ties in Finnish urban families.* Paper presented at the 62nd Annual Meeting of the American Sociological Association, San Francisco, August 1967.

Sussman, M. B. (Ed.). *Sourcebook in marriage and the family.* Boston: Houghton Mifflin, 1968.

Part 2

Fundamental Concepts
in Chronic Illness

Chapter 5

Career

The term "career" has been traditionally reserved for an individual's long-term involvement and advancement in a respectable profession. In a broader sense, however, the term may be applied to any social strand of any person's passage through life. The concept of career is uniquely suited to the task of describing the subjective and objective experiences of chronic illness. Such a description is the focus of this chapter. We first discuss the concept of career and the related concept of time from a theorectical viewpoint, using the outline of Lyman and Scott (1970) and adding selected concepts from Roth's (1963) theoretical and empirical writings on patients with tuberculosis. We then discuss various applications of the concept to the study of chronic illness. Specifically, we examine research on patients with polio, nursing home patients, and mental patients. In the third section of the chapter we present two case studies in which we analyze a chronic illness from a career standpoint. The first is the case of transsexual adolescent; the second is the case of a middle-aged man with a myocardial infarction.

CAREER AND TIME: A THEORETICAL POINT OF VIEW

Structure reduces anxiety. Because of this, people are constantly trying to structure events, especially those that are uncertain or ambiguous. One way to structure uncertainty is to structure the time periods in which uncertain events occur. To do this, one uses personal experiences as well as information derived from other people in similar situations. Suchman (1965) refers to this phenomenon as the "lay referral system." An important result of group comparisons is that group norms develop regarding the timing of certain events. When many people go through the same series of events, the phenomenon is termed a "career" and the sequence of timing of the events is called the "career timetable" (Roth, 1963, p. 93).

Lyman and Scott (1970) speak of "time tracks" in much the same way that Roth speaks of the career timetable. Time tracks are the time periods used by individuals or groups to designate the beginning or the termination of events. A person's life span is the most culturally universal example of a time track, in which the periods of life are benchmarked by childhood, adolescence, adulthood, and old age. Time tracks can also delineate periods in history that are characterized by social events, types of activity, or a dominant thought. We refer to such time periods as the Tragic Era, the Jazz Age, the Great Depression, and the Roaring Twenties (Sorokin and Merton, 1937). Similarly, we indicate durations of time by such expressions as "for a semester" or "for a Christmas season." This reference to time indicates its importance as a *social* phenomenon rather than an astronomical phenomenon (Moore, 1963). Two days during a Christmas vacation are experienced quite differently from two days during a regular work period, even though both time periods consist of 48 hours.

One way to study how people experience time is to examine how they construct the "out there," that is, to examine the way in which they structure time periods in which uncertain events occur. The studies of Roth (1963) and Lyman and Scott (1970) are two notable examples of such analyses. Roth, in a study of patients with tuberculosis, found that people involved in a career try to define when certain salient things will happen to them. By pooling their observations in an unsystematic way, career participants develop time norms against which to measure their individual progress. The benchmarks of this timetable are the significant events that occur in an average career. Both tubercular patients and their health care personnel are career participants, and the norms of these two groups are sometimes different since their criteria for progress and their ideas of proper timing are different (Roth, 1963, p. 107). Bargaining occurs when the patient tries to bring the authority judgment figure into line with his own more optimistic view of his status on the timetable.

Lyman and Scott (1970) outline the analystical features of a career through the concepts of time track and time-track movement. In the following pages, we use their analytical constructions to organize our theoretical discussion of career timetables. Within this organization, we also discuss the concepts of Roth (1963).

Humanistic-Fatalistic Dimension

The first pair of concepts that denote events and their passage along a career or time track are embodied in the humanistic–fatalistic dimension (Lyman & Scott, 1970, p. 191). A humanistic career is one in which a person believes that events are being governed by his personal decisions. He feels in control of himself and the world around him. He enters into events with a sense of mastery. A fatalistic career, on the other hand, is one in which everyday activities are a matter of obligation, are outside one's control, and are vehicles of conformity rather than personal expression.

A person whose career is fatalistic experiences the inconvenience of time; he feels himself to be a slave to an activity and uses such terms as "rat race" and "treadmill" to describe his occupation or state of life. Lyman and Scott (1970) point out that not all social groups are equally vulnerable to a fatalistic career since their different social statuses result in a different degree of access to social power and social freedom. The urban poor and minorities are examples of social groups with greater vulnerability to a fatalistic career occupationally. In a less direct way they are also more vulnerable to a fatalistic career of chronic illness since social class and race are associated with various states of health and illness (Hollingshead & Redlich, 1958).

Several responses to the awareness that one is living out a fatalistic career have been observed; Lyman and Scott (1970, p. 192) believe that people frequently respond by trying to experience some control over and freedom from everyday events. Thus, a prison inmate may challenge the powerful staff to a fight in order to gain control. A wife who feels trapped in her marriage may have an affair to free herself. Another woman may seek employment at a midlife crisis.

Roth (1963) emphasizes that an integral aspect of *any* response to a fatalistic career is one's attempt to assess how long the inconvenience of time will last. One makes this assessment by comparing oneself with others in a similar situation. An important subjective aspect of this comparison is the process of choosing the person with whom one compares oneself. Thus, a tubercular patient develops norms not only for the entire group of hospitalized patients, but also for subgroups. He divides the patient groups into categories according to his predictions about their course of illness and treatment. He can then identify himself with anyone in any of the categories. The result is a subjectively more precise notion of what might happen to him in the course of his fatalistic career and how long the inconvenience of time will last; in short, he feels more in control of his fate.

Continuous-Episodic Dimension

The continuous–episodic dimension of a career refers to the fact that the length of time involved in the career is inversely proportional to the pace of behavior associated with it. In occupational careers that involve a long-term accumulation of skills and honors, there is a slow but steady build-up of confidence and prestige. By contrast, episodes are characterized by an intensity of activity and more frantic behavior. An example of this dimension is the love affair versus marriage (Lyman & Scott, 1970). It is easier to be a lover than a husband or wife since it is more difficult to show intelligence every day than to make pretty speeches from time to time. Simmel (1959, p. 252) states that love has two standards of time: the moment of passion and the eternal element, which cannot pass. The erotic moment has a definite beginning and end in a single time period. Marriage, however, has a more careerlike duration.

Chronic illness represents a fatalistic and continuous career. An interesting aspect of the chronic illness experience, however, is that patients cannot conceptualize the entire career as a total unit (Roth, 1963). Instead, they break the career into smaller episodes, which are experientially manageable; this gives them more control over their situation by providing greater structure to their lives. A patient with tuberculosis does not think of his hospitalization as a totality but rather focuses on the time that will be spent on a certain unit. He divides the period of hospitalization into the time before surgery and the time after surgery, the time spent at each level of graded exercises, or the time spent at each level of increasing privileges. The thought of managing a fatalistic career until promotion to the next level of activities is easier than the thought of managing a fatalistic career until discharge from the hospital.

Pace and Sequence

All careers are governed by norms of pace and sequence. Pace norms govern the rate at which social interactions take place, whereas sequence norms govern the sequence of events around which the interactions happen. For example, there are norms that govern the pace and sequence of events in a courtship and there are norms that govern the pace and sequence of events in race and ethnic relations. Two people are not expected to marry until they have known each other for a certain amount of time; and the second generation of every immigrant group is expected to do better than the parent generation.

The pace and sequence of a tubercular patient's career are governed by the hospital personnel and hospital regulations. Consequently, the only control the patients has consists of determining the normal sequence of events along the career and identifying the appropriate benchmarks against which he can compare his progress. The ultimate focus of the timetable career is discharge from the hospital; as mentioned earlier, however, to make the fatalistic career manageable, other events along the way are measured.

The benchmarks in the career of a hospitalized tubercular patient consist of a series of restrictions and privileges. How soon after admission (or some other reference point) is the patient allowed to go to the bathroom or to the dayroom? When is he allowed to go outside for walks? Such privileges are important and desired not merely for the sake of the activities themselves; they also have symbolic value for they indicate that one's treatment is progressing and that one is closer to discharge.

In her very early writings about the experience of being a tubercular patient, Betty MacDonald (1948, p. 142) showed how a particular sequence of events outlined a patient's career:

> The only way we could tell whether we were getting well or dying was by the privileges we were granted. If we were progressing satisfactorily at the end of one month we were given the bathroom privilege and 15 minutes of reading-and-writing time. . . . At the end of three months we were given a chest examination, along with other tests, and if all was still well we were given three hours' time up, one hour occupational therapy time and could go to the movies.

One of the ways in which a patient attempts to control the pacing of events is to take privileges surreptitiously before they are officially granted. For example, a patient will increase his own "up time" or reading time. However, he still looks forward to being granted these privileges officially because they lend validity to his belief that he is making progress. A patient with two hours of "up time" may actually be spending eight hours each day out of bed. At the same time he may be pressuring the physician to give him four hours of "up time."

A second means of gaining control over the pacing of career events is bargaining. When the respective opinions of the patient and hospital personnel are not in agreement, the patient tries to bring the judgment of the hospital personnel into line with his more optimistic view of the pace and sequence of events leading to discharge. Physicians regard bargaining as unpleasant and occasionally become angry with patients. The fact remains, however, that patients who exert this pressure are often successful in that they obtain the desired results sooner than they would had if they simply waited (Roth, 1963, p. 49). Physicians vary widely in their submission to patient pressure; the job of the patient is to find the physician's breaking point or weak spots.

Another important concept is that of career failure, which applies to individuals who do not successfully keep pace with others on the career timetable (Roth, 1963, pp. 105–107). A tubercular patient whose career exceeds the expected timetable is considered a failure since his progress is judged in terms of the common timetable. He is considered unlucky rather than unsuccessful, however, since he has less control over the situation than someone in an occupational situation. Nonetheless, the feeling that he is far behind schedule is the same. The reaction of tubercular patients to failure vary greatly. Some regard a few days' delay as a tragedy, whereas others consider a few months' delay unimportant. Each individual, however, talks in terms of the career timetable and considers his own position against this norm. Such phrases as "I should have received surgery earlier," or "I am supposed to have bathroom privileges by this time" are indicative of the patient's attempt to keep pace with the general timetable (Roth, 1963).

Determinateness-Indeterminateness Dimension

The degree of determinateness of a career indicates the degree of specificity. Some careers, such as a jail sentence or a college course, are very specific. A particular length of time is specified, and a person can plan with a high degree of accuracy how long the activity will take and what it will consist of. There is a definite beginning and end, both of which are clearly visible. There are also definite benchmarks along the way to indicate how far someone has come and how far he has to go.

The determinateness–indeterminateness dimension of career analysis has heuristic value for the study of chronic illness since this fatalistic career is often indeterminate in nature. Although a chronically ill person has benchmarks against which to compare his progress, they are rarely precise. Roth (1963) found that a tubercular patient generally stayed in the hospital for about a year and usually went through progressive stages toward recovery. However, the timetable varied somewhat for each person at each stage. The most indeterminate stage was discharge from the hospital. Supposedly the physician made a decision about discharge on the basis of laboratory tests and X-ray examinations. However, these criteria were not as simple as one might suspect. Both these tests and the physician's interpretation of the tests were subject to error. For example, different physicians disagreed on the interpretation of an X-ray and some physicians even disagreed with their own earlier interpretation of the same X-ray.

An important aspect of the bargaining was that physicians and patients dealt with the indeterminate nature of the illness in the same way; that is, both developed conceptions of an appropriate timetable, although the patient's timetables were shorter than the physicians' and considered by the patients to be more precise. Consequently, time was a major consideration whenever a physician had to decide whether to grant a pass. Each time a patient requested a pass, the physician's first question was likely to be, "When did you have your last pass?" Clearly, this question would be pointless unless the physician had in mind some notion of how long patients should wait between passes. Similarly, whenever the physician had to decide whether a patient could return to fulltime work, he always asked, "How long has he been out of the hospital?" rather than "What is his present physical condition?" which was considered only secondarily.

APPLICATIONS OF CAREER TO THE STUDY OF CHRONIC ILLNESS

The Polio Patient

In a longitudinal study of the psychological and social impact of paralytic poliomyelitis on children and their families, Davis (1956, 1963) examined the ways in which hospital personnel managed the patient's and family's definition of time in the recovery process. The recovery process of a polio patient is similar in many respects to that of a tubercular patient; and although both of these chronic illnesses are rare today, the sociological implications of their careerlike nature have important applications to other chronic illnesses. For example, the patient and family have different definitions of time in the initial stages of the recovery process than do health care personnel. When the stricken child is first admitted to the hospital in an acute stage of poliomyelitis, the family bombards the physicians, nurses, and other attending personnel with such questions as "How long will it be?" and "When can I have my child back?" Invariably, the initial *episodic* perspective on the hospital confinement, with associated expectations of rapid recovery, is replaced within a few weeks by a long-term, *continuous* perspective wherein the extent of ultimate recovery from the disease is viewed in a more qualified and ambiguous fashion. What was initially seen as an episodic and determinate career is soon viewed as continuous and indeterminate. "When they come in here, the children think in terms of days. Very soon they're thinking in terms of weeks and not long after that in terms of months" (Davis, 1956, p. 583).

Davis studied how the change in time perspective was brought about. That is, he studied the situational and institutional contexts of communication between professionals and patients to understand how hospital personnel psychologically lengthened the time perspective for the patient and family. The first variable analyzed in this bargaining situation was the power discrepancy between the physician and patient. The complete dependence of the patient and family on the physician constitutes an important point of leverage for the physician as he begins to redefine the time perspective.

A second variable is the indeterminate nature of the polio career since so little is known about polio. The practitioner is thus confronted by significant areas of therapeutic uncertainty related to the socially crucial questions of rate of recovery and ultimate extent of disability. It is necessary for the physician to communicate to the parents that the uncertainty stems from the nature of the disease itself and not from his own incompetence or unwillingness to speak the truth. He uses such phrases as "much is unknown" and "only time will tell" to convince the parents. "Time" in this sense connotes a long and indeterminate amount of time.

A third variable in lengthening the time perspective is the gradient approach to recovery that the hospital institutes. As in the case of a tubercular patient, treatment procedures are progressively arranged and serve to indicate the sequence of benchmarks on the road to recovery. The pacing and sequence of time begin to be conceived of as measured intervals in the striving toward a goal of wellness. The implications for the parents are many. For example, parents are permitted to visit their children in the hospital only once or twice each week at regularly scheduled times. This in itself frequently imparts to them a time perspective with attenuated periodicity. In the course of these visits they soon become aware that they are able to observe only slight changes from week to week and come to believe anew that recovery is a long and slow process. This belief is reinforced by the physician, who cautions them not to expect too much too quickly. Optimism is not completely discouraged, however, for an attitude of restrained hopefulness is typically regarded by hospital personnel as most conducive to establishing a proper therapeutic environment (Davis, 1963). One parent who called daily to ask about her child's progress was told, "Mrs. Smith, if you call me every day, there's not much progress I can report in Harry's condition. But if you would call me every other week, I think I'll be able to give you a good report" (Davis, 1956, p. 584).

A fourth variable in lengthening the time perspective is the manner in which hospital personnel structure the patient's recovery career. Because the recovery career is indeterminate, the patient and family can see progress only from implicit cues in the treatment procedures and the explanations of hospital personnel, which, in the case of the tubercular patient, are symbolic benchmarks along the recovery career.

A child with extensive muscle damage in one leg that permits him neither to stand nor walk may begin on a stretcher bed, where a physiotherapist bends and manipulates the paralyzed leg to the point of pain. This procedure indicates to the child that the leg is potentially of use, something that a passive regime of bed rest would not make evident so early. Several days later the child may be suspended in a hydrotherapy pool, where the buoyancy of the water permits him to move the damaged leg more easily. Although this in itself is a rewarding experience, it is also rewarding as a symbol of progress. In the course of several months the child may progress from moving the leg to and fro while he lies prone on a floor mat, to standing up while he is being held, to ambulating up and down a ramp while he supports himself on arm rails, to taking his first tentative steps with the aid of braces, crutches, or both. As each phase of treatment is being mastered, the child is prepared by the hospital personnel for the next phase. The progression defines the recovery career for him; and his progressive mastery of new movements indicate that he is "getting well."

A fifth variable in lengthening the time perspective is the loosening of the child's effective ties with home and immersion in the hospital's subculture of sickness. Rapid immersion proceeds on many well-charted fronts. It is accomplished by restricting parents' visits to once or twice each week; by the hospital personnel assuming many parental functions; by duplicating in the hospital many of the activities and diversions of home; and by implementing a reward and punishment system, both formal and informal, that sanctions good behavior and cooperative attitudes. Most importantly, immersion occurs simply by virtue of the fact that the child is living in a milieu in which sickness is the norm rather than the deviation. This norm enables the child to relate in a more thorough and structured fashion to a common universe of special meanings, goals.

In general, lengthening the time perspective has positive consequences for the polio patient and his family. It allows them to shift their attention from the ultimate hope of walking, running, and playing ball to such shortrange goals as sitting up in bed, moving a specific muscle, or using a wheel chair. Managing the fatalistic career until promotion to the next level of activities is not as difficult as managing the career to wellness. Not all of the consequences of a lengthened time perspective are positive, however. Because a subjective aspect of managing a fatalistic career involves choosing a person with whom to compare oneself, immersion into the hospital subculture provides the polio child with a new set of comparisons and values. However, the values of the hospital are not the values of society to which the child will one day return. A severely paralyzed child who after long treatment is able to get out of bed and move about on crutches has, in the eyes of hospital personnel, made marked progress. Naturally, the child is encouraged by his achievement, but to outsiders, who may include the parents; he may just be another "poor crippled kid" (Davis, 1956, p. 585). Hence, some of the recovered polio patients in Davis's study, unlike the tubercular patients, were reluctant to leave the hospital at the time of discharge.

The institutional management of the fatalistic, continuous career of stroke victims (Hoffman, 1974) contrasts sharply with that of tubercular and polio patients. Like tuberculosis and polio, a stroke results in an indeterminate career since the nature of the stroke is deceptive. First is the great variety of patterns of recovery from a stroke. Some patients are left with only a slight slur in speech, whereas others may lose almost all of their motor capacities. Without a full understanding of the physiological aspects of stroke, patients may aspire to the recovery level of persons who have suffered less neural damage. They may compare themselves with inappropriate role models. A second deceptive aspect of a stroke is that recovery is often very rapid in the first few days, and patients have a false impression about the speed of recovery.

A major difference in the career of a stroke patient and that of a tubercular or polio patient is the fact that the stroke patient is initially hospitalized in an acute-care general hospital. This experience contributes to the stroke patient's unrealistic expectations. In the case of tubercular and polio patients, hospital personnel consciously lengthen the time perspective for the patients. They help to provide concrete benchmarks along the recovery career, and they encourage patients to choose appropriate role models (other patients) with whom to compare themselves. This is not the case for a stroke patient in a general hospital, which is oriented toward episodic, fast-paced illness careers. Hospital personnel in a general hospital are less apt to lengthen the time perspective for the patient and family. Moreover, because there are seldom other stroke patients on the unit, patients do not have a group norm against which to measure their own progress; they have to identify and evaluate their own benchmarks. Without an appreciation of what is "normal," one can never really be behind schedule; hence, a lack of significant improvement can always be explained by "giving it time."

The Nursing Home Patient*

Gustafson (1972) applies the career concept to the experience of elderly people in convalescent hospitals and nursing homes. The career for some nursing home patients is one of dying. Except in cases in which the patient is severely incapacitated intellectually, the patient, family,

---

*We recognize that the objective of nursing home placement often is to rehabilitate and discharge the individual to home or an alternate community living site. The purpose of the discussion in this section is to illustrate the concept of a declining career.

and staff almost always know that a permanent placement means an institutional death. There exists, therefore, what Glaser and Strauss (1965) call an open-awareness context (although not a shared awareness). This is true whether the patient is suffering from a rapidly progressive disease of which he will soon die or from the chronic diseases of old age, in which case he may linger indefinitely.

A nursing home is the last recourse for some old people who have tried to maintain their social independence as long as possible and for their families (Jacobs, 1969, Kahana, 1961). Admission to a nursing home is widely considered the ultimate failure in one's social career. In Roth's (1963, p. 105) terms it is a career failure. Thus, Gustafson (1972) refers to the career of a nursing home patient as "regressive" rather than "progressive," distinguishing it from the career of a tubercular, polio, or stroke patient. In the case of the latter chronic illness conditions, minimizing treatment time constitutes success. For a nursing home patient, however, success is the maximum delay of passage from one stage to the next.

For most chronic illness conditions, the passage of significant events and bargaining efforts move in the same direction—toward recovery. In a nursing home patient's career, events progress in one direction (toward death), whereas bargaining efforts pull in the other direction (toward health). This tension makes life very difficult, but it is essential for the maintenance of any kind of life at all. Thus, during most of a nursing home career, a patient is fighting social death, which is operationalized by social isolation.

A person moves through his career as a nursing home patient according to a timetable informally defined by the patient and nursing home personnel. Gustafson (1972) outlines two types of benchmarks (physical and mental) along a regression scale. Physical deterioration is measured by degrees of social activity, mobility, and functional control. Mental deterioration is measured by declining mental control.

The informal career of these four indicators is even more indeterminate than the formalized system of classification of tubercular, polio, or stroke patients discussed above. Since there is no standard duration for each stage of the nursing home career, the norms for pace and sequence of events are confused. Improved health and relapses occur frequently and cause constant shifts in the patient's time perspective. There is no guarantee that every patient will move in an orderly way or at a similar pace through the regressive career.

One reason for the generality and indeterminateness of the benchmarks is that there is often limited communication between nursing home personnel and patients and limited communication among the patients themselves. More elaborate and concrete benchmarks are impossible to construct without clear communications. Several authors (Glaser & Strauss, 1965; Kübler-Ross, 1969; Quint, 1967) have shown that patients' unresolved anxieties about impending death prevent nursing home personnel from having honest discussions with patients about their conditions. Communications among patients are also minimal since some patients may be disengaging from social interactions (Cumming & Henry, 1961) and others may be unable to speak as a result of a stroke or other impediments. Because patients have so many different experiential and social backgrounds, they may have little in common to talk about.

The indeterminate nature of the benchmarks makes them unreliable indicators for approaching death. The patient thus sees death as something that could unexpectedly overtake him at any time, or after a long time. This indeterminateness also has a positive consequence, however (Gustafson, 1972). When his situation seems bad, the patient can find fault with the benchmarks. When his situation seems good, he can remind himself that death does not always "follow the rules" implied by the timetable career. Objectively speaking, the norms are not reliable but, psychologically speaking, they are comforting. Working out one's position on a career timetable is in itself a lively, hopeful, and social activity.

Previously we saw that the career of a tubercular or polio patient was most indeterminate around the time of discharge from the hospital. In contrast, it is toward the end of the nursing home career that the benchmarks become *more determinate*. Early in a nursing home patient's career, norms are vague and the patient is kept busy evaluating his status and bargaining for a sense of social viability. At the end of the career, perhaps within a week or two of death, the signs are much more dependable and the imminence of death cannot be avoided. Confinement to bed, accompanied by extreme lassitude or coma, is a fairly certain sign of impending death. Transfer to a general hospital, except for the repair of fractures of routine treatments, also suggests that death is near.

We saw previously that bargaining is a crucial aspect of a chronic illness career. Bargaining is also crucial for a nursing home patient career, but it has a subtly different meaning. Tubercular or polio patients bargain for a change in their official position: they want those in authority to do something to change their status in the hospital. Patients in a nursing home are not assigned to any official status. Thus, nursing home patients bargain for moral and social support of their self-images (Gustafson, 1972). They want the authorities as well as their peers to do and say things that are assuring to them and help them maintain a lively social status. They want to be needed and to be important to other people so that *social death* will not precede their biological death.

As in the case of tubercular or polio patients, nursing home patients sometimes use extraneous criteria to improve their bargaining position. Provision with glasses, hearing aids, dentistry, occupational and physical therapy, and other aids and services that the staff may consider nonessential are often highly valued by patients since they are status symbols. They indicate that a patient has social value and possibly a long future. For example, an old lady may never read but may indignantly fight for new glasses; by getting them for her the staff shows that they consider her to have a future. For some patients private possessions assume great importance as signs of viable social life; this accounts for some of the compulsive hoarding of "junk," such as bingo prizes, greeting cards, and holiday decorations.

A second major difference in the bargaining of nursing home patients and patients with other chronic illnesses is that the process works in reverse. Whereas patients with chronic illnesses generally increase their bargaining activity as they move toward the end of their hospital career (Davis, 1956; Roth, 1963), nursing home patients start out actively bargaining and often give up this effort toward the end of their career. In both cases, the change in bargaining intensity is related to a change in pace and sequence and timing. Patients with tuberculosis or polio and nursing home patients all start their careers with the idea that it will not take long to get cured (Davis, 1956; Roth, 1963) or to die (Gustafson, 1972). In almost all cases, the patients soon learn that the goal is much farther away than they first thought. This realization discourages patients with a chronic illness from bargaining intensely until the chances for success seem the greatest—at the end of the progressive career. The same realization is a kind of reprieve for nursing home patients, however, and encourages them to fight for the maintenance of their social life. When the end does come into sight, bargaining is no longer worth the effort.

In her study of Parkinson patients, Singer (1974) used the concepts of *social death* and *social aging* in much the same way that Gustafson did. She found that the social consequences of Parkinson's disease are equivalent to a condition of premature social aging in the sense that the activity levels of Parkinson patients correspond to those of people who are chronologically older. Because this artificial aging process is superimposed on the natural processes of growing older, its effects are different for people of different ages. That is, it impinges more heavily on younger patients since these patients compare themselves with younger persons of the general population.

The Mental Patient
Goffman (1961) uses the concept of career to describe the experience of the mental patient. He points out that a major advantage of this concept is its two-sidedness. One side is linked to a person's internal mat-

ters, whereas the other side concerns his official or public position. The concept of career allows one to move back and forth between these two aspects of the self (Goffman, 1961, p. 127).

Like Davis and Roth, Goffman (1961) uses an institutional approach to the study of self. Thus, the self is a reflection of the values of society. As such, the self is not so much supported by societal values as it is determined by them. Specifically, Goffman analyzes two institutional arrangements crucial to the self-definition of the mental patient. The first is the extent to which the patient believest that his next of kin will remain loyal to him. The second concerns the protection the patient requires to keep intact the version of himself that he presents to others.

A unique aspect of a mental patient is the wide variation in the kind and degree of illness that he is imputed to be suffering. This diversity results in a continuous career that is the most determinate of those discussed thus far. Once started on this career, all mental patients are confronted by similar responses from people. The core of the problem of mental illness is the stigma of being mentally ill, not the illness itself. Despite the fact that there are many kinds of mental illness, with different symptoms and prognoses, the public response to mental illness is uniform. Being mentally ill becomes the dominant social status of the affected individuals. The uniformity of this social status may ensure a dissimilar group of people a common fatalistic career.

A second unique aspect of a mental patient is that the indeterminate nature of his career has a retroactive element. Because mental illness is a vague concept, behavior that is considered indicative of mental illness is vague. It is also value-laden in that the judgment of one or more other people is involved. The specific kinds of behavior that define a person as mentally ill and require him to be hospitalized are considered to differ from the everyday actions of a mentally healthy person. However, there is no clear-cut definition of these differentiating factors. Moreover, when one studies actual hospital commitments, one finds that a patient's seemingly similar actions have different outcomes. (Goffman, 1961).

The diagnosis of mental illness is based on a psychiatric view of the patient's past. This case history is not meant to be a rough average or sampling of past conduct; rather, the purpose of the history is to show that the patient is "sick" and to show why it was necessary to commit him to a mental institution. This is done by extracting from his entire life a list of incidents that have or might have had "symptomatic" significance and early acts in which the patient appears to have shown bad judgment or emotional disturbance (Goffman, 1961, p. 156). Misbehavior that could be common to a wide variety of people is considered to substantiate the need for hospitalization.

The term "career contingencies" (D'Arcy, 1976; Grove, 1970; Lemert, 1946) is used to explain those aspects of a mental patient's makeup and behaviors that affect the type of career that he follows. Some of the career contingencies that have been studied are socioeconomic status (Hollingshead & Redlich, 1958) the visibility of the offense (Mechanic, 1978), and the community regard for the type of treatment given in available hospitals (Meyers & Schaffer, 1954).

A third unique aspect of the mental patient career is that bargaining for this status begins *before* hospitalization (the prepatient phase), and the prepatient and family may not bargain for the same outcome (Goffman, 1961). Bargaining in the prepatient phase involves three sets of people: the next of kin or family member, that is, the person on whom the patient is most dependent; the complainant, the person whose complaint in retrospect appears to have started the person on his way to the hospital; and the mediators, the agents to which the prepatient is sequentially referred and through which he is relayed and processed on his way to the hospital.

In the prepatient's progress from home to the hospital, bargaining frequently results in the prepatient becoming a third person in an alienating coalition. His next of kin may urge him to talk things over with a health professional counselor. Disinclination on his part may result in threats of desertion, disownment, or other legal action. Typically, the next of kin will have set up the interview. This move effectively establishes the next of kin as the responsible person to whom pertinent findings can be divulged while effectively establishing the other as the patient. Unlike patients in the other chronic illness careers discussed thus far, the pre-"mental" patient is in a powerless position since he and his next of kin are bargaining on *different* sides. The prepatient may go to the interview with the understanding that he is an equal of someone who is so bound to him that a third person could not come between them. Upon arrival at the professional's office the prepatient suddenly finds that he and his next of kin do not have the same roles or the same power since a prior agreement was made between the professional and the next of kin in an effort to hospitalize the prepatient. The experience of being a third man in such a coalition often embitters the prepatient, especially since his troubles have probably led to some estrangement from his next of kin already.

Like the nursing home patient career, the mental patient career is by definition a career failure. The mental patient career is more degrading, however, since the patient's behaviors have to be controlled and the patient may have to be "locked up." The hospital setting thus has restrictive rules that make clear to the patient that he is a mental patient who has suffered some kind of social collapse, that he has failed in some major way. This humiliation is most keenly felt by middle-class patients, since their former life gave them little preparation for affronts such as these. All patients, however, feel some downgrading. Just as any normal member of his outside subculture would do, the patient often responds to this situation by telling a sad tale to prove that he is not sick, that he had a little trouble, that it was someone else's fault, that his past life has some honor, and that the hospital is unjust in forcing the career of mental patient upon him. Each patient generally volunteers relatively acceptable reasons for his hospitalization while at the same time accepting the "acceptable" reasons from other patients. Goffman (1961, pp. 152–153) found such stories as the following given and overtly accepted by other patients:

> *I was going to night school to get an M.A. degree and holding down a job in addition, and the load got too much for me.*
>
> *The others here are sick mentally, but I'm suffering from a bad nervous system and that is what is giving me these phobias.*
>
> *I got here by mistake because of a diabetes diagnosis, and I'll leave in a couple of days. [The patient had been in the hospital for seven weeks.]*

The reality and at times degrading conditions of the hospital setting belie many of the patient's stories; the very fact that they are in a mental hospital is evidence against these tales. Thus, a patient's difficulties are closely tied to his version of what has been happening to him. If cooperation toward recovery is to be secured, health care personnel consider it helpful if this version is discredited. The patient must attain "insight" and adopt the hospital's view of himself. Consequently, the staff denies the patient's rationalizations.

As in each of the chronic illness careers examined thus far, the mental patient's status is assessed through graded benchmarks, which indicate progress toward discharge (Goffman, 1961, p. 148). The worst level of privileges may involve confinement in a seclusion room, whereas the best may be a private room with the freedom to walk around the grounds or leave the hospital to go shopping or to go home on a pass. The meaning of privileges or benchmarks in a mental patient career differs from that in other chronic illness careers in two fundamental ways. First, the restrictions of the mental patient result from the institutionalization, not from the illness itself. Thus, the mental patient cannot take privileges prematurely. Second, to a greater degree than in other chronic illnesses, the mental patient enjoys the privileges not only for the freedom they offer, but for their symbolic meaning, Symbolically the privileges indicate the worthiness of the patient's public self. When a patient asks for additional privileges, he may be told that they will be granted when the staff feels he is "able to manage" or will be "comfortable" with a higher level of privileges. Being assigned more privileges is presented not as a reward but as an expression of the patients general level of social functioning, as the extent of recovery from his previous career failure.

AN ANALYSIS OF CHRONIC ILLNESS FROM THE STANDPOINT OF CAREER

In this section we present two case studies of individuals with chronic conditions. These case studies illustrate the way in which the negotiations and interactions of clients and health care providers are similar to those described by the career concept and show how this concept clarifies the process of adjusting to a chronic illness.

Case Study I: Transsexualism

Basic to an understanding of transsexualism is a knowledge of the difference between the terms "sex" and "gender." "Sex" refers to anatomical characteristics; "gender" describes emotional feelings of being male (masculine) or female (feminine). Transsexualism is a chronic illness that occurs when a person's sex and gender are *incongruent.* Specifically, transsexualism in a biological male is a chronic illness in which the male has gender feelings of being female and considers himself "trapped" in the body of a biological male.

Transsexualism follows a careerlike orientation which begins shortly after birth. In this case history, we study the careerlike nature of the development of a transsexual syndrome in Ms. Shiela Williams, a biological male who has gender feelings of being female.

Prepatient Phase. Shiela Williams was born John Williams in 1960. He was the third sibling of five children, having two older sisters. The underpinnings for Shiela's transsexual career were established soon after birth, when he was in many ways treated as a female. His career was quite vague and indeterminate at this early stage; nevertheless, the result was confusion and disorientation for the child. He was given his older sisters' toys to play with and was dressed in their clothes since the family was too poor to buy male clothing for the first male child. In other, more direct ways, however, the mother treated the male child as female. His hair was allowed to grow long and was frequently tied with ribbons. He was taught to avoid rough activities. In short, all-feminine behavior was reinforced by the mother. The father, a construction worker, was quite upset with the mother and at times "tried to make a man of the boy." The father's participation in the child rearing was sporadic, however, because he worked long hours and was frequently away from home.

An important benchmark in Shiela's transsexual career involves Goffman's (1961) notions of the public and private self. Shiela's effeminate behavior and treatment like a girl were largely private until she entered school; then, when the effeminate behavior was discovered, the private feminine career became public. Shiela was labeled a sissy, and her fatalistic career began to take shape.

Shiela's career became more and more uncomfortable as she grew older; consequently, she began to associate with others who, like herself, were considered deviants. She discovered the "gay" subculture, a community of people who shared her sexual preferences. Transition from the straight community to the gay community was a relief. Shiela no longer felt isolated. She liked the gay world and learned from it. When she entered the gay community she was an uncertain person; now she had a rationale for her behavior. As a result she became far more sure of herself and far more wise. She was also more *determinate* on her female identification.

Shiela was 16 when she first heard about sex reassignment surgery. With this new knowledge she began to think differently about herself. Before this, she had considered herself to be gay; now she considered herself straight; that is, she considered herself a female trapped in a male body. At the age of 19 she applied to a transsexual clinic requesting sex reassignment surgery.

The Patient Phase.   The patient phase of Shiela's transsexual career began with her application to a transsexual clinic. Because transsexualism indicates mental illness, the transsexual career is by definition a career failure. However, there are differences. Other mental patients are considered to have behavioral problems that necessitate hospitalization so that they will be protected from harming themselves or others. Shiela's was a career failure in that she simply failed at being male. What other males took for granted, Shiela could not do. She was obsessed with her male body, repeating over and over that she was a female trapped in a male body.

A unique aspect of Shiela's transsexual career is that she sought treatment and eagerly entered the health care system. Thus, her career and those of other mental patients differ in two ways: the bargaining coalitions are different, and the indeterminate nature of the illness has different implications. We saw that in other mental illness careers bargaining involves three sets of people: the next of kin or family, the complainant, and health care personnel. For Shiela there are only two sets of people; a complainant is not invloved since Shiela voluntarily applied to the transsexual clinic. Moreover, although the family and health care personnel are generally on the same side (as in other mental illness careers), they are trying to talk Shiela out of treatment rather than into treatment. They tell her that changing sex will not solve all of her problems, that there are no magic solutions, and that she will still have the same personality even if she has a body of a different sex.

There is a retroactive element in Shiela's transsexual career , just as there is in other mental illness careers. However, for Shiela this retroactive element has different implications. We saw previously that in taking a mental patient's case history a professional culls early behaviors that are considered to have symptomatic significance, whereas the patient attempts to deny or hide deviant behaviors. For Shiela, the situation is the reverse. She boasts of her lifelong effeminate tendencies. She anwers questions at length to convince the interviewer that she is indeed a transsexual desperately in need of sex reassignment surgery. She even fabricates part of her history to convince the interviewer of her desperate situation.

An important aspect of Shiela's treatment is lengthening the time perspective of the treatment process. When she applied to the clinic, she was thinking in terms of months before she might have sex reassignment surgery. The initial treatment process consists of questioning whether sex reassignment surgery is the best treatment for Shiela and, if so, lengthening the time perspective from Shiela's point of view. Several of the strategies for lengthening the time perspective are similar to those used with polio or tubercular patients. For example, as soon as Shiela applied to the clinic, she was given a brochure outlining specific criteria for sex reassignment surgery, which included being in psychiatric treatment for a minimum of two years, being over the age of 21, and being in stable emotional health. Outlining these criteria has two functions in lengthening the time perspective for Shiela. It provides a minimum of time before sex reassignment surgery can be performed, thus serving as a very determinate benchmark against which Shiela may measure her progress in the clinic program. It also leaves the exact time of surgery open to interpretation since the criterion of emotional stability is indeterminate; the exact behaviors that distinguish emotional stability are difficult to define. We saw previously that a polio patient's X-ray at the time of discharge can be interpreted differently by different physicians. Even more so for transsexuals, when the two-year treatment minimum and age requirement have been met, physicians may differ in their opinions regarding the patient's emotional stability.

A second approach whereby health care personnel can lengthen Shiela's time perspective is by capitalizing on the indeterminate nature of transsexualism. Little is known about the cause and best treatment of the syndrome. Professionals prefer to proceed cautiously. They believe that quick decisions are unwise since there are so many aspects of the illness that are not well researched. If they wait a few years, more will be known and the treatment is likely to be more successful.

A final strategy for lengthening Shiela's time perspective involves a gradient approach to treatment. As in the case of tubercular or polio patients, treatment procedures are progressively arranged to indicate a specific pace and sequence of benchmarks in the treatment process. For example, Shiela may first enter an individual therapy program and subsequently enter a group therapy program, in which she will meet other pre- and postsurgery transsexual patients. As in other chronic illness, each benchmark has significance in and of itself and also for its symbolic meaning. For Shiela, an important benchmark is being prescribed female hormones since they enhance her feminine features and make it easier for her to pass as a female. The symbolic meaning of the hormones, however, is equally important since they indicate *progress* along the career to sex reassignment surgery.

We saw previously that one way in which patients attempt to control the pacing of events is to take privileges surreptitiously before they are officially granted. Before Shiela applied to the transsexual clinic, she was taking "street hormones," that is, female birth control pills, which were easy to purchase in the gay or transsexual community. However, she still looked forward to being prescribed hormones in the clinic because this would legitimatize her belief that she was making progress. Thus, when she aplied to the program she immediately began asking for hormones, even though she had been taking hormones for over a year.

Case II: Myocardial Infarction
A myocardial infarction (MI) is the most acute and potentially lethal stage of heart disease and, as such, is accompanied by a proportionate amount of medical urgency and disruption for the patient and family. However, in a physiological sense, an infarction is but a critical moment in the slowly developing, multidetermined disease process of artherosclerosis or arteriosclerosis. For many people, it is the point at which the silent chronic disease precipitates into an illness and the patient career begins. For most victims of a heart attack, the onset of the patient role is sudden and unexpected, even though the potential and the developing momentum of the disease stretch across the patient's lifetime. Many of the aspects of a person's life style, many of the attitudes and values that are associated with the onset and progression of heart disease, later influence the course of the post-MI

period and the nature of the careerlike pattern during recovery. In this case study, we examine the pre-MI period in which the foundations for the post-MI career are found.

Pre-MI Phase. Richard Crane was the last of three children of Kevin and Michelle Crane. Richard's father was a struggling, yet successful tradesman in a small tool-and-dye shop. As he moved up the ranks into management and then partnership, the family not only progressed materially, but also changed its attitudes and values. Richard was young enough when the changes in his father's career occurred that he grew up in the midst of the family's new way of life. When he began first grade, it was assumed that he would someday go to college and reap the benefits of his father's hard work, sacrifice, and careful planning.

When Richard was 17, his father, 48 years old, died suddenly of a heart attack. Richard's older brother and sister were already married and settled, and the father's business left Richard and his mother comfortably cared for. In fact, there were few overt changes in Richard's life as a consequence of his father's death. His ambition to succeed in college and to fulfill his father's expectation grew even stronger. Underlying this drive and ambition, however, was a new construct resulting in part from the loss of his father: hard work and control were not so much a guarantee of success as they were the only safeguard against devastating failure.

Richard did well in college and later in law school. He married shortly after law school and worked for a while at the bottom of the ladder in a large law firm. He moved up in the firm quickly by working overtime and being involved in many projects at once. He was often overextended but managed to accomplish all that he set out to do.

When he was 35 years old, he decided that working for someone else was a waste of his time and talent; and so, with the help of his wife and some friends, he began his own law firm. With Richard's drive and endless energy, the decision paid off well. At first the firm required every moment of Richard's attention and all of his talent; but after a number of years and a few expansions, he had developed a smoothly running operation. By this time, however, Richard had a deeply engrained pattern of thinking and style of work. What would appear to some as a well-organized business capable of absorbing some temporary losses or setbacks, Richard saw as a business teetering on the brink of disaster. Thus, Richard continued to work long hours and to keep constant vigilance, and he always felt the pressure of time.

When Richard was 45 years old, a number of events occurred. His mother died in the summer at 75 years of age. In the fall, the law firm underwent another expansion; Richard took on a new partner and at the same time an increase in contracts. At Christmas, Richard's wife forced him to take a long-overdue trip to Mexico for a rest. He had put it off so often in the past that he felt compelled to go—with the understanding that he would take some work along. As it turned out, he cut the trip short partly because of the epigastric pain he kept feeling, ostensibly from spicy food.

Richard returned to an onslaught of work and a flu epidemic, which had reduced his staff to a skeleton crew. After two weeks of nearly nonstop work, Richard decided to take a few days off with his wife and son and enjoy some skiing. The next day, after shopping and a celebration dinner at a steak house with his family, Richard went to bed early feeling full and bloated and sensing that he was coming down with the flu.

Onset of the Patient Role. During the night Richard awoke with dyspnea, crushing chest pains, and mainly a sense of dread. When neither aspirin nor antacid relieved the worsening symptoms, Richard's wife called their family physician and good friend, who sent them directly to the emergency room. At 4:30 A.M., Richard was admitted to the coronary care unit with a probable anterior wall infarction.

Richard's case illustrates some characteristics of heart disease that give it a distinctive career orientation. The onset of symptoms often marks the first period of bargaining. When Richard awoke with chest pains, he bargained for time and control by first using home remedies that he knew were inappropriate for the severity of his discomfort. Although he was aware that something was dreadfully wrong, he felt that the best way to deal with it was "to will it away or just ignore it." Through this bargaining, he hoped to convert a potentially fatal incident into one that was under his control.

The bargaining for time at the onset of an infarction has several forms. First, there may be a testing of the severity of the problem, in which case the person may continue to perform his usual activities until he is prevented from doing so. Second, bargaining may be used to delay the acceptance of the patient role and to maintain control for a while longer: the person completes the work day or waits until a family member has gone home or to college after a weekend visit before disclosing the symptoms to others and seeking help. There is one feature of this bargaining that distinguishes it from the type that occurs at a later time in the illness and from the type that was described for the tubercular patients. During the onset of the infarction, the patient's bargaining is constrained by progressively debilitating symptoms. The physiological changes that usually accompany an MI rapidly bring the bargaining and resistance to the patient role to an end, and the hospital phase of the chronic disease begins.

Acute Hospital Phase. The hospitalization and disease course for an MI patient is not a uniform one. For most patients, there are three distinct phases, each with its own career task. The first is the acute hospital phase, during which the patient's task is to learn and accept the diagnosis of heart attack. The acute hospital phase is marked by the same dramatic and fast pace that accompany the onset. The critical care period has all the hallmarks of an acute illness, with the severe symptoms of illness—chest pain, nausea, palpitations, and anxiety—paralleled by specialized care measures. As the symptoms abate, the care moves into a phase of quiet observation in which rest and comfort are maintained. The acute period has a number of closely spaced benchmarks. Moves within the coronary care unit, relaxation of visitor and activity restrictions, and progression to solid foods signal improvement. For many patients the sense of feeling better provides the best evidence that they have survived. It is also at this point that the meaning of the diagnosis begins to have an impact.

Richard went through the whirlwind period without remembering much about the first days. The pain had been so severe by the time he had arrived at the emergency room that his major focus had been on its relief. For the first day on the coronary care unit, he had been frequently medicated with morphine and had slept off and on. He had been disoriented a few times on awakening but for the most part was drowsy and free of pain. On the second day, the staff cardiologist told Richard and his wife that enzyme studies had confirmed the diagnosis of a moderately severe MI and that, although there was heart muscle injury, his heart had stabilized well. The physician's report removed what little doubt remained for Richard. He had suspected the trouble before coming to the hospital but had at the same time believed that it could not be happening to him. Being in a coronary care unit had confirmed his fears, and now the diagnosis was certain. The assimilation and acceptance of the diagnosis had already begun, but now the process was accelerated. Richard and his wife discussed everything that had led to the MI. To make the event more un-derstandable and seem less a matter of fate, they speculated as to its cause and how it might have been prevented. They discussed the close call Richard had had, each reliving their feelings and thoughts. They talked about the excellent care he was receiving and how magnificent modern medicine was. They reviewed all aspects of what had occurred and how effectively it had been handled. Patients often use this process to regain a sense of control over an event that has given little warning. If one can find the cause, one might be able to prevent it from occurring again.

Richard accepted the diagnosis fairly readily; at the same time any thoughts about the future gave way to an appreciation for having survived the ordeal. This "here-and-now" response is typical of many patients and facilitates the transition to the next phase of the illness.

There is another typical response during this phase, which is one of greater reluctance to accept the diagnosis. The patient questions the validity of the tests or of the physician's diagnostic expertise, tries to minimize the extent of the disease, or selectively misinterprets what is being said. (For example, "I had a heart attack but the doctor said there was no damage." "I had a myocardial infarction but no heart attack." "I'm just here for observation.") These methods of handling the illness might be considered another example of bargaining, or a type of plea bargaining. The patient strikes a deal with himself and his family and physician on the level of disease that he will accept. This type of bargaining is often more difficult for the patient to maintain. It is difficult, for example, to continue to believe that one has not sustained a heart attack in the presence of beeping monitors, intravenous lines, and other MI victims. Most patients finally accept the diagnosis by the time the acute phase of the illness and the care end.

The Convalescent Phase. On the fifth day after admission Richard was transferred to a surgical floor, the unit used for the convalescence of MI patients. He was feeling better and considered the move to be certain evidence that he had survived; he was, in his words, "on the way home."

Entry into the convalescent phase marks the beginning of the discharge process for many patients. It forms a striking contrast to the acute phase. It is slowly paced, and only vague and indeterminate benchmarks of improvement are visible. Most of all it is a period of contradictions: just as it marks the end of a major hospitalization, it marks the beginning of the patient's new life as an MI survivor. The task that the patient faces during this phase is the recognition and acceptance of the chronic illness.

On the new unit, Richard began to feel a return to normal life. His family and friends visited regularly, and his interest in the outside world and particularly in his firm began to stir. However, amid these familiar activities and feelings, remnants of the disease remained. The bland, salt-free, low-fat diet and nitroglycerin paste that had seemed to him appropriate on the coronary care unit followed him to the new unit. He was not allowed to take a shower and had his most basic activities monitored by a physical therapist, who checked his pulse rate and taught him to do the same. Friends told him he looked fine, almost too healthy to have had a heart attack, but for all his appearances of health, Richard felt weak and tired. He was aware of sensations in his chest that he had not noticed before. There was a new sense of vulnerability, and he faced his forthcoming discharge with both eagerness and dread.

For Richard this period of hospitalization was the most difficult. He was familiar with the kind of problems that could be analyzed, broken down into specific issues, and then solved. This situation and his anxiety and ambivalent feelings were new and difficult to face. Moreover, there were fewer indications by which he could gauge his progress and a growing sense that things would never be the same.

To regain some sense of control Richard began to make plans for his new life through a process of bargaining. In this phase of a cardiac patient's career, bargaining can have an all-or-none quality. Some patients, including Richard, accept the disease role under their terms and bring it under their control. The fatalistic dimension of a career is converted to a humanistic one. Richard decided that it was time he made the necessary changes to ensure that he would never have another heart attack. He approached the role with the same vigor and urgency with which he had approached his precardiac career. He collected as much information as he could about exercise, diet, and relaxation. He had a dietitian draw up a month-long diet. He mapped out a route and time for his daily walks, and from his hospital bed he began to organize cardiopulmonary resuscitation and exercise classes for members of his firm. Richard was striving to be as successful in his cardiac career as he was in his business.

The response of some patients in this phase is very different from Richard's: it is a complete rejection of the new career. Rejection of the role begins even within the confines of the hospital. Sneaking a cigarette, walking down the hall, using the stairs, having forbidden food brought from home, and conducting business from the hospital bed are ways in which patients maintain control through noncompliance. This behavior also tests limits, a mechanism some patients use to make the nebulous heart disease more understandable and real.

The bargaining that is carried out during the convalescent phase of the illness still occurs within the confines of the hospital system. A person develops an understanding of the disease, including the restrictions connected with it, while he is still a patient. It is after discharge, in the rehabilitative phase, that he faces the task of incorporating the disease into his former life style.

The Rehabilitative Phase. Although rehabilitation ideally is begun just after the acute phase of the illness, the process is often restricted to the patient's learning factual information and making plans for discharge. Most patients cannot anticipate what it will be like to be home or to have a chronic illness career.

Richard was discharged from the hospital just less than two weeks after admission. He was eager to get home and had cajoled the staff cardiologist into discharging him several days ahead of schedule. He had made all the necessary arrangements for his follow-up visits and for care at home well in advance. He joked as he left the hospital about his speedy recovery and his new slim stature—he had lost seven pounds during the illness.

Once he was at home, the euphoria lifted, and Richard felt depressed and weaker than he had felt in the hospital. He had not anticipated this lack of energy and so had to cancel a reunion with some friends and business associates. For the first week, the fatigue continued and Richard had problems sleeping; he would awaken early in the morning, thinking about how much his life had changed, and then find it difficult to fall back asleep.

By the third week, Richard had begun to regain some energy, and his sleeping improved. He went on daily walks with his wife and slowly began to turn his attention to former interests. In general, however, Richard faced the resumption of each activity with a mixture of eagerness and fear. His sense of vulnerability remained, and was even heightened, as his former strength returned. His family shared his anxiety. His wife was reluctant to leave him at home alone, even for brief shopping trips. When she did, she called him frequently to see if he was well. His son cancelled a number of dates and social events but at the same time was reluctant to spend much time actually visiting with his father.

On discharge, Richard had been instructed not to return to the office until after a follow-up visit six weeks later. He had protested vehemently that this length of time away from work would be very disruptive to his business. Now, however, he was facing the end of the six-week period with increasing anxiety. He was worried about stepping back onto the treadmill that he felt had been responsible for his heart attack.

Richard's response during the first few weeks after discharge represents one pattern that has been described in heart patients. The initial period after discharge is marked by depression and anxiety. The lack of overt symptoms of illness (except, in some cases, episodes of angina) and, therefore, of improvement enhances the patient's feelings of vulnerability and lack of control. The threat of a possible recurrence of an attack is heightened each time an activity brings on angina or even chest flutter. For many patients during the first months of recovery, a sense of resolution evolves as physical strength returns.

Resolution occurs when the patient achieves a balance between the restrictions and limitations created by the illness and his goals and values before the onset of illness. It includes shifting values, adjusting priorities, and regaining security and confidence in spite of the threat of sudden death. The bargaining that the cardiac patient uses to bring about this resolution has been called the "calculus of cutting back." This is a type of cost–benefit analysis of meeting the demands of the disease and the subsequent effect on the quality of one's life.

In Richard's case, the bargaining began with the reestablishment of his sense of control. In some ways, the possibility of another insidious and "unscheduled" attack or death was the major source of stress and depression for Richard, who always weighed consequences and alternatives before taking action. Now faced with the possibility of an incontrollable event, Richard began to exercise increasing control over the consequences. He drew up a new will and updated and ordered many of the financial and insurance matters that he had planned to put off until retirement. He contracted out a number of home improvements that would result in a maintenance–free house for his family in case of his death. He made changes in the law firm, making one associate a partner and selling the part of the firm that had been least successful. He turned over the responsibility for his mother's estate to his brother-in-law and called a meeting with his wife and son and their lawyer to go over in detail his own affairs. It is important that Richard and his family did this with no sense of dread or morbid premonition. In fact, Richard felt a returning sense of order and with it a lifting of depression and anxiety. He was once again in control. His family recognized his lifting spirits and shared in his sense of returning normalcy.

The next step of bargaining includes the calculated risks. Richard complied with diet, exercise, and medication regimens. At the same time he returned to his work with the same urgency and drive as before. Richard considered it an unacceptable demand of the illness to have to compromise on his profession. He and his wife recognized and accepted that his work must be experienced in its fullest. Richard now spends more planned time with his wife and son. They enjoy this time, and his wife is slowly dealing with her own fears that he is working too much. Richard's physician at first insisted that Richard cut back to half-time work, but now he, too, accepts Richard's assessment of his need for achievement.

It has been three years since Richard's MI. He has maintained his weight at slightly below the recommended figure; he has given up smoking, drinks only occasionally, and follows a strict low-salt and low-cholesterol diet. He exercises several times each week and walks two miles each day. Generally, he feels better than he did before his

MI. He continues to work ten or twelve hours per day, including some weekends. Recently, he has added a number of new cases and a new associate to the firm.

In considering Richard's resolution and the compromises he has made, we can recognize some elements of his pre-illness period. He has bargained for control and for adding a stronger humanistic dimension to his chronic illness career.

REFERENCES

Cumming, E., & Henry, W. *Growing old.* New York: Basic Books, 1961.

Darcy, C. The contingencies and mental illness in societal reaction theory: A critique. *Canadian Review of Sociology and Anthropology,* 1976, **13**, 873-884.

Davis, F. Definitions of time and recovery in paralytic polio convalescence. *American Journal of Sociology,* 1956, **61**, 582-87.

Davis, F. *Passage through crisis: Polio victims and their families.* New York: Bobbs-Merrill, 1963.

Glaser, B. G., & Strauss, A. L. *Awareness of dying.* Chicago: Aldine, 1965.

Goffman, E. The moral career of the mental patient In E. Goffman (Ed.), *Asylums: Essays on the social situation of mental patients and other inmates.* Chicago: Aldine, 1961.

Gove, W. R. Societal reaction as an explanation of mental illness: An evaluation. *American Sociological Review,* 1970, **35**, 873-884.

Gustafson, E. Dying: The career of the nursing home patient. *Journal of Health and Social Behavior,* 1972, **13**, 226-235.

Hoffman, J. E. Nothing can be done: Social dimensions of the treatment of stroke patients in the general hospital. *Urban Life and Culture,* 1974, **3**, 50-70.

Hollingshead, A. B., & Redlich, F. C. *Social class and mental illness: A community study.* New York: Wiley, 1958.

Jacobs, R. Adjustment to a home for the aged. *Gerontologist, 1969,* **9**, 268-275.

Kahana, E. Emerging issues in institutional services for the aging. *Gerontologist,* 1961, **11**, 51-58.

Kubler-Ross, E. *On death and dying.* New York: Macmillan, 1969.

Lemert, E. Legal commitment and social control. *Sociology and Social Research,* 1946, **30**, 370-78.

Lyman, S. M., & Scott, M. B. *A sociology of the absurd.* New York: Appleton, 1970.

MacDonald, B. *The plague and I.* Philadelphia: Lippincott, 1948.

Mechanic, D. *Medical sociology (2nd ed.).* New York: Free Press, 1978.

Meyers, J. K., & Schaffer, L. Social stratification and psychiatric practice: A study of an outpatient clinic. *American Sociological Review,* 1954, 14, 207-310.

Moore, W. *Man, time and society.* New York: Wiley, 1963.

Quint, J. *The nurse and the dying patient.* New York: Macmillan, 1967.

Roth, J. *Timetables: Structuring the passage of time in hospital treatment and other careers.* New York: Bobbs-Merrill, 1963.

Simmel, G. The adventure. In K. H. Wolff (Ed.), *Georg Simmel, 1858-1918.* Columbus: Ohio State University Press, 1959.

Singer, E. Premature social aging: The social-psychological consequences of a chronic illness. *Social Science and Medicine,* 1974, 8, 143-151.

Sorokin, P., & Merton, R. K. Social time: A methodological and functional analysis. *American Journal of Sociology,* 1937, 42, 615-29.

Suchman, E. A. Stages of illness and medical care. *Journal of Health and Social Behavior,* 1965, 6, 114-128.

Chapter 6

Social Support

The help provided by family and friends in times of distress is a power-ful source of comfort and courage. Health care providers are becoming increasingly aware of social support as a factor in both health and ill-ness. One of the difficulties of using this concept in client assessment and treatment is that it is not well defined either conceptually or operationally. The purpose of this chapter is to begin to clarify social support: what it is, how it functions, and its effects. The case studies at the end of the chapter illustrate how knowledge of this concept can be used to assess and assist people with chronic illness.

CONCEPTUALIZING SOCIAL SUPPORT

As soon as one attempts to define "social support," it becomes appar-ent that it is not a single concept, but a set of concepts. Although there are areas of agreement regarding definitional aspects of social support, none of the leading writers supports a single definition. A review of two theoretical positions on social support will demonstrate the major similarities and differences among the definitions in the literature.

One of the earliest systematic conceptualizations of social support was that of Weiss (1969, 1974). Weiss defined "support" as the quality

of feeling sustained through the gratification of needs. His categoriza-
tion was based on empirical investigations of two groups of individuals: recently divorced or separated people and women who had
recently made geographic moves to accommodate their husbands' occupational requirements. Two findings of these studies suggested the
distinctive provisions of various types of relationships. Friendships,
even though close and important, did not diminish the loneliness experienced by many formerly married people. What seemed to be lacking for them was an intense and intimate relationship with another
person. On the other hand, the geographically uprooted married
women seemed to suffer from a lack of access to a social network or
community of friends with whom to share interests and social activities. Weiss described the condition of the formerly married individuals
as the loneliness of emotional isolation and that of the geographically
displaced women as the loneliness of social isolation. He hypothesized
that "different types of relationships make different provisions, all of
which may be required by individuals at least under some conditions"
(Weiss, 1974, p. 21).

The state of social support can be defined, according to Weiss, as a
combination of six categories of relational provisions, each ordinarily
associated with a particular type of relationship (Weiss, 1974,
pp. 23-24). *Attachment,* or a sense of security and place, a sense that
one is cared for and loved, is provided by intimate dyadic relations
such as one finds in marriage or very close friendships. A lack of this
type of relationship results in emotional isolation and loneliness.
Social integration is provided by the less intense, less intimate sharing
found in group relationships. In these situations one has the opportunity for companionship, participation in social events, and exchange of
services. The absence of these relationships may result in social isolation and a sense that life is dull and boring. *Opportunity for nurturance* is provided by relationships in which an adult takes responsibility
for the well-being of a child. In this relationship the individual has a
sense of being needed, of being depended on. A lack of this type of relationship may give rise to a sense of meaningless in life. *Reassurance of
worth,* a sense that one is competent in a social role, that one is respected or admired, that one is valued for one's skills or competence, is
provided by work relationships and certain family relationships. In the
absence of such relationships one may develop a low regard for oneself
or a sense of uselessness. *A sense of reliable alliance* is usually provided by kin relations in which there is an expectation for continuing
assistance whether or not there is mutual affection or reciprocation.
Weiss suggests that a lack of this type of relationship may lead to a
sense of vulnerability and abandonment. *The obtaining of guidance,* or

access to a trustworthy and authoritarian figure who can furnish emotional support and assist with the formulation of a line of action, is found in relationships with professional people during times of acute stress or crisis. The absence of this kind of relationship may result in hopelessness or despair.

A second conceptualization of social support is provided by Cobb (1976, p. 300), who defines social support as "information leading the subject to believe that she/he is cared for and loved, esteemed and a member of a network of mutual obligations." There are, according to Cobb, three classes of information. First, information that one is cared for and loved, like Weiss's attachment dimension, is exchanged in intimate situations involving trust. This kind of information is often referred to as emotional support. Second, information leading the individual to believe that he is esteemed and valued reinforces the individual's sense of worth or competence and is particularly effective when it is communicated in public situations. Cobb refers to this as esteem support and is in some respects similar to Weiss's reassurance of worth dimension. Third, information that one belongs to a network of communication and mutual obligation is common to everyone in the network and shared in the sense that each member is aware that every other member knows. This class of information is analogous to two dimensions outlined in Weiss's conceptualization of social support, i.e., social integration and sense of reliable alliance.

Recent studies of health and illness have begun to include the concept of social networks as an analytical tool. A "social network" is defined as a specific set of linkages among a defined set of individuals that can be of use in evaluating the social behavior of the people involved (Mitchell, 1969). Social networks can be considered from at least two broad perspectives: structural properties and functional properties or process. Mitchell (1969) describes the former as the "morphological" properties of networks, or the links in the network. He identifies the functional properties of network (one of which is the provision of social support) as "interactional" properties describing the nature or quality of the links in the social network.

Walker, McBride, and Vachon (1977, p. 35) draw on the work of Mitchell (1969) to define five characteristics of the structure of social networks most relevant to the provision of social support:

1. *Size:* The number of people with whom the individual maintains some social contact, including those contacts that are renewable in case of need.
2. *Strength of ties:* A combination of characteristics that are likely to be intercorrelated, e.g., the amount of time, the emo-

tional intensity, the intimacy (mutual confiding), and the reciprocal services that characterize the tie (Granovetter, 1973).

3. *Density:* The extent to which the members of an individual's social network know and contact one another independently of the individual.

4. *Homogeneity of membership:* The extent to which network members share social attributes including demographic characteristics, such as age, sex, ethnicity, and social class, and attitudinal and behavioral characteristics, such as social values and life styles.

5. *Dispersion of membership:* The ease with which network members can make face-to-face contact.

Characteristics of the structure of social networks that differ slightly from those described by Walker et al. (1977) are identified by Mueller (1980) and Pilisuk and Froland (1978). Mueller (1980, p. 149) suggests the following seven characteristics: size, density or connectedness, frequency of contact, multiplexity (relationships in more than one content area, e.g., recreational, economic, religious, sexual, and political), ratio of kin to non-kin in the network, directionality or reciprocity of links, and geographic distance of the focal person from network members. Pilisuk and Froland (1978, p. 277) describe the structure of social networks by the following dimensions: reachability (the average number of links needed to connect any two network members by the shortest route), density, range (the number of members in the network), homogeneity, clusters (cliques of dense links within the network), and dispersion.

The structural properties of an individual's social network provide some evidence of the availability of social support. However, they are not, in themselves, evidence of the *quality* of relationships that exist within the structure. In order to determine this, it is necessary to consider the interactional properties of the network (Mitchell, 1969). Mitchell (1969, pp. 20–27) suggests three dimensions of interaction within social networks:

1. *Content:* The meanings that people give to their relationships, feedback from others that encourage self-esteem, validating behaviors, and telling others their strengths. This dimension incorporates aspects of social support suggested by Weiss (1974), Cobb (1976), and Kahn (1978).

2. *Directedness:* The amount of reciprocity of supportive behavior between individuals. The implication of this dimension is that supportive interactions between individuals cannot long

be sustained in a situation of unidirectionality. The exchange of supportive behavior between individuals is described in Weiss's (1974) taxonomy as "reassurance of worth" and/or "opportunity for nurturance." The capacity or opportunity to give (as well as receive) enhances an individual's sense of usefulness and competence.

3. *Intensity:* The degree to which individuals are prepared to honor obligations or feel free to exercise the rights implied in their link to some other person.

The extent to which reciprocity exists in any relationship depends, in part, on the strength of the bond between the two people and the willingness with which they are prepared to forego other considerations in carrying out the obligations of their relationship.

The dimensions of content, directedness, and intensity proposed by Mitchell (1969) and the characteristics of networks described by Pilisuk and Froland (1978) and Mueller (1980) are synthesized by Walker et al. (1977) in their discussion on the relationship between individual needs and network characteristics. These authors assert that the structure or configuration as well as the interactional properties of networks determine the extent to which individual needs are met in the course of human events. Drawing from a large body of social–psychological literature, Walker et al. (1977, pp. 35–36) suggest the following hypotheses:

1. *Social identity* is best maintained by a network of small size, strong ties, high density, high homogeneity, and low dispersion.
2. *Emotional support* is best provided by a network of high density, high homogeneity, and low dispersion.
3. *Material aid and services* are best provided by a network of high density, large size, and strong ties.
4. *Diversity of information* is best secured in a network in which there are some weak ties that serve as "bridges" to other networks.
5. *New social contacts* are best made through networks with bridging ties to other networks.

Although these hypotheses are grounded in the literature, very little research has been done to determine the extent of empirical support that exists for each one. The authors make an interesting observation about the kinds of networks through which new information and new social contacts are secured. A small, dense, highly homogeneous network is likely to circulate the same information and attitudes among its members and also to resist the entry of new members. However, one or more weak ties to other networks permits different attitudes and information to enter and provides the opportunity for new social contacts (Walker et al., 1977, p. 37). Granovetter (1973, p. 1371) notes that "the fewer indirect contacts [weak links to other networks] one has the more encapsulated he will be in terms of knowledge of the world beyond his own friendship circle." Access to new information and new social contacts is a critical factor in the adjustment to long-term illnesses and other transition situations (unemployment, bereavement, and relocation, marital separation, and divorce).

In summary, the foregoing review of social support provides some evidence of the theoretical diversity surrounding this construct. There are, however, several points at which the ideas of social support converge. Unquestionably, the area of major agreement centers on the *communication of positive affect*. In a supportive relationship the principals have a sense of warmth and caring, and express their concern for each other. They know that others believe in them and respect them. There is feedback that encourages self-esteem and affirms or endorses one's behavior or one's attributes. A second area of agreement centers on *social integration*. It is supportive to belong to groups, to have an opportunity for exchange with others, to share common experiences, and to know that there are others who will come to one's aid in time of need. A third area of agreement, albeit somewhat less emphatic, relates to *instrumental behavior*, the provision of material or tangible aid. The final area of agreement is *reciprocity*, or directedness in interactions. The likelihood that human needs will be met has been suggested to be related to both the structure and function of social networks (size, density, homogeneity, intensity, dispersion, and strength of the ties). It is also agreed that human beings need social support, that it contributes to well-being and the ability to withstand stress, and that the need for social support persists throughout life.

THE ROLE AND FUNCTION OF SOCIAL SUPPORT

Social support buffers or protects individuals from the effects of many kinds of stressors. However, a network structure that effectively meets one need may not effectively meet all needs. To suggest that one kind of support is appropriate in all stressful situations is to ignore the diversity of needs an individual may experience under stress (Walker et al., 1977, p. 37). Three factors influence the kind of support that is appropriate during periods of crisis: the nature of the stressful situation, the point in the crisis at which support is provided (timing); and the individual's resources.

Nature of the Situation

A common characteristic of stressful situations is discontinuity with the past. The problems a person confronts defy familiar ways of behaving. There is a high degree of ambiguity, and there is a need for information or feedback from supportive others that one's behavior is appropriate. There are at least three distinct forms of situational distress, each of which is likely to require a different kind of social support (Weiss, 1976, p. 214):

1. *Crisis:* A severely upsetting situation of limited duration in which an individual's resources must be hastily summoned to cope with threats of emotional and social (and sometimes physical) stability. The key features of this definition are suddenness, limited duration, and severe distress, e.g., an intense marital quarrel, news of serious or fatal illness in oneself or a loved one, or death of a spouse or close friend.

2. *Transition:* A period of relational and personal change. Parkes (1971, p. 103) defines "transitions" as "major changes in life-space which are lasting in their effects, which take place over a relatively short period of time and which affect large areas of the assumptive world. The key features of transitions are that they involve major changes and have lasting effects, e.g., chronic illness, retirement, divorce, or bereavement. A transition ends, according to Weiss (1976, p. 215), with the establishment of a new, stable life situation, which may be adequate to meet the individual's needs or may in some way be deficient.

3. *Deficit situations:* A state in which a relational provision important to well-being is unobtainable. An example of a deficit situation is the case of a lonely widow who may become involved with children, grandchildren, and various group activities in her neighborhood but still experience profound loneliness.

There may be forms of stressful situations in addition to these three, but Weiss (1976) suggests that this triad is particularly important since each represents the sequelae of loss. Crisis occurs on first awareness of the imminence of loss; transition follows if the loss is unavoidable; and transition may give rise to a reorganized life that in some way is deficient (Weiss, 1976, p. 215).

The most useful kinds of social support are likely to be different for each distressful situation. Although there are overlapping characteristics of support in each case, one might suggest that, in general, emotional support (empathy, understanding) is more useful during crisis, that information, orientation, and concrete assistance are more appropriate during transitional periods, and that compensation for specific deficiences, e.g., a person acting as a confidant for a widower or, in the case of a single female parent, a male helping to deal with an adolescent boy's developmental needs, is most appropriate in deficit situations.

Timing

The needs of an individual who is experiencing distress will most likely change with time. For example, when a person is undergoing diagnostic tests to determine the nature of an illness, appropriate support will be that which reduces anxiety and the distress of uncertainty. Once a diagnosis is made social support is related to managing treatment and assisting the patient in reorganizing his life style as necessary or coming to terms with the need to change his life goals and priorities. Supportive behavior that provides relief and comfort initially may be inappropriate, or even harmful, at later states in the adjustment process.

Personal resources

Social support should fit the situation, utilizing and capitalizing on the individuals existing resources and adding or changing only when there are deficits in the existing support structure.

EFFECTS OF SOCIAL SUPPORT

A large body of literature is accumulating on the relationship between stressful life events and social support. Taken alone, no one study is completely convincing; taken together, however, the results are impressive. This is true particularly in view of the fact that study designs have varied, conceptual and operational definitions of support and stress differ, and outcome measures have been widely diverse. In nearly every study a positive finding in the predicted direction has been demonstrated. This is sufficiently encouraging to warrant further investigation (Cassel, 1976, p. 121).

The Family as a Source of Support

We know very little about how the family impedes or facilitates rehabilitation or adaptation to long-term illness in one of its members. Parsons and Fox (1952) note that "the optimal balance between permissive-supportive and disciplinary facets of treating illness is peculiarly difficult to maintain in the kind of situation presented in the American family." The family, according to Waller and Hill (1951), as a group of interacting people is composed of individuals of different age and sex, each with different needs and desires, each growing at a different rate and having a different level of comprehension about how to handle the problems of living together as a family. As a problem-solving group the family is at a decided disadvantage compared with other groups, precisely because of this inequality in its members (Hill, 1965). Contrary to what might be commonly believed about families and their capacity to provide support to one another, Waller and Hill (1951, p. 27) state, "At rare times during the family life cycle, the family members are sufficiently reciprocal in their need to love and be loved . . . to mutually support one another."

In spite of the fact that the family might be a less than competent group for handling stresses and that our measures of family functioning are crude, the family is an important arena of study for as Litman (1974, p. 495) points out:

> The family constitutes perhaps the most important social context within which illness occurs and is resolved. Family is involved in the process of defining illness, providing preliminary validation to the sick role, precipitating initial steps in seeking out and utilizing necessary available care, including participation in care.

In a study of family influence on the course of chronic schizophrenia, Brown (1962) verified his hypothesis that a patient's behavior would deteriorate if he returned to a home in which, at the time of discharge, "strongly expressed emotions or hostility, or dominating behavior was shown towards the patient by a member of the family." Simmons, Klein, and Simmons (1977) found adaptation after kidney transplant to be positively related to perceived family closeness. The adaptation measures in this study were (a) the patient's perceived level of physical rehabilitation (his feelings of health and physical well-being); (b) satisfaction with major role relationships, self-esteem, happiness, and depression; and (c) ability to perform occupational or school roles. The findings suggest that marital status made little difference, although perceived rejection by one's spouse appeared to be associated with long-term maladjustment. In addition, those patients who rated their families closer one year after transplant demonstrated lower anxiety, higher self-esteem, greater stability, and more feelings of control over their destiny.

The importance of including family environment measures in studies of adaptation to long-term conditions is clearly demonstrated by the study of Bromet and Moos (1977) assessing the post-treatment functioning of alcoholic patients in relation to the presence or absence of what the authors call "marital resources" and the type of social environment provided by this resource, if present. These authors refer to a rather impressive body of literature which shows that married people seem to have an advantage over unmarried individuals in a variety of illness situations. However, Bromet and Moos note that the dichotomous measure of married versus not married is too crude to reveal anything about the quality of relationships that may develop within a marriage, that is, the components of family climate. These investigators used the Family Environment Scale (Moos & Insel, 1974) as the measure of family resources. Functioning after discharge from the hospital was measured on four dimensions: behavioral impairment, subjective rating of drinking problems, psychological well-being, and social functioning. In general, the findings were as follows. The post-treatment functioning of patients in stable marital situations was better than that of patients without these resources. Among the married patients, the more positively the family environment was perceived in terms of cohesion (high) and conflict (low), the more positive was the functioning of the alcoholic member. It appears from this study that the level of a patient's adjustment is clearly associated with particular patterns of cohesion and integration in the family unit.

Not all attempts at relating family integration to adjustment are as neat as that of Bromet and Moos (1977). Noting the vexing problem of differential responses to treatment by the orthopedically disabled, Litman (1966) hypothesized that there would be a direct relationship between patients' responses to rehabilitation and the degree of family integration or solidarity. However, as the author noted, "the absence of family ties seemed neither to aid nor hinder therapeutic performance, nor incentive" (Litman, 1966, p. 214). One explanation offered by Litman is that, while an individual is in a rehabilitation program, the family has little direct responsibility for his care and therefore measures of family process probably have no bearing on the outcome of the rehabilitation program. This may be so, and it might be further suggested that the support provided by the professional staff in this case could be the most powerful factor in rehabilitation success.

In a study of adjustment after first myocardial infarct, Garrity (1973) considered the role of support in vocational adjustment. He suggested that work adjustment occurs in two stages: the decision to return to work and the decision as to how much work to do. One factor that was significantly and inversely correlated with the second stage was "the amount of worry of the family" as perceived by the patient. As the amount of worry perceived by the patient increased, the number of hours that he worked decreased.

Most of the literature suggests that social support is a positive factor. However, this study points out another important effect of social support. Behavior on the part of others that is often referred to as kind, sensitive, solicitous, and concerned (and assumed to be good) does not necessarily have a benign influence on a person's adaptive behavior. Both Hyman (1971) and Lewis (1966) suggest that disability might increase in the presence of overprotective or preferential treatment by important or significant others. Hyman (1971) suggests two mechanisms through which preferential treatment might operate to produce disability. The first one is secondary gain, or the acquisition of love, affection, or exemptions from responsibility that are unavailable to the individual outside the sick role. The second is one of socialization, in which preferential treatment modifies self-conceptions to include the concept of self as sick. The internalization of the expectations or social norms of the sick role that prescribe some form of disability reduces the patient's attempts to rehabilitate or to return to his normal social roles (Hyman, 1971, p. 330).

In an examination of the social factors that influence disability after myocardial infarct, Reif (1975) demonstrated the profoundly important effect of others on postcoronary men's conceptions of themselves as normal or disabled. The behavior of the wives of the men in the sample was not much different from that which falls under the general rubric of emotional support, for example, expressions of concern, worry, warnings about overexertion, and generally solicitous behavior. However, the effects of this kind of behavior were not uniformly positive. Often the men came to hold concepts of themselves as sick and disabled. Reif attributed this to a convergence of definitions, so that some wive's beliefs that the men were disabled came eventually to be the definitions held by the men themselves. When physicians and employers concurred with a wife's behavior and beliefs, husbands were even more likely to define themselves as disabled than when one of these individuals was not in agreement.

The importance of such studies as those by Reif (1975), Hyman (1971), Garrity (1973), and Lewis (1966) is not only the refinement of the concept of social support, but also the sensitizing effect of these studies on other investigators: the assumption that the effects of social support are always good must be questioned. Furthermore, until we pay more attention to the processes through which support operates, the conditions under which it is or is not present, and the stances under which it has either positive or negative effects, we will not begin to understand the powerful influence of this phenomenon or the direction and course of adaptation to stressful or challenging conditions.

It seems clear that, despite the diversity of conceptualizations and measures of the family as a source of support, it is an important factor to consider in the investigation of adaptative processes. However, it is equally important to consider other interpersonal transactions.

Friends and Others as Sources of Support

Although the definition of "friend" is empirical (Bott, 1971), Adams (1967) notes the distinction between properties of friendship and properties of kinship. The former are characterized by consensus, or shared interests, and are manifest in voluntary activities, whereas the latter are characterized by positive concern and obligation expressed as mutual aid. These two categories are not mutually exclusive, and Adams points out the conceptual and empirical overlap. For the most part, however, studies dealing with the supportive behavior of friends do not define "friendship" any more rigorously than to state that a friend is an important "other" with whom the individual has no relational ties.

Lowenthal and Haven (1968) call attention to the absence in the social science literature of studies on the potentially positive effect of an intimate relationship on health and well-being. Their own study provided evidence that a confidant, someone with whom one could share the burdens or stresses of life, had a significantly positive effect on the morale of older people who had suffered the loss of a spouse through death or the loss of a job through retirement.

Social integration and social involvement are frequently cited as empirical indicators of the presence of support opportunities. Less frequently, social isolation is studied as the absence of social support. Hyman (1972) used three levels of social isolation to assess the relationship between isolation and functional improvement after a stroke: alienation or feelings of loneliness, number of relatives and friends available in time of need, and degree of isolation in living arrangements. All three levels of isolation were found to impair progress in rehabilitation. Hyman (1972) hypothesized that the relationship between social isolation and successful rehabilitation could be explained in several ways. First, if an individual's social isolation is distressing, and if social satisfactions are available in the rehabilitation center but are not available in the "real" world, then there will be little motivation to become rehabilitated and return to one's former life. Second, a lack of encouragement from family and friends and an absence of relatives or friends to pressure medical personnel for needed care, or the fact that no one needs or depends on the patient, might well be factors in retarding rehabilitation. Finally, the internalization of the role of aging as one of withdrawal and inactivity could also militate against successful stroke rehabilitation.

It is apparent that family and friends can have a profound influence on the course of long-term illness. In the literature general social support has been shown in both long- and short-term illnesses to:

- Reduce the number of complications of pregnancy for women under high stress (Nuckolls, Cassel, & Kaplan, 1972).
- Reduce the need for steroids in adult asthmatics in periods of stress (DeAraujo, Van Arsdel, Holmes, & Dudley, 1973).
- Aid recovery from congestive heart failure and tuberculosis (Chambers & Reiser, 1953; Chen & Cobb, 1960).
- Protect against clinical depression in the face of adverse events (Brown, Bhrolchain, & Harris, 1975).
- Reduce psychological distress and physiological symptoms following job loss and bereavement (Cobb, 1974; Gore, 1978; Maddison and Walker, 1967).
- Protect against the development of emotional problems that can be associated with aging (Blau, 1973; Lowenthal & Haven, 1968).
- Reduce the physical symptoms of those working in highly stressful job environments (Cobb, 1974; Gore, 1978; LaRocco, House, & French, 1980).
- Help keep patients in needed medical treatment and promote adherence to needed medical regimens (Baekeland & Lundwall, 1975; MacElveen, 1972).

Additional studies have shown that the support network is more likely to be mobilized among medical patients than among psychiatric patients (Tolsdorf, 1976). The disruption of social networks is a particularly important factor in the onset and course of depression (Mueller, 1980). The incidence of angina pectoris among men with high levels of anxiety is significantly reduced by the presence of a supportive spouse (Medalie & Goldbourt, 1976). Adaptation to maintenance dialysis is related to several different kinds of social support: family closeness, spouse support, and the presence of a confidant (Dimond, 1979). Finally, empathy correlates with the rate of progress of stroke patients (Robertson & Suinn, 1968).

Underlying most of the studies of social support, stress, and illness outcomes are one or more of the following hypotheses (Hamburg & Killilea, 1979, p. 257):

1. Social support has a direct effect on health; the presence or absence of social support is crucial.
2. Social support provides a buffer against the effects of high-level stress; the interaction between stressors and social support is important.
3. Social support has a mediating effect that stimulates the development of coping strategies and promotes mastery over one's situation; social competence may account for the absence of ill health.

4. The lack of social support exacerbates the impact of stressful events.

ASSESSMENT OF THE ROLE OF SOCIAL SUPPORT IN CHRONIC ILLNESS

In this section we present two case studies of individuals with chronic illness. Our purpose is to indicate the importance of assessing the social environment of a client with a long-term illness and to suggest that the role of social support may differ according to both the nature of the chronic condition and the individual's developmental stage.

Case Study I: Chronic Renal Failure

Michael, age 27, has been on maintenance hemodialysis for three years. He lives with his wife, Mary Ann, age 26, and two children, Jennifer, who is 4, and Jimmy, who is 8. Michael dialyzes at home three times weekly for six hours at a time. In spite of meticulous compliance with the medical regimen, Michael's physical problems are getting worse. He suffers from hypertension, fluid overload, pulmonary edema, and profound anemia, which contributes to extreme fatigue. In addition he has insomnia and experiences severe leg cramps during and after dialysis.

Because of his physical problems, Michael has had to reduce his work as a tax consultant for several local firms to part time. His wife has gone back to work part time as a licensed practical nurse on the 3 P.M. to 11 P.M. shift to supplement the family income. Mary Ann's return to work has necessitated a change in dialysis time from evenings to early morning. Moreover, since the family can't afford a babysitter for Jennifer, Mary Ann's mother comes in on those days that Mary Ann works. She prepares the evening meal and helps Michael get the children to bed. Both Jennifer and Jimmy are healthy, happy children, who enjoy their grandmother very much. Recently Jimmy has begun to ask why his father does not come to watch his soccer team play.

In the past year Michael's ability to cope with his condition has appeared to be deteriorating. He is clinically depressed and reports angry exchanges with his mother-in-law, who "drives me crazy!" He and Mary Ann argue about the need for her to work; he does not like to dialyze in the morning because it "wipes him out" and he misses a half-day of work. He is very worried that Jimmy is not getting enough of his time, not just during soccer games, but at home as well. He simply does not seem to have the time or energy to spend with the children. He spends an increasing amount of time wondering if his wife and children would be better off without him.

Discussion. Chronic illness is not common among young adults, but its presence can create problems for young people and their families. Chronic renal failure and maintenance hemodialysis represent a particularly difficult situation because the individual is completely dependent on a machine for life itself. Michael, moreover, is dependent on his wife to help him manage home dialysis and on his mother-in-law to help him manage the children. Dependency is difficult for most people, but for Michael it comes at a time when all of his energies are focused on achieving independence, managing family affairs, raising children, and succeeding in the work world.

Michael's is a very complex situation and would require an approach on the part of the health care provider that took into account the multiplicity of factors involved. We shall summarize briefly the role of social support in this case.

First, we have seen that the family is a major source of support in health and illness (Chapter 4). To a great extent, the capacity of a chronically ill person to cope is a function of his familial environment. The family's response and the kind of supportive environment it provides depend on the interpretation and meaning of the illness to family members, the resources available within the nuclear and extended family, and the shared goals and values. In Michael's case there is some evidence that the family is rallying to help. However, we do not know the meaning of Michael's illness to other memebers of the family, which probably influences the manner in which they provide help.

Second, there are several types of support, all of which are important but not equally necessary in any given situation. Michael appears to have sufficient tangible assistance from his wife in operating the machine and from his mother-in-law in baby-sitting and home management. However, we know nothing about his need for informational or cognitive assistance in understand the disease and its sequelae. Nor do we know the extent of emotional support needed or provided by the members of the family.

Third, Michael's wife and mother-in-law may think that they are providing all the help that is necessary or possible, but if Michael does not perceive it as such, it is not very useful. The important distinction here is between subjective perception of support (Michael's point of view) and objective support (Mary Ann and her mother's point of view).

It is very important, in cases such as Michael's, to determine the family's ability to provide help, the family members' understanding and interpretation of the illness, the kind of support needed, and the perception of support by the individuals involved. Sustained communication between family members and between the family and the health care provider is essential for the effective functioning of social support and the achievement of maximum independence for a young adult with a chronic illness.

Case Study II: Cerebrovascular Accident

Mrs. Esther Long is a 78-year-old widow who is recovering from a cerebrovascular accident that occurred ten months ago. The "stroke" left her with moderately slurred speech and right hemiparesis. She has lived alone for three years in a small home, which she and her late husband purchased shortly after their youngest child was married and which she refers to as her "dream house." Mrs. Long made an excellent recovery from the stroke. She was diligent in the rehabilitation process, learning how to cook and manage her home as a "left-handed" person. She seemed to adjust well to the fact that she could no longer drive her car, being assured of transportation by a daughter whenever necessary (to go to church, the grocery store, or doctor's appointments). What bothers Mrs. Long the most is her appearance; her face droops on the right side and she can not control a slight drool, which occurs periodically. In spite of this Mrs. Long is a charming and gracious woman. She has returned to many of her former activities: reading, telephone visiting with "shut-ins" in her church, and hosting a monthly luncheon for her bridge club.

Two months ago her best friend died suddenly. Since then her daughter has noticed a profound change. She is not eating well; she has cancelled her bridge club luncheon and seems to spend most of the day just sitting. Sometimes she does not get dressed, fix her hair, or put on her make-up. Her daughter has noticed diminished mobility and increased drooling. Even more distressing to the daughter are the calls she gets in the middle of the night from her mother who seems confused and frightened. The daughter cannot understand why her mother is acting this way and is thinking about putting her in a nursing home.

Discussion. The case of Mrs. Long is not atypical. As we noted earlier (Chapter 3), chronic illness is quite common among older adults. However, in assessing this case, the health care provider must consider much more than the residual effects of a stroke. In addition to the loss of certain physical capacities, Mrs. Long has experienced other significant losses in a relatively short period of time: the death of her husband, the loss of physical attractiveness due to weakened facial muscles, the loss of her ability to drive a car, and finally the sudden loss of a dear driend. It is in this framework of multiple losses that Mrs. Long's situation must be evaluated.

The multiple losses experienced by older adults have been likened to the piecemeal loss of self (Dimond, 1980, Kastenbaum, 1969). Older people are frequently faced with multiple losses, and the elderly may lack the social, personal and economic resources to cope effectively with these realities. Friends, spouse, and health all influence self-concept and self-esteem, and when they are lost in a short period of time, the result may be profound depression bereavement "overload," unresolved grieving, and giving up. For Mrs. Long, the support provided by family and health professionals could be the critical factor in determining whether her earlier coping strengths will be reestablished.

If we consider Mrs. Long's case in the context of social support, it is clear that with the death of her husband and her best friend she has lost the kind of relationship that provided intimacy and a sense that she is cared for and loved. Weiss (1974) refers to this as attachment, and Cobb (1976) calls it emotional support. It is generally believed that this kind of support is provided in dyadic relations such as one finds in marriage or very close friendships. Finding a replacement for this kind of relationship is not a very viable option for Mrs. Long. One of the tragedies of advanced age is the ever-diminishing circle of intimates and chance of replacement. There are, however, other aspects of social support that can be reinforced, and this would be one goal of care for Mrs. Long.

It is important in situations such as Mrs. Long's, in which there has been noticeable and rapid deterioration of function, to a completely assess physical, emotional, and social status. Health practitioners, in the course of this assessment, not only gain important information on which to build a plan of care, but by their presence and confident manner also provide the kind of support Weiss (1974) refers to as "obtaining guidance". In times of stress, professionals assist with the formulation of a line of action and by so doing convey hope to the individual.

Mrs. Long's family should be included in the plan of care. Very often family members are uncertain about how to help their elderly members and prematurely resort to solutions such as placement in a nursing home. In the case of Mrs. Long, family members might be encouraged to consider other options first: making periodic visits during the day to share a meal with Mrs. Long (to eat with, not merely prepare and leave or prepare and watch her eat); going for a ride with Mrs. Long just for the enjoyment of it (this would be in addition to visiting the physician or grocery shopping or attending to other necessary business); spending nights with Mrs. Long (or arranging for an aid from a service pool to spend the night) for a while to assure her of company when she awakens. Gradually involving Mrs. Long's bridge club friends would be important for restoring her sense of belonging and also for enhancing her opportunities to develop closer friendships with individuals in this group. Perhaps this small group, or some member of it, could perform exercises with Mrs. Long.

These are only some of the activities that might be planned with Mrs. Long, her family, and friends. We know from her earlier response to the stroke that she was once capable of mobilizing her energies to cope with difficult situations. The goal now is to provide the social and emotional supports to help Mrs. Long recapture the vitality, sense of worth, and competence that are necessary to deal with the losses she has recently experienced.

REFERENCES

Adams, B. *The family: A sociological interpretation.* Chicago: Rand McNally, 1967.

Baekeland, F., & Lundwall, L. Dropping out of treatment: A critical review. *Psychological Bulletin,* 1975, **82**, 738-783.

Blau, Z. *Old age in a changing society.* New York: Viewpoints, 1973.

Bott, E. *Family and social networks (2nd Rev. ed).* London: Tavistock, 1971.

Bromet, E., & Moos, R. Environmental resources and the post-treatment functioning of alcoholic patients. *Journal of Health and Social Behavior,* 1977, **18**, 326-338.

Brown, G. Influence of family life on the course of schizophrenic illness. *British Journal of Preventive and Social Medicine,* 1962, **16**, 55-68.

Brown, G., Bhrolchain, M., & Harris, T. Social class and phychiatric disturbance among women in urban populations. *Sociology,* 1975, **9**, 225.

Cassel, J. The contributions of the social environment to host resistance. *American Journal of Epidemiology,* 1976, **104**, 107-123.

Chambers, W., & Reiser, M. Emotional stress in the precipitation of congestive heart failure. *Psychosomatic Medicine,* 1953, **15**, 38-60.

Chen, E., & Cobb, S. Family structure in relation to health and disease. *Journal of Chronic Diseases,* 1960, **12**, 544-567.

Cobb, S. Physiological changes in men whose jobs were abolished. *Journal of Psychosomatic Research,* 1974, **18**, 254-258.

Cobb, S. Social support as a moderator of life stress. *Psychosomatic Medicine,* 1976, **3**, 300-314.

DeAraujo, G., Van Arsdel, P., Holmes, T., & Dudley, D. Life change, coping ability, and chronic intrinsic asthma. *Journal of Psychosomatic Research,* 1973 **17**, 359-363.

Dimond, M. Social support and adaptation to chronic illness: The case of maintenance hemodialysis. *Research in Nursing and Health,* 1979, **2**, 101-108.

Dimond, M. Caring: Nursing's promise to the elderly. *Geriatric Nursing,* September-October, 1980, 196-198.

Garrity, T. Vocational adjustment after first myocardial infarction. *Social Science and Medicine,* 1973, **7**, 705-717.

Gore, S. The effect of social support in moderating the health consequences of unemployment. *Journal of Health and Social Behavior,* 1978, **19**, 157-169.

Granovetter, M. The strength of weak ties. *American Journal of Sociology,* 1973, **78**, 1360-1365.

Hamburg, B., & Killilea, M. Relation of social support, stress, illness, and use of health services. In *Healthy People: The Surgeon General's Report on Health Promotion and Disease Prevention.* Washington, D.C.: U. S. Department of Health, Education, and Welfare, 1979, (Publication No. 79-55071A).

Hill, R. Generic features of families under stress. In H. Parad (Ed.), *Crisis intervention.* New York: Family Services Association, 1965.

Hyman, M. Disability and patients' perceptions of preferential treatment. *Journal of Chronic Diseases,* 1971, **24**, 329-342.

Hyman, M. Social isolation and performance in rehabilitation. *Journal of Chronic Diseases,* 1972, **25**, 85-97.

Kahn, R. *Aging and social support.* Paper presented at the meeting of the American Association for the Advancement of Science, Washington, D.C., May 1978.

Kastenbaum, R. Death and bereavement in later life. In A. Kutscher (Ed.), *Death and bereavement.* Springfield, Ill.: Thomas, 1969.

LaRocco, J., House, J., & French, J. R. P. Social support, occupational stress, and health. *Journal of Health and Social Behavior,* 1980, **21**, 202-218.

Lewis, C. Factors influencing the return to work of men with congestive heart failure. *Journal of Chronic Dieases,* 1966, **19**, 1193-1209.

Litman, T. The family and physical rehabilitation. *Journal of Chronic Diseases,* 1966, **19**, 211-217.

Litman, T. The family as a basic unit in health and medical care. *Social Science and Medicine,* 1974, **8**, 495-519.

Lowenthal, M., & Haven, C. Interaction and adaptation: Intimacy as a critical variable. *American Sociological Review,* 1968, **33**, 20-30.

MacElveen, P. Cooperative triad in home dialysis care and patient outcomes. In M. Batey (Ed.), *Communicating nursing research* (Vol. 5). Boulder, Colo.: Wichen, 1972.

Maddison, D., & Walker, W. Factors affecting the outcome of conjugal bereavement. *British Journal of Psychiatry,* 1967, **113**, 1057-1067.

Medalie, J., & Goldbourt, U. Angina pectoris among 10,000 men: Psychosocial and other risk factors as evidenced by a multiple analysis of a five year incidence study. *American Journal of Medicine,* 1976, **60**, 910-921.

Mitchell, J. *Social networks and urban situations.* Manchester, England: Manchester University Press, 1969.

Moos, R., & Insel, P. *Family, work and group environment scales.* Palo Alto, Calif.: Consulting Psychologists Press, 1974.

Mueller, D. Social networks: A promising direction for research on the relationship of the social environment to psychiatric disorder. *Social Science and Medicine*, 1980, **14A**, 147-161.

Nuckolls, K., Cassel, J., & Kaplan, B. Psychosocial assets, life crisis, and the prognosis of pregnancy. *American Journal of Epidemiology*, 1972, **95**, 431-441.

Parkes, C. M. Psychosocial transitions: A field for study. *Social Science and Medicine*, 1971, **5**, 101-115.

Parsons, T., & Fox, R. Illness, therapy, and the modern American family. *Journal of Social Issues*, 1952, **8**, 31-44.

Pilisuk, M., & Froland, C. Kinship, social networks, social support and health. *Social Science and Medicine*, 1978, **12B**, 273-280.

Reif, L. Cardiacs and normals: The social construction of a disability (Doctoral dissertation, University of California, San Francisco, 1975). *Dissertation Abstracts International*, 1976, **36**, 7003A. (University Microfilms No. 76-8246)

Robertson, E., & Suinn, R. The determination of rate of progress of stroke patients through empathy measures of patient and family. *Journal of Psychosomatic Research*, 1968, **12**, 189-191.

Simmons, R., Klein, S., & Simmons, P. *The gift of life*. New York: Wiley (Interscience), 1977.

Tolsdorf, C. Social networks, support, and coping: An exploratory study. *Family Process*, 1976, **15**, 407-417.

Walker, K., McBride, A., & Vachon, M. Social support networks and the crisis of bereavement. *Social Science and Medicine*, 1977, **11**, 35-41.

Waller, W., & Hill, R. *The family: A dynamic interpretation*. New York: Dryde, 1951.

Weiss, R. S. Fund of sociability. *Transactions*, 1969, **9**, 36-40.

Weiss, R. S. The provisions of social relationships. In Z. Rubin (Ed.), *Doing unto others*. Englewood Cliffs, N.J.: Prentice-Hall, 1974.

Weiss, R. S. Transition states and other stressful situations: Their nature and programs for their management. In G. Caplan & M. Killilea (Eds.), *Support systems and mutual help*. New York: Grune & Stratton, 1976.

Chapter 7

Identity

In Chapter 1, we made several distinctions between the concepts of disease, illness, and sickness. In this chapter we elaborate these distinctions by focusing on the concept of identity. Personal identity is integrally involved in the manner in which disease, illness, and sickness are defined, both by chronically ill people and by the health professionals caring for them. Different forms of chronic illness have different effects on a person's identity; similarly, the same chronic illness may have a different impact on a person's identity at different stages of his life.

In this chapter, we first discuss the concept of identity from a theoretical view point using the outline provided by James (1910). We delineate the social and internal determinants that are important in the formation of personal identity and then examine personal identity in relation to the life span. We turn then to a discussion of a chronic illness identity. Using the concept of ambiguous or stigmatized identity, we show how a chronic illness or disability affects an ill person's identity as well as his social interactions. In this section we emphasize the importance of the attitudes and behavior of health care professionals toward a chronically ill person in determining identity. Finally, we present two case studies illustrating the role of identity in chronic illness.

IDENTITY: A THEORETICAL VIEWPOINT

Identity Defined

A person's identity is that experience which he regards as essentially "me." One develops a conceptualization of oneself and labels the experience of existing (Gergen, 1971). Since the process of self-conceptualization is necessarily internal, no commonly agreed upon description of the process has been found. Thus, although the importance of identity has never been questioned, the exact meaning of the concept has been the subject of countless works in social psychology (Epstein, 1973). Here we present the approach developed by James (1910), in which one's identity is considered to have five components.

The *material self* is perhaps the most obvious since we are located inside a physical body that is uniquely ours. Although we are attached to a material body, our sense of identity is composed mainly of the stream of sensations that relate to our bodies. Most of the time we are not aware of these sensations, but together they form a basic picture, or schema, of ourselves. Usually, our picture of our own body, that is, our body image, corresponds to objective reality so that we are not aware of the complexities of the picture. However, if the reality and the personal perception diverge (for example, there are different disease and illness definitions), the complexity of our experience of ourselves becomes very clear. A radical example of divergence between the objective (disease) and perceptive (illness) levels is the phenomenon of "phantom limb." Someone who has had a limb amputated may continue to feel the limb in its usual position and to experience movement there for years (Simmel, 1966).

The experience of a material identity is closely related to a specific location in the body. A number of studies have been done to ascertain which part of the body is most often associated with one's identity. Most people believe that the "me" resides in an area midway between and slightly behind the eyes (Middlebrook, 1974).

The *psychological self* is what a person thinks of when he thinks of "me." It may be thought of as a set of attitudes, beliefs, and judgments. The psychological self provides a frame of reference or standard against which all information is judged or interpreted. Each evaluation is determined by one's past experiences and ideals as to what ought to be. We saw earlier, for example, that patients with chronic illness such as polio or tuberculosis compare themselves not with "normal" people but with other hospitalized patients. They have thus taken on a new psychological identity—that of a chronically ill person with tuberculosis or polio.

The *cognitive and affective self* consists of one's own experience of the process of experiencing. In contrast to the psychological component, which focuses on the end result of our thinking and emotional processes, here the emphasis is on the actual process of our thinking, imagining, and sensing. This phenomenon has been described as the "stream of consciousness" (Middlebrook, 1974, p. 62). This aspect of identity is "the very core and nucleus of our self, as we know it, the very sanctuary of our life" (James, cited in Gordon & Gergen, 1968, p. 43).

A person's social interactions have the most significant influence on the formation of his identity, as will be discussed later. A person's *social self* is a consequence of the roles that he plays in society. The social self is constructed of labels that are both assigned by others and self-imposed. A person's identity can be modified by his interactions with others in the social enviroment and by the labels that others impose on him. For example, Preston (1979) found that patients enacted roles complementary to that of the nursing staff in that they generally accepted the staff's supposition's. Patients who were treated as invalids acted as invalids, whereas those treated as responsible individuals acted accordingly.

The *ideal self* is what each of us would like to be. A person's ideal self may change, depending on his level of aspiration and goals and on extenuating circumstances. Strauss and Glaser (1975, p. 64) describe "downward trajectories and new levels of normality" for the chronically ill. This is a new conceptualization of the ideal self from the viewpoint of the chronically ill. Many chronic illnesses have characteristically downward trajectories and the ill person must come to terms with his present situation. If he continues to act and live as if his condition is only temporarily bad and will soon improve, then sooner or later his arrangements for coping will prove inadequate.

Development of Personal Identity
Although it is helpful to examine the individual components of identity, it is doubtful whether most people think of their self-experience in this way. Identity is a cohesive whole that presents a single image to those who view it at any given time. In the remainder of the chapter, therefore, we focus on identity as a unitary concept.

Social Determinants of Identity.
Probably the most popular concept of identity formation is that one's identity is the product of one's interactions with significant others. This concept is embodied in a number of social-psychological theories about identity. The earliest of these was that of Cooley (1902), who believed that the self reflected the imagined reactions and appraisals of others, which he termed the "looking-glass self." The looking-glass concept referred to an individ-

ual perceiving himself in the way that others perceive him. Mead (1934) expanded and made more explicit the looking-glass concept by stating that a child's identity is determined by his imitation of reactions of significant others and by their reactions to him. He suggested that an individual's identity is formulated from his concerns about how others react to him. In order to anticipate other people's reaction so that he can behave accordingly, an individual learns to perceive the world as they do. By incorporating his expectations of how the "generalized other" would respond to certain actions, the individual acquires a source of internal regulation that guides and stabilizes his behavior in the absence of external pressure. According to Mead, a person has as many identities as he does social roles. Some of the roles are relatively broad and of considerable significance, whereas others are specific to particular situations and are of little significance in the formation of identity.

For Sullivan (1953), as for Cooley and Mead, a person's identity stems from social interactions of the child with a particular significant other, namely, particularly the mother, rather than with society at large. He identifies significant others as those who provide rewards and punishments in a person's life. On the basis of these rewards and punishments, a person forms a "reflected appraisal" of himself. In other words, the way in which a person is treated or judged by significant others determines the way in which he sees himself. For example, if a mother sees her child as weak and frail and incapable of undertaking tasks that require strength, the child will view himself in that manner.

Another theory emphasizing the social determinants of the self is reference group theory. According to this theory, an individual identifies with the standards and beliefs of certain groups termed reference groups (Middlebrook, 1974). He then defines and evaluates himself in relation to these. For most people, groups to which they actually belong, called "membership groups," rather than groups they merely observe, serve as the measuring standards or reference groups. For a chronically ill person, other chronically ill serve as the reference group.

Occasionally, a group that an individual does not belong to may fulfill the measuring function. Any group against which the individual evaluates himself, whether or not he actually belongs to it, is a reference group. An individual may have more than one reference group, and some of the groups may have conflicting standards—for example, a family and a group of hospitalized patients.

Once an individual has identified with a group, how does the group influence his behavior? First, through its "normative function," it places subtle and not so subtle pressures on the individual to conform to the others in the group (Kelley, 1952). Second, through its "comparative function," the group becomes source of information against which a person can judge his beliefs about many aspects of reality—including himself. Even if the members of the group make no overt attempts to influence a person, he looks to them to decide what is correct. To make a judgment about his own physical attactiveness, for example, a person may compare his appearance with that of others or that of television personalities. Even if a person has no desire to be liked or accepted by the other people, he uses them as a source of information.

Although the normative and comparative functions of reference groups can be distinguished theoretically, empirically they are closely interrelated. The normative function may mediate what seems to be a comparative function and vice versa. However, both of these functions make the reference group an important source of one's beliefs and values.

Internal Determinants of Identity. It has become evident that social interactions are crucial in the formation of one's identity. Parent-child interactions are generally considered to form the core of a child's identity. Later interactions with others, as in reference groups, further influence one's identity. However, social determinants do not operate alone in identity formation. Two important internal variables in identity formation are one's perception of one's actual abilities and the active role of the self.

Perceived competency has been emphasized as an important determinate by several theorists. For example, it has been argued that a sense of competency is basic to the development of self-esteem, a factor closely associated with one's identity (White, 1959). Research in this area, although not extensive, supports the importance of perceived competency. For example, in the 1940s and 1950s a number of "level of aspiration" studies suggested that perceived failure on uninvolved experimental tasks influenced an individual's goals. It was consistently found that, when subjects were made to think that they had succeeded, their level of aspiration rose; when they thought that they had failed, the level fell (Pepitone, 1968). Success or failure at a more involved task also has an effect on one's level of self-esteem (Koocher, 1971). In a study at a YWCA summer camp, where the ability to swim was considered important, success in learning to swim was related to a significant increase in the learner's level of self-esteem.

Nevertheless, competence as evaluated by others does not always correspond to an individual's own view of his abilities. Also important is the active role of the self. People whom others consider highly competent may view themselves as incompetent and thus have a low level of self-esteem. The reverse may also occur. However, not all individuals accept their socially rated self; some judge themselves by their own internal standards, which may be either more or less demanding. Several studies have confirmed the independence of self-evaluations from the reaction of others. Kohlberg (1969) believes that the most advanced stage of moral development involves an individual judging his actions by his own ethical principles rather than acting in a manner that will please his peers.

It is apparent from our discussion that social determinants provide the basis for the development of one's identity. Although most of the theoretical formulations agree on the importance of others in this process, they differ in their emphasis on who is crucial and on the way in which the process occurs (Roy, 1976). A person's perception of his own competence and his own identity can also determine the evolution of his identity. Both the social and internal explanations overlap, and any complete theory of identity formation must take both into account.

Personal Identity Throughout the Life Span

A person's identity is not fixed once and for all in childhood but rather continues to evolve throughout the life span (Morse & Gergen, 1970; Sarbin, 1954; Sherif & Cantril, 1947). As noted in Chapter 3 it is important to recognize the changes in a person's identity that take place thoughout his life. It would seem, for example, that the youth orientation of American society would create potential conflicts for those in later stages of the adult life cycle (Lowenthal, Thurnher, & Chiriboga, 1975). An apparent corollary of the emphasis on youth is the negative image of aging and the aged reportedly held by those still in the younger life cycle (Bunzel, 1972; Rosenfelt, 1965). It consequently seems reasonable to predict that a person's identity changes in such a way that his self-esteem decreases as he grows older. Evidence for this hypothesis is equivocal, however. Although several research studies found an age-related shift to self-depreciation (Geidt & Lehner, 1951; Wallach & Kogan, 1961; Ziller, 1967), other studies (Mason, 1954; Thomae, 1970) found that the aged may actually have a more positive self-identity than do those who are younger. Sex differences also appear to be a confounding variable influencing identity over time (Grant, 1969).

Lowenthal et al. (1975) explored the difference in the identities of 216 men and women in successive stages of adult life. Those represented were high school seniors, newlywed individuals, middle-aged individuals and adults in the preretirement phase. These researchers found that a person's identity definitely changed over the life span and that the changes in men differ from those in women.

In terms of the instrumental behavior of these individuals there was improved efficiency with time; e.g., there was a decline in absent-mindedness, disorderliness, laziness, and restlessness. In the area of interpersonal relations there was a decline in vulnerability, e.g., suspicion and embarrassment. There was a decline in the need for misrepresentation and manipulation, such as guile, shrewdness, and drama, along with an increase in frankness. In conflict-evoking behavior there was a decline in sarcasm and stubbornness. Finally, there was an increase in overall self-reliance; e.g., there was less timidity, helplessness, indecisiveness, dependency, and self-control. Overall, the change was positive: as people grew older, their personal identity becomes more positive.

Differences found in the identities of men and women supported earlier findings (Grant, 1969) that women, more than men, ascribe expressive attributes (both positive and negative) to themselves. At all stages in the life cycle, the men were classic examples of the instrumental role player. They described themselves as ambitious, assertive, calm, competitive, confident, guileful, hostile, reasonable, self-controlled, shrewd, sophisticated, unconventional, and versatile. Women rated themselves higher than men on the characteristics of being charming, cooperative, easily embarrassed, easily hurt, friendly, helpless, sincere, sympathetic, and timid.

These researchers (Lowenthal et al., 1975) explored further the meaning of sex differences thoughout the life span by constructing two indexes, one of masculine and one of feminine traits. As expected, men scored higher on the masculinity index and women higher on the femininity index. In addition to the sex differences, however, it was found that the feminine identity of women changed over the life span. Women in the later stages felt less feminine than younger women. The identities of preretired women more closely approximated those of their male counterparts than did those of the older women in the study. Whereas women ranked consistently higher than men on the femininity index in high school, newlywed, and midlife stages, the preretirement men and women were not significantly different.

Overall, the patterns that emerged from the analysis of identity change over the life span in men were clear-cut. The stage differences were in basic accord with theoretical developmental statements such as those of Erikson (1963), Cumming and Henry (1961) and Neugarten (1968). As the men proceeded through the successive stages of life, they passed from a stage of insecurity and discontentedness in self-identity (high school) through a buoyant and sometimes uncontrolled phase (newlywed), through a stage of control and industry (middle age), to a later point of decreased demands on the self and greater acceptance of others and the environment (preretirement) (Lowenthal et al., 1975).

The patterns of identity change in women over the life span were less clear-cut. The identities of the high school girls were similar to those of the boys in their negative content. The girls, like the boys, questioned their ability to lead an independent life. At the newlywed stage, however, the men's identities differed markedly from those of the women. The men's identities were distinguished by high energy, whereas the women's were distinguished by its very lack. Middle-aged women also differed from middle-aged men in that they reported greater absentmindedness and unhappiness. Also, middle-aged women were more negative than women at other stages of the life cycle. However, they were not as one might conjecture, distressed by the pending departure of their last child (Lowenthal & Chiriboga, 1972), and few seemed disturbed about menopause. The reasons for their diminished sense of well-being were complex but often centered on relations with their spouse. Their identities again stand in sharp con-trast to the generally postitive ones of the middle-aged men. Moreover, the women seemed to feel deficient in the very areas in which men re-garded themselves as strong. The men reported a heightened sense of orderliness, whereas women reported a heightened sense of absent-mindedness. It was at the preretirement stage that the women finally seemed to be functioning at their peak. The earlier problems with com-petence, independence, and interpersonal relations appeared to be resolved. The preretired women saw themselves as less dependent and helpless and as more assertive. They more resembled the middle-aged men than the preretirement men. Changing patterns of dominance were found in the preretirement stage for both men and women. Both agreed that, in the later life stages, fewer men are "boss" in the family and that more women are.

Research has consistently shown that men are more likely to deny problems than are women (Grant, 1969; Lowenthal & Chiriboga, 1972). Lowenthal et. al. (1975) reported similar findings in their life span identity analysis of men and women. Men generally admitted to fewer shortcomings and appeared to be more accepting of and comfortable with themselves. Their concerns with identity change were more stage-specific, and no negative identity traits presented a problem for all men in all stages. Those negative traits most commonly acknowlegded were laziness and disorderliness, which were mentioned by all except middle-aged men. High school boys were most troubled by their ab-sentmindedness and dependency. Newlywed men wished that they were less easily hurt and less stubborn, defensive, sarcastic, and im-pulsive. Middle-aged men also admitted to being easily hurt, stubborn, and defensive. The preretirement men wished they were less touchy and more shrewd.

The women generally admitted to a greater number of shortcomings than did the men (Lowenthal et al., 1975). Women at each life stage focused on questions of social vulnerability and of mastery. They wished that they were less easily hurt and touchy, as well as more confident and shrewd. Other negative attributes that they (with the exception of preretirement women) admitted to were easy embarrassment, stubbornness, absentmindedness, worry, laziness, and indecision. The women also mentioned other stage-specific concerns. High schools girls wished they were less dissatisfied. Newlywed women wished they were less selfish but also that they were more energetic, ambitious, and less dull. Middle-aged women felt that they should be more introspective, persevering, reserved, and poised. One-third of the middle-aged women stated a need to be more imaginative. The preretirement women resembled the middle-aged women in their concern for more social personality, but they seemed closer to their goal. Rather than desiring a social barricade of poise and reserve, they wished for greater charm and sophistication. They were also unique in their focus on assertiveness and competitiveness (Lowenthal et al., 1975).

INDENTITY AND CHRONIC ILLNESS

Development of Ambiguous or Stigmatized Identity

We stated in Chapter 5 that, because structure reduces anxiety, people are constantly trying to structure events, especially uncertain or ambiguous events. The purpose of Chapter 5 was to show how people structure the common events, which we termed career, that occur in various types of chronic illness. In this section we discuss one occurrence in the career of chronic illness: the formation of an ambiguous or stigmatized identity (Goffman, 1963; Preston, 1979).

A basic need of human beings is to be oriented to the world around them. To maintain this orientation, they develop "typifications" of the perceptual and experiential world. We might say that in this way knowledge is the typification of things and events (Preston,1979, p. 25). For example, the defining of the properties of a lemon comprises its typification: its color, odor, shape, size, texture, and taste. Each event is typified by such qualifications as time, place, purpose, actors, dress, and ritual.

Although individuals do not expect the world to conform completely to explicit typifications or ideals, they do expect some normal range in variation. "There are large lemons and small lemons, but generally no mature lemon is the size of a pea or a watermelon" (Preston, 1979, p. 25). One consequently expects a mature lemon to be some shade of yellow, and all real lemons have a unique color, odor, shape, size, and texture. No event, regardless of how typified, is exactly like another; yet there are limits to what constitutes a given type of event. As Preston states, "Weddings differ from funerals, and both differ from storms, sailing or bookbinding" (Preston, 1979, p.25).

Ambiguity occurs when an individual encounters an element that does not fall within a specified range of normal variations and there is no alternate typification to account for the diversion. The incongruence is the source of ambiguity (Preston, 1979, p. 26). If one finds a lemon the size of a watermelon and knows of no other lemonlike fruit that is that size, then one has found an ambiguous lemon, something that both seems to be a lemon and seems not to be a lemon. The most severe ambiguity does not arise from blatant incongruities but rather from situations that border on meeting yet not meeting a typification. Because the boundaries that delimit the characteristics of an entity are not definitive, it is not at all certain where the lines of normal and abnormal cross. The lines of normality are bands of ambiguity. Thus, it is not certain how large a lemon must be before it becomes a freak, or how much larger it must be before it becomes a nonlemon.

Goffman's concept of stigma is closely related to Preston's (1979) concept of ambiguity. Goffman (1963, p. 1) defines stigma as the incongruence between the virtual social identity (the ideal) and the actual social identity (the real). Like Preston, Goffman emphasizes the relative nature of defining a social object so that the most severe stigma results when situations border on the nomal but are not normal.

Both Preston and Goffman point out that social human beings take an active part in the development of ambiguity. Nature does not just present us with amgibuities and stigmas; we assist in this presentation. When westerners first confronted flying fish, they confronted an ambiguity arising from nature. Most ambiguities, however, are not of this sort. Most arise from incongruities in the personal and social order; that is, human beings attempt to superimpose a social order on nature through physical labor. We seek to maintain conditions that are essential for our survival. We try to restrict humankind to comparable typifications of a normal range. Regardless of his effort, however, there are human beings so disparate that they are not normative, yet they are still human beings; they are ambiguous or stigmatized human beings. In society we have the mindless, the paralyzed, the stunted, the deformed, the insane, and the dead. More normative human beings must deal with these ambiguous beings if the former are to build for themselves some security and structure in the world.

As stated above, an important aspect of the concepts of ambiguity and stigma is their relativity. Anything can be clean or dirty (Preston, 1979, p. 30). Soil in the ground is earth, but on the floor it becomes dirt.

Shoes on a floor are clean but become dirt on the dining room table. Hair on the head is clean but becomes dirt on a champagne glass. Even space, such as a missing tooth or the absence of a proper greeting, can be dirt. The point is that it is not the "dirt" that is ambiguous but the incongruence of the situation with that which is normal. Thus, earth can spoil the identity of an object and render it stigmatized.

The relationship between deviation from the normal and degree of stigmatization is curvilinear. The apex of this relationship represents the demarcation between the perception of an entity with incongruent elements and the perception of something else with elements of the entity. Before the apex, increasing deviation increases the stigmatization; after that point, the increasing deviation decreases the stigmatization. Thus, a man with grotesque features who still resembles a man would be more stigmatized than a man so grotesque that he does not resemble a man.

Because we are always trying to structure events, ambiguity is fearsome for us. A result of this fear is that underlying uncertainty may result in prejudices. Preternatural evil has been attributed to deformed people, delapidated houses, wrecked ships, and even ladders. Dead birds have been construed as omens. Monsters represent the terror of the uncertainty. They do not symbolize concrete expectations but are combinations of the incongruous (Preston, 1979). If death is their theme, and it often is, they do not lie still in their graves as ordinary beings but walk around manifesting a most ambiguous death.

We saw earlier that human beings learn their identities through social interactions; yet there is no clear definition of a human being, nor is there an explicit description of "normal" human beings, although we have norms of beauty and norms of ugliness. To the eyes of each of us, there are always ambiguous and stigmatized people. They display characteristics that are incongruent with those norms that we have of beauty. Some characteristics are more central than others in rendering someone ambiguous. For example, the face is probably the most significant aspect of the human form. Deformities of the face are more stigmatizing than comparable deformities of other parts of the body. Generally, the upper part of the body is more central to human identity than the lower part. A mermaid is less startling than a woman with a fish head. Perhaps this is because personality is so closely inter-wined with human identity. A personality disorder is generally more damning than a comparable motor disorder.

The concepts of ambiguity and stigma are important in a book on chronic illness because several chronic illnesses render a person ambiguous and stigmatized. The most common form of ambiguity occurs in the process of what Strauss and Glaser (1975, p. 60) call "identity spread." That is, when the symptom of the chronic illness is intrusive, other people assume that the ill person cannot work, act, or be like ordinary mortals. A common complaint of the blind and physically handicapped is that people are continually rushing to help them do what they are quite capable of doing or that people treat them as if they were more handicapped than they actually are. These people overgeneralize the sick person's visible symptoms. The visible stigma and ambiguity tend to dominate social interactions unless the sick person uses tactics to normalize the situation.

Normalizing a situation by the chronically ill consists of attempting to hide the intrusive symptom. A deformity may be covered with clothes, or a trembling hand may be held under the table during conversation. An epileptic person stated that she chose church people as her friends and that she had coached them to continue talking during her seizures. Afterward, they would offer her a drink of water but otherwise would go on as usual (Glaser & Strauss, 1975).

To understand the process of normalizing a situation, one must understand the distinctions between disease, illness, and sickness. Normalization involves an incongruence in definitions of the situation by the chronically ill person and those around him. As noted in Chapter 2, parties can theoretically disagree in two ways. The ill person can believe that he is more ill than others believe, or the ill person (who normalizes the situation) can believe that his condition is more normal than others believe. In this situation, the ill person conceptualizes himself as having a more normal identity than do those around him, who conceptualize him as having a sick identity.

In summary, ambiguous human beings remind normal people of their human frailties and the possibility that they too could become ambiguous. In the following section we discuss various reactions and adaptations by normal individuals to ambiguous and stigmatized individuals.

Reactions to Ambiguous and Stigmatized Human Beings
Although normal people are frightened by ambiguous people, they are also fascinated. This fascination is evidenced by numerous works of art depicting expressions of horror as well as by public reaction to horror. People will crowd in to view the gore from an automobile accident; they will almost fight to get to the head of the crowd—only to become sick.

All reactions to ambiguous and stigmatized human beings entail both ambivalence and denial. The ambivalence arises from the mystery of human identity that ambiguous people represent, an identity that both frightens and fascinates. Normal people fear ambiguous individuals' threat to the boundaries of human identity, and yet they are drawn by a promise that, if they can subdue the threat of human ambiguity, they can resolve their own human uncertainty. Thus, persons adopt means for assuaging human ambiguity both for defense and for strength. Preston (1979, pp. 50–61) describes ten means by which both professional and lay people assuage their perceptions of human ambiguity through denial and avoidance.

1. *Impulsive reaction:* The impulsive reaction is the least sophisticated. It is an impromptu reaction to a surprise encounter with human ambiguity. The individual is startled, and thus his reaction manifests an uncertainty and ambivalence so acute as to preclude any denial but flight. Temporarily a blend of horror and curiosity can transfix the individual, but ultimately he is most likely to flee.

2. *Prejudiced reaction:* A reaction is prejudiced when it is governed by a protective preconception that is not integrated with a developed ideology. Prejudices include folk conceptions, superstitions, and distorted fragments or religious rationales. These reactions assume two forms: taboo reaction (in which ambivalence is prominent) and aversion reaction (in which denial is prominent).

A taboo reaction is planned and thus is a safe experience. An ambiguous human being is seen to be mysterious, disgusting, and powerful but not dangerous as long as he is treated according to the prescribed regimen. He becomes a witch, an oracle, or a freak in a sideshow. Association with an ambiguous individual as taboo fosters a sense of power since it allows for expression of the uncertainty of human identity and enables one to affirm one's normality through contrast. An aversion reaction protects a normal individual by distinguishing the ambiguous person from humankind. Curiosity is transformed into aggression. Hate, fear, rage, horror, attack, and mockery dominate. Normal people hound and torment the cripple so that they can assure themselves that they are different.

3. *Obscenity reaction:* A person's reaction is obscene when he is obsessively drawn to mingle with an ambiguous individual. The compulsive and private nature of the obscenity reaction distinguish it from both forms of prejudiced reaction. It is an attempt by the normal individual to calm his concerns with regard to his own identity. Thus, the ambiguous individual serves as a prop between the normal person and his uncertainties about himself.

4. *Ritual separation:* Ritual separation is based on a developed ideology and is a sublimation of aversion reaction. Death rites are the ultimate form of ritualistic separation. Funerals are religious rites by which the dead are ritualistically removed from humankind. Medicine also entails rites of ultimate separation. Standardized tests are administered to the deceased so that he may be pronounced dead and deprived of the considerations due living persons.

As a hedge against confusion, normal human beings define categories of human abnormality. Medical professionals diagnose; they certify that ambiguous individuals are suffering from various maladies that set them apart from healthy people. At times, formal banishment follows the diagnosis. In the past, lepers were forced to leave society. Currently, people judged insane, are, with due process, placed in mental hospitals; paraplegics are confined to rehabilitation centers. Once these ambiguous and stigmatized people are hidden, the general public is spared the ordeal of dealing with them.

5. *Humanitarianism, or a broadening of perspective:* Unlike the previous reactions, this is one by which ambiguous individuals are bound to humankind. Here the definition of humankind is broadened to include all but the dead. Humanitarians locate human essence in the invisible realm of the spirit; the actual form of the body does not matter. A variation of this reaction is that all people are imperfect, some more than others.

6. *Spiritual transcendence:* Like humanitarianism, spiritual transcendence locates the human essence in an intangible spirit. Spiritual transcendence differs from humanitarianism in that the former is concerned with the dead and the possibility of death, whereas the latter is concerned with living ambiguous people. Rituals prepare normative mortals for positive immortal identities and usher the dead into heaven. Funerals are rites not only of temporal separation but also of spiritual transcendence.

7. *Normalization:* Normalization is an effort to reduce the ambiguity of ambiguous individuals by making them more humanlike. Surgery, therapy, and the like are used to correct the source of human ambiguity. The appeal of this reaction is that the confrontation and assuagement take place in the present. Normalization binds ambiguous people to humanity through reform or rehabilitation.

8. *Diversionary focus and actions:* Perceptions of ambiguity can be attenuated by attention to other concerns, such as one's home or family. Job-related activities are an excellent diversion. For example, a housekeeper may maneuver around a bed, scrubbing away and daydreaming as she quells the impact of the contracted body and drooling mouth of the ambiguous person in the bed.

More elaborate forms of normalization can actually be diversionary. Normalization can become so ritualized that a displacement of goals may result in an individual becoming more intent on the proper administration of a cure than on its actual effect. Preston (1979, p. 57) quotes the old adage to illustrate the point: the surgery was a complete success but the patient died.

9. *The M*A*S*H effect and method:* The M*A*S*H effect is named after the movie *M*A*S*H*, which depicts the events in an army

field hospital in Korea during the Korean War. Humor and antics are mixed with carnage and danger. M*A*S*H nurses and doctors are irreverent and cavelier, yet this relentness and frantic comedy is steeled with muted desperation. The antics seem essential for coping with the stress of the war. Seriousness in the face of so many deformities and so much surgery would be impossible. Stress evokes the M*A*S*H effect, which serves to ease the stress with diversion and release.

10. *Induration:* Induration is an unconscious diminishing of the impact of human ambiguity. In the face of threatening ambiguity, the mind protects the self through a selective myopia, in which the stigma is seen but the implications are not felt. Indurations develop gradually as a shield against chronic exposure to human ambiguity. The most severe form of induration is indifference. Complete indifference is rare, yet an element of indifference is essential to this form of assuagement.

The Impact of Professional Reactions to the Identity of Ambiguous Individuals

Several theorists and researchers (Goffman, 1963; Preston, 1979; Scott, 1970) provide convincing arguments that a health care professional's reaction to ambiguity such as chronic illness can affect a patient's identity. There is ample evidence that a chronically ill person may take on the identity imposed by the professional; however, not all professional's define the chronically ill in the same way. Scott (1970) used the example of blindness to illustrate the point. Blindness is a condition in which an absence of vision prevents a person from relating directly to his environment. People who cannot see cannot navigate on unfamiliar environments without mechanical aids or assistance from others. If they are completely blind, they cannot read or directly experience such things as distant scenery, paintings, or structures, such as buildings, that are too large to be apprehended by touch. A blind person cannot perform such activities as flying an airplane or playing tennis. There is little else, however, that can be predicted about blind people from the nature of the condition alone.

In the United States, workers for the blind espouse many different theories about blindness, most of them psychological in nature. The focus is on the impact that blindness is thought to have on one's identity and personal adjustment (Carrol, 1961). Many experts believe that the loss of vision is a basic blow the the identity, so that deep shock follows the onset of this condition. Grief and depression are likely to occur. A basic goal of rehabilitation is adjustment to the blindness. In most theories, a blind person is considered to be adjusted when he has faced and fully accepted the fact that he is blind. Only then is he ready to learn the skills and attitudes that enable him to compensate for the losses he has suffered. The final product of rehabilitation is the evalution of a new identity: that of a blind person who accepts the condition, having learned to live with it.

Professional health care workers for the blind in other countries have defined the meaning of blindness differently. Leading experts in Sweden, for example, regard blindness as little more than the loss of one sense modality. They believe that blindness does not change one's identity or abilities. Rather, blindness is a technical handicap that can be overcome by the mastery of new techniques and use of technical aids (Scott, 1970). There is great reliance on equipment such as travel guides and special devices for the home and for personal grooming. Rehabilitation is viewed as a process of learning to use the new devices most effectively. Psychiatric counseling and clinical therapy, which are an integral part of U.S. rehabilitation programs, are played down or omitted in most Swedish programs.

In England, ideologies about blindness among leading workers for the blind are cast in terms of "mood states" (Scott, 1970). These workers feel that the blind are vulnerable to depression and are constantly in danger of becoming more handicapped by their plight. One of the chief goals of working with the blind is to lift their spirits. To this end, rehabilitation centers have been established to which many blind people return for a few weeks each year. These centers are usually located in pleasant surroundings, for example, near the sea, and they have a distinctive air of cheerfulness. Music is everywhere, and much of the day is spent in diversionary social and recreational activities. Training in mechanical aids, such as Braille or the white cane, is undertaken primarily because it provides workers with opportunities to cheer up the clients. In the United States and Sweden a goal of rehabilitation is to make blind people as independent as possible. In England, however, this is not necessarily the case. Many of the blind to whom the leading experts point with admiration are unable to walk about unless they are guided by someone who can see. These workers have constructed an identity for the blind that is one of good-naturedness and cheerfullness in the face of adversity.

In many ways the professional attitudes of health care personnel determine the identities of chronically ill ambiguous people in relation to their illness. Preston (1979) found that patients at a general hospital adapted to the suppositions of the staff. Although a newly disabled person knows, phenomenologically, that he is the same person that he was before the injury or illness occurred, he is sometimes coerced by the professional health care personnel into wondering whether he has become a different person with a different identity (Kerr, 1970). The illness and disability experience places him in such new psychological identity situations in which his customary behavior may stimulate responses so radically different from what he is accustomed to that he may often consciously or unconsciously question who he is, what roles are appropriate for him, and what he can expect to be able to do. Kerr (1970) believes that the most critical answers to such questions about identity come from professional health care personnel in everyday situations during treatment. In these situations, they can help the chronically ill to develop an invalid identity or the identity of a responsible individual who can function in everyday life.

In summary, the expectations of the health care staff are useful if they help a patient to gain or regain maturity and a positive identity. They hinder if they impede the patient's progress. Kerr (1970) believes that the best kind of help is like that of a blocker on a football team, who runs interference, clears the path, creates the opportunities, and makes it as easy as possible for another player to take the ball and run with it. That, perhaps, is the major task of health care professionals. It is the patient's ball game and, by their appropriate or inappropriate expectations and behavior, health care workers can help or hinder the formation of a positive identity.

MAINTAINING A POSITIVE IDENTITY IN THE FACE OF CHRONIC ILLNESS

Case Study I: Spinal Cord Injury

John was a senior in high school and was in most ways typical of an adolescent his age. He was active in sports, had a steady girlfriend, and looked forward to graduation. John's fondest memories of high school were associated with sports: he was on the varsity swim team and played football, although he had never made the first team. Like most adolescents, John was preoccupied with his physical identity and stature; he jogged three miles per day faithfully to stay in shape. He often dreamt of winning a swimming scholarship to a well-known university. He believed that a swimming scholarship would provide his only opportunity to attend college since his family could not afford to send him and he had never been outstanding academically.

John came from a working-class family with traditional values. Both his mother and father worked at an automobile plant: his father in the foundry and his mother in the office. John was the second of four children. Nancy, his older sister, was married and had one small child. Tom was two years younger than John and was a sophomore in high school. Judy, the youngest, was 13 and would enter high school next year. All of the children held part-time jobs to earn spending money. John worked at the corner gas station.

In the spring of his senior year John went on the senior class trip, which consisted of a two-day tour of New York City and two subsequent days at a summer resort in upstate New York. During the second day at the resort John and several other friends went on a picnic and swimming outing. That afternoon a tragic accident happened. John dove off a large rock into the shallow waters of the lake. His head hit the bottom, and instantly he felt that he could not move his legs. He was taken by ambulance to a nearby hospital, where, after a few days, a final diagnosis of a severed spinal cord was made. John was paralyzed from the waist down; his new identity was that of a paraplegic.

Discussion.   As will be noted in Chapter 8, it is not easy for a person to shift from complete autonomy to complete dependence. During the first few days in the hospital John was completely paralyzed and totally dependent on other people. He could only lie in traction on a frame and stare at the ceiling for four hours and then at the floor for four hours. As with many patients, the frustration grew and, after the first few days of denial passed, John became very depressed.

A person's identity is a product of his social interactions as well as his own perception of himself. John's perception of himself began to change as he gradually acquired the ability to move his arms. He at least felt like a person again. The new movement gave him hope, which allowed him to change the image of his ideal self and to some extent allowed him to adjust to the physical disability of no movement in his legs. When John was transferred to the rehabilitation hospital, other events further enabled him to adjust gradually to the new disability. At the rehabilitation hospital he saw others with his type of injury, or with even worse injuries, so that his reference group changed. His goal of becoming a championship swimmer changed to one of being an independent adult who could manage for himself despite his physical disability.

The aspect of one's identity that is most easy to conceptualize is the material self, since this aspect of the identity is visible. A physical disability is one type of chronic illness that has the greatest impact on one's material self, which in turn has an impact on one's psychological self. John's change in physical appearance was drastic, and he became aware of it on three occasions. Four months after his accident, John was told that he would see the gym at the rehabilitation hospital. He was shocked when he was assisted into his clothes and realized that they were two sizes too big; he had gone from 195 pounds to 145 pounds. Later, while being pushed in his wheelchair into the gym, he caught a glimpse of himself in the full-length mirror. For the first time he saw what he now looked like; he was skinny, pale, and his clothes were oversized. Finally, when John was given his own wheelchair, he was shocked to realize that it symbolized his permanent disability. The chair would limit him for life, but it was the only thing that could give him independence.

It has been evident throughout this text that the role of family is important in the rehabilitation process of a patient with a chronic illness. At the end of his several-month stay in the rehabilitation hospital, John did not want to go home, despite the fact that he had gained strength in his arms and could maneuver his wheelchair with relative ease. He felt secure in the center surrounded by people who were in the same situation as he or in situations even worse, which made him feel better. When he needed something done, there were workers to help him who were being paid just for that purpose. The fact that they were being paid eliminated any guilt feelings he had about being a burden. Once John was home, however, some of the pessimism that had built up in his mind was removed. A crucial variable in the rehabilitation process is the extent to which the family allows the chronically ill person to adjust to an active role within the family. John's family allowed him to make this adjustment by providing the support and encouragement to feed the dog, participate in daily chores and by resuming the activities for which he had been previously responsible. As a result of this active role, he was treated as a responsible person, and he responded as one.

Adjusting to the outside world consists not only of adjusting to one's family's but to society in general. It consists of presenting one's new disability identity to the world. We discussed earlier the various adaptations of normal people to ambiguous or stigmatized individuals. We also discussed the strategies of the chronically ill to normalize their situation. Such adaptations and strategies were present in John's relationships. His biggest problem was that he tried to look and act normal even though he was constantly being reminded, through interpersonal relationships, architectural barriers, and vocational goals, that he was not normal. For example, his future occupation could not be dictated by what he wanted to do or even by his intellectual ability; it would be dictated by what he was physically capable of doing. This conflict between personal identity and society, however, did not force John into isolation. Although all social interactions are important, the most important are those with the family. Because of John's supportive family, he was able to retain a positive personal identity, maintain a feeling of independence, and maintain interpersonal relationships.

This discussion highlights the importance of the family in the formation of the self-concept of a newly disabled individual. For the health care worker this brings out the importance of considering the family in formulating the plan of care. The goal of the health care worker is to maximize communication between the chronically ill person and the family so that social and emotional supports are maximized. Only in this way can a person retain a positive personal identity in the face of chronic illness.

Case Study II: Juvenile Diabetes

Elizabeth is a 9-year-old who lives with her parents and 7-year-old sister, Katie, in a small university town. Both of Elizabeth's parents teach at the college: her father in the mathematics department and her mother in the school of education.

Before the onset of diabetes last February, Elizabeth was an active child and a leader among her peers. She excelled in school, scoring in the 97th percentile on national achievement tests. She was also inquisitive and sensitive, seeking full explanations for the events that occurred around her or those she heard her parents discussing. Often, long after an event was past, she would comment on it again or go over some element of the explanation she had been given.

Although she was a good student and enjoyed learning, she spent relatively little time working on school subjects. She most enjoyed being with her friends and seemed to fall naturally into a role of advisor, instigator, planner, and general leader. In the neighborhood, there were a number of children Elizabeth's age or younger, and they and Elizabeth became the pacesetters for the rest.

Elizabeth's leadership was especially evident at home, where she relished the role of big sister, both protecting and socializing Katie as she grew. She was a precise but gentle taskmaster; consistent with latency age development, she adhered strictly to rules and regulations, social norms and form. She worked very hard at blending in with the others and took on the responsibility of helping others blend in as well. For all of her attention to detail and concern over propriety, she was easy going. Although she had a slightly quick temper, she rarely pouted and could be easily cajoled into a better mood.

In February, Elizabeth caught an upper respiratory tract infection. In less than a week the acute symptoms subsided, but she remained irritable and lethargic. She was also losing weight despite an increasingly voracious appetite. Shortly after returning to school, Elizabeth had several emotional outbursts, during which she cried with very little provocation. She began withdrawing from her friends, and her performance in school slipped. At this time the teacher observed that she squinted to see the blackboard and sent a note home suggesting an eye examination.

At home, Elizabeth had frequent crying fits after school. She lost interest in family activities and quarreled with Katie when she interacted with her at all. Her weight continued to decrease, although her appetite continued to increase and she demanded between-meal snacks and drinks. She began waking in the night and had two episodes of enuresis, an experience that was extremely humiliating for her.

All of these changes occurred in a relatively short period of time. It was just over a month after Elizabeth had contracted the cold that her mother took her to a pediatrician, who diagnosed diabetes. It was routine practice to admit newly diagnosed diabetic children to the hospital in order to establish insulin control of the disease and to begin an intensive teaching program for the child and parents. Shortly after admission, with the administration of insulin, Elizabeth quickly regained her energy and old disposition. She seemed eager to learn about her disease; she quickly mastered urine testing, using the same preciseness she had exercised in her games and school activities. She seemed to understand the interaction among diet, insulin, and activity and was eager to show off her new knowledge and skills to her parents, Katie, and her grandparents.

On the unit, Elizabeth quickly became a favorite among the staff and a leader of the other children. She was frequently involved in organizing playroom activities or helping younger children. Toward the end of her hospitalization, another child with diabetes was admitted and Elizabeth had an important role in his learning experience. "It's easy," she would tell him. "Watch me," as she did the fractional urine tests and once, encouraged by his admiration, even gave herself an injection.

Elizabeth paid a great deal of attention to the other children, asking repeatedly about their disorders and prognosis, how the disease developed, how it felt, and what would happen to them. She made a clear distinction between herself and the other patients: "They are here because they are sick; I'm here to learn things."

The hospital experience went by quickly and smoothly. Elizabeth's parents were incredulous at how quickly she learned and readily accepted the major changes in her life. In contrast, it was more difficult for them to accept the permanency of a major disease that had appeared so unexpectedly.

By the time of discharge, Elizabeth was ready to leave. She was beginning to miss her friends and showed renewed interest in school and activities. Her friends were glad that she was back, although in the ever-changing lives of 9-year-olds, new alliances had formed and interests developed while she was away. They were things to which Elizabeth quickly caught on. Besides, Elizabeth had new things to talk about as well. As a way of helping her return to school, Elizabeth's teacher invited her to talk about the hospital and diabetes during show-and-tell time. Eagerly Elizabeth talked about her hospital stay and showed the children what she had learned about insulin and injections. They watched intently, but this was not something in which they could share; in fact, the "blending-in" process did not work in this case. At one point during the demonstration, one of Elizabeth's friends remarked that she did not like to watch.

In the next few weeks, Elizabeth regained her old energy and drive. She gained weight and again excelled in school. Her initial enthusiasm for being the model diabetic, however, had greatly diminished. In fact, as she resumed her old activities, she began to reject her diabetic role. She balked at testing her urine. "It's yukky and disgusting," she would argue, mimicking an observation made by one of her classmates. She no longer showed any interest in giving herself injections and protested whenever her mother rotated the injection sights on her arms or legs because she felt the marks would show. On several occasions her mother found discarded candy wrappers in her pockets, always after Elizabeth had been out with her friends.

As hard as Elizabeth was trying to reject her new illness, others were forcing her into the role, often unnecessarily. At school, the teacher would warn Elizabeth not to play in active competition and often made her sit on the sidelines. Her friends excluded her, on the advice of the teacher and sometimes their parents, from many of their games and trips. On one occasion, two of her friends told the teacher Elizabeth had candy. When Elizabeth explained that her doctor had told her to carry lifesavers (in case of unexpected hypoglycemia), the teacher was not convinced and called her mother, who verified the story.

Out of school, Elizabeth's activities also changed. One Saturday morning she found all of her friends at one house, playing after a Friday night slumber party. She ran home, crying bitterly about her friends who no longer liked her. Later in the day, the mother who had hosted the party called Elizabeth's parents. She explained that they had missed Elizabeth but that she had been afraid that Elizabeth might get sick, eat the wrong things, or require insulin. "Frankly," said the mother, "I know nothing about diabetes except the horror stories, and I'm scared to death that something will happen to Elizabeth while she's here."

By midsummer, Elizabeth had changed significantly. Her diabetes remained under good control, and she was growing at a rate appropriate for her age. There were, however, changes in her personality. She was less sure of herself, avoiding new situations and meeting new people. She no longer wanted to spend the night away from home and rarely accepted invitations to eat with her friends. Although she seemed to be avoiding many of the things she had enjoyed in the past, she was not interested in, and did not accept, the things associated with her illness. At first she had been proud of her ability to test her own urine and prepare her insulin injections but now avoided any of the trappings of the disease. She frequently had temper tantrums at the time of the injections, over meals, and over doctor appointments. In contrast, however, it was more often Elizabeth than others who would evoke diabetes as a reason for restricting her activities or as an explanation for a failure. It was as if Elizabeth were rejecting an identity she felt incapable of escaping. With the identity of diabetic came an ill-defined yet pervasive sense of vulnerability.

In August, Elizabeth's parents enrolled her in a day camp for diabetic children, a program sponsored by the hospital. She went reluctantly and concealed her attendance at camp from her friends, giving a variety of excuses for being away each day. The camp was an active one near a lake. Activities included tennis, riding, and swimming lessons in addition to diabetic classes and group activities dealing with disease management. For the first time since her diagnosis, Elizabeth was in contact with other diabetics, who shared her concerns and feelings and at the same time were very much like her other friends. At home and at school, she was the only diabetic she knew, and whatever it meant to be a diabetic had been left for her to figure out. At camp, she was able to sort out other children according to what she liked or did not like about them, not according to whether or not they had diabetes. She belonged and fit in. Twice during the day everyone gathered together and tested urine. The children complained and joked about it, and learned tricks and twists, but they all did it together. At camp this activity was something that made Elizabeth belong, not something that isolated her.

As the summer progressed, Elizabeth became much more confident and assertive. With the regular and scheduled activities, her insulin needs decreased and became more stable. She was happy and excited about what she was doing. Because she belonged to a close group at camp, her absence from neighborhood friends did not matter. During the last week of camp, the children were encouraged to invite their families and selected friends to attend special picnics and events. Once again, Elizabeth was eager to show off what she had learned and mastered. This time the activities were not disease-related but focused on the children's normal development and talent. The special friends Elizabeth had invited felt the privilege, and her reintegration into her group at school had begun.

In the fall Elizabeth would be returning to an ordinary environment. The camp experience had been artificial, but by experiencing a reference group relatively early in the course of her illness Elizabeth was able to learn which characteristics belonged to her disease and which to herself.

By the time that Elizabeth returned to school, much of the maintenance care of diabetes had become routine and no longer an issue. Her confidence had returned, and her sense of self and identity had become more fully determined. After all, she had met many diabetics, some of whom were tall and others short; some pretty, others not; some friendly, some less amiable. The variety among the children had made them much like others Elizabeth knew.

In the case of diabetes, there is no disfigurement. Elizabeth learned more about the real vulnerability: she saw children who got sick when the illness went out of control, and she saw those for whom the disease was more severe. She also learned what she could safely do. She saw children being active; she herself engaged in tough competition and sometimes won and sometimes lost. The outcome was less a product of the disease than of her natural ability and effort.

It is important to understand that the "learning" referred to in this discussion is the learning acquired through experience, in the sense of learning attitudes, social norms, likes, and dislikes. The latency age is a time during which important socialization into the family and society occurs. The natural development bent, at this time, toward rules and structure facilitates the process. At the same time, a child's conceptual and verbal abilities are still limited. Elizabeth knew that she was a diabetic and could precisely "feed back" her instructions concerning insulin, exercise, and diet. However, no one will ever know what Elizabeth's conceptualization of diabetes was. During the latency age the ability to reason abstractly develops, and there is an active exchange between concrete and abstract representation. How did Elizabeth understand the fact that the islets of Langerans were not functioning?

The major way in which school-age children learn is by experience and exploration. They begin to develop abstract concepts from a collection of concrete experiences and to categorize the world. The structure that school-age children create for themselves provides the framework through which this information is processed to produce an identity and sense of self. The peer group is very important during this time, for as a reference group it provides further stability. Peers become an extension of the secure base that parents provide younger children. Peers provide the feedback, models, and information through which children learn. They learn what it means to be a boy or girl, an athlete, a student, or a friend. They learn who they are: an American, a country or a city dweller; a Lutheran, a Catholic, or a Jew; a Yankee or Red Sox fan; a student of a particular grade school. They learn about social traits: kindness, generosity, intelligence, talent, and style. School-age children therefore pay a great deal of attention to labels.

When the onset of a chronic disease adds a new label during the latency period, a child's peer structure is disrupted until representatives of the child's new category can be found. Because Elizabeth was the first diabetic that either she or her peer group had ever known, everything that she was and did became part of the diabetic role. That label set her apart. Because a latency-age child is just forming an identity, experiencing and "trying on" different ways of behaving and thinking, any label that is introduced during this period will have a great impact on his later sense of self. As the child grows, given enough varied experiences, his perspective on the multitude of roles and labels will shift, and the contribution of the disease label to his identity will be less dominant. When Elizabeth was first diagnosed, she quickly became a female diabetic who was good in school. After the camp experience and several months of struggling with her feelings, she emerged as a girl, an excellent student, who had diabetes.

REFERENCES

Bunzel, J. H. Note on the history of a concept—gerontophobia. *Gerontologist*, 1972, 12(2, Pt. 1), 116; 203.

Carroll, T. J. *Blindness: What it is, what it does, and how to live with it.* Boston: Little, Brown, 1961.

Cooley, C. *Human nature and the social order.* New York: Scribner's, 1902.

Cumming, E., & Henry, W. E. *Growing old: The process of disengagement.* New York: Basic Books, 1961.

Epstein, S. The self concept revisited. *American Psychologist*, May 1973, pp. 407–416.

Erikson, E. H. *Childhood and society* (2nd ed.). New York: Norton, 1963.

Gergen, K. *The concept of self.* New York: Holt, Rinehart, 1971.

Giedt, F. H., & Lehner, G. F. J. Assignment of ages and on the draw-a-person test by male neuropsychiatric patients. *Journal of Personality*, 1951, 19, 440–448.

Goffman, E. *Stigma: Notes on the management of spoiled identity.* Englewood Cliffs N.J.: Prentice-Hall, 1963.

Gordon, C., & Gergen, K. Introduction to Volume I. In C. Gordon & K. Gergen (Eds.), *The self in social interaction.* New York: Wiley, 1968.

Grant, C. H. Age differences in self concept from early adulthood through old age. *Proceedings of the 77th Annual Convention of the American Psychological Association*, 1969, 4, 717–718.

James, W. *Psychology: The briefer course.* New York: Holt, 1910.

Kelley, H. Two functions of reference groups. In G. Swanson, T. Newcomb, E. Hartley (Eds.), *Readings in social psychology* (2nd ed.). New York: Holt, Rinehart, 1952.

Kerr, N. Staff expectations for disabled persons: Helpful or harmful? In J. Stubbins, (Ed.), *Social and psychological aspects of disability.* Baltimore: University Park Press, 1970.

Kohlberg, L. Stage and sequence: The cognitive development approach to socialization. In D. Goslin (Ed.), *Handbook of socialization theory and research.* Chicago: Rand McNally, 1969.

Koocher, G. Swimming, competence, and personality change. *Journal of Personality and Social Psychology,* 1971, 18, 275–278.

Lowenthal, M. F., & Chiriboga, D. Transition into the empty nest: Crisis, challenge, or relief? *Archives of General Psychiatry,* 1972, 26, 8–14.

Lowenthal, M. F., Thurnher, M., Chiriboga, D. & Associates. *Four stages of life: A comparative study of women and men facing transitions.* San Francisco: Jossey-Bass, 1975.

Mason, E. P. Some correlates of self-judgments of the aged. *Journal of Gerontology,* 1954, 9, 324–337.

Mead, G. *Mind, self, and society.* Chicago: University of Chicago Press, 1934.

Middlebrook, P. N. *Social psychology and modern life.* New York: Knopf, 1974.

Morse, S., & Gergen, K. J. Social comparison, self-consistency, and the concept of self. *Journal of Personality and Social Psychology,* 1970, 16, 148–156.

Neugarten, B. L., & Gutmann, D. L. Age–sex roles and personality in middle age: A thematic apperception study. In B. L. Neugarten (Ed.), *Middle age and aging.* Chicago: Chicago University Press, 1968.

Pepitone, A. An experimental analysis of self dynamics. In C. Gordon & K. Gergen (Eds.), *The self in social interaction.* New York: Wiley, 1968.

Preston, R. P. *The dilemmas of care: Social and nursing adaptions to the deformed, the disabled and the aged.* New York: Elsevier, 1979.

Rosenfelt, R. H. The elderly mystique. *Journal of Social Issues,* 1965, 21, 37–43.

Roy, Sister Callista. *Introduction to nursing: An adaptation model.* Englewood Cliffs, N. J.: Prentice-Hall, 1976.

Sarbin, T. R. Role theory. In G. Lindzey (Ed.) *Handbook of social psychology.* Reading, Mass.: Addison-Wesley, 1954.

Scott, R. A. *The making of the blind.* New York: Russell Sage, 1970.

Sherif, M., & Cantril, H. *The psychology of ego involvements.* New York: Wiley, 1947.

Simmel, M. Developmental aspects of the body scheme. *Child Development,* 1966, 37, 83–95.

Strauss, A. L., & Glaser, B. G. *Chronic illness and the quality of life.* St. Louis: Mosby, 1975.

Sullivan, H. S. *The interpersonal theory of psychiatry.* New York: Norton, 1953.

Thomae, H. Theory of aging and cognitive theory of personality. *Human Development,* 1970, 13, 1–16.

Wallach, M., & Kogan, N. Aspects of judgment and decision making: Interrelationships and changes with age. *Behavioral Science,* 1961, 6, 23–36.

White, R. Motivation reconsidered: The concept of competence. *Psychological Review*, 1959, **66**, 297–334.

Ziller, R. *Self-other orientation: Theory and communication.* Paper presented at the meeting of the American Research Association, New York, February 1967.

Chapter 8

Personal Control

Independence, personal control and self-determination are basic values of human life. Throughout the life span, people struggle to gain, enhance, and maintain control of themselves and their lives. Chronic illness presents a serious threat to these fundamental values. As noted in Chapter 2, the successful management of chronic illness depends to a large extent on clients' opportunities to control and direct their treatment regimen. Several dimensions of concept of control are important to understand in relation to chronic illness. In this chapter we discuss locus of control and health locus of control, as well as related or similar concepts: learned helplessness, attribution, and fatalism. This theoretical discussion is followed by a review of empirical evidence relating personal control to developmental stages and the management of stress and illness. The chapter concludes with two case studies that demonstrate the relevance of the concept of personal control in a toddler with hemophilia and an older adult with arthritis.

LOCUS OF CONTROL

Among the most widely cited dimensions of personal control is the concept of locus of control developed by Rotter (1966) and subsequently refined, specified, and measured by many others (for reviews, see Arakelian, 1980; Lefcourt, 1966b). Social learning theory provides the theoretical framework for this concept (Rotter, 1954). The definition proposed by Rotter (1966, p. 1) is as follows:

> When a reinforcement is perceived by the subject as following some action of his own, but not being entirely contingent upon his action, then it is typically perceived as the result of luck, chance, fate, as under the control of powerful others, or as unpredictable because of the great complexity of the forces surrounding him. When the event is interpreted in this way by an individual, we have labeled this a belief in *external control*. If the person perceives that the event is contingent upon his own behavior or his own relatively permanent characteristics, we have termed this a belief in *internal control*.

Expectancy and value are two important aspects of locus of control. Expectancy refers to the belief that certain behavior of an individual will result in a particular reinforcement. With time, and having had multiple and diverse life experiences, the individual comes to expect that certain outcomes will or will not follow upon his behavior. Value refers to the extent that reinforcement is important to an individual. In general, the more value an individual places on a particular outcome, the greater will be the relevance of the individual's capacity to influence the outcome. For example, to be able to influence the occurrence of symptoms in a chronic illness is likely to be a valued outcome for most people, and thus the belief that one's own actions can accomplish this is important.

Locus of control, as conceptualized by Rotter (1966), is a generalized expectancy that functions over a broad range of situations and predicts the extent to which individuals believe that they have or do not have the power to control what happens to them. This construct describes individuals according to the degree to which they accept or claim personal responsibility for what happens to them (Lefcourt, 1966a). Although the assessment that an individual makes of his control in a specific situation (situational expectancy) is determined by the particular set of circumstances, it is also true that individuals draw on past experiences (generalized expectancies) to make determinations about the present (Arakelian, 1980). In the following section we discuss a situation-specific dimension of locus of control.

Health Locus of Control

In recent years the debate over whether locus of control is a generalized or situational expectancy has become more pronounced. The general I–E (internal–external) Scale developed by Rotter (1966) does not seem to predict health behaviors (Tolor, 1978). In fact, Rotter (1975) has admitted that how broad a measured of generalized expectancies can be in order for it to include the expectancies relevant to multiple and diverse situations is somewhat arbitrary. Some writers suggest that the narrower the sampling and the more situationally specific the items, the closer will be the prediction to specific situations (Reid, Haas, & Hawkings, 1977). Others note the faulty assumption that people are consistent in their behaviors in all situations and that global, nonspecific measures of personality, such as Rotter's I–E Scale, can predict behaviors in highly specific circumstances (Mischel, 1968). Any personality measure must take into consideration an individual's developmental stage, the event to which the measure is supposed to apply, and the value that the individual places on the event.

In an attempt to achieve more sensitive predictions of health behavior and perceived control Wallston, Wallston, Kaplan, and Maides (1976) developed a Health Locus of Control Scale. These authors noted the mixed and contradictory findings reported by Marston (1970) in her review of the literature on perceived control and physical health and well-being. One of the reasons for contradictory results is found in a basic premise of social learning theory. According to this theory if an individual has repeated experiences in a specific situation, he will learn what to expect. Therefore, the generalized expectancies measured by the Rotter I–E Scale do not necessarily predict specific health behaviors. Thus, Wallston et al. (1976) developed a specific measure based on the assumption that health-related locus of control would more precisely predict the relationship between perceived control and health behavior. The dimensions of expectancy and value are maintained in the health locus of control measure, but the content is specific to health and illness.

Misconceptions About Locus of Control

Rotter (1975, p. 59) has suggested that a number of misconceptions about the concept of a generalized expectancy for internal versus external control of reinforcement have arisen, at least as he developed the concept and its operational measures. The first has resulted from the failure of most investigators to treat reinforcement value as a separate variable. In order to determine the predictive capabilities of internality versus externality, one must either control value or measure it separately. It makes no sense to explore the influence of internality versus externality unless the outcome or behavior being measured is known to be valued by the individual. Although health is assumed to be a universal value, there is evidence that the value of health, and thus health and illness behavior, may be relative when compared with other desired outcomes or competing needs, as mentioned in Chapter 1 and supported by the literature (Becker, 1974; Fabrega, 1973; Mechanic, 1978).

The misconception (alluded to in the above discussion of health locus of control) relates to the specificity or generality of the concept. Rotter (1975) states that the more structured, familiar, and unambiguous a situation is, the less reasonable it is to assume that a generalized expectancy will predict behavior. In these situations more reliable information about behavior can be predicted by more specific measures of perceived control.

The third misconception is the pervasive, implied or explicit notion that being internal is good but being external is bad. As discussed in some detail in a later section of this chapter, one's perception of control may be very stressful, whereas the belief that one is not in control and thus not responsible for the outcome may be much less stressful.

Concepts Related to Locus of Control

Investigators have tried to understand a person's ability (or lack of ability) to control his personal environment from many conceptual perspectives. Among those similar to locus of control are self-efficacy (Bandura, 1977), personal sense of mastery (Coleman, Campbell, Hobson, McPartland, Mood, Weinfield, & York, 1966), competence (Moos & Tsu, 1976; White, 1959), powerlessness (Seeman, 1959), hopelessness (Beck, Weissman, Lester, & Trexler 1974), feeling the "pawn" versus the "origin" (deCharms, 1968), learned helplessness (Seligman, 1975), fatalism (Wheaton, 1980), and learned inflexibility (Kohn, 1972).

Bandura (1977, p. 191) postulates that expectations of personal efficacy determine whether coping behavior will be initiated, how much effort will be expanded, and how long it will be sustained in the face of obstacles and aversive experiences. Bandura distinguishes two kinds of expectation. Outcome expectancies refer to "a person's estimate that a given behavior will lead to certain outcomes." An efficacy expectation is the conviction that "one can successfully execute the behavior required to produce the outcomes." In other words, if an individual believes that certain behaviors will result in certain outcomes, but does not believe that he can perform the required activity, then his behavior will not be influenced. The stronger the perceived self-efficacy, the more effort the individual will put forth to achieve some outcome.

Two decades before Bandura experimented with the concept of self-efficacy, White (1959) described competence in terms of feelings of efficacy. Competent human beings experience the power of initiative and a sense of being the causal agent in their own lives. Moos and Tsu

(1976) suggest that, for competent people, transitions and life crisis may be defined as opportunities and challenges rather than threats to self-integrity.

Learned helplessness theory states that the expectation that an outcome is independent of responding (a) reduces the motivation to control that outcome and (b) interferes with learning that responding controls outcome in other contingencies (Maier & Seligman, 1976). Learned helplessness is an inability to respond instrumentally after experiencing inescapable aversive events in which instrumental behavior had no effect on outcome. This phenomenon has been demonstrated in both animals and human beings (Seligman, 1975). Helplessness is a three-step process: (a) information about reinforcement contingency is received; (b) cognitive representation of the contingency in the form of learning, expectation, or belief occurs; and (c) behavior follows. If the individual learns that he can control aversive events his fear is reduced and may disappear. If, on the other hand, the individual learns that he cannot control the trauma, his fear will decrease with time and be replaced by depression (Maier & Seligman, 1976).

Several conceptual variations on helplessness have appeared in the literature. One of these is pessimism or hopelessness, in which an individual fails to make any effort to change his life circumstance. Although many clinical investigators have defined hopelessness as a diffuse feeling state and consequently too vague and amorphous to test, Stotland (1969) suggests that hopelessness can be defined as a system of negative expectancies concerning one's current and future life. As such, it is similar to learned helplessness.

At issue in much of the research dealing with personal control is the question of whether the critical factor is control as such or predictability. This is important in situations in which a person may not be able to control the occurrence of an event but can predict when the event will happen and plan strategies to manage its occurrence. For example, the symptoms of some chronic conditions might be managed with greater ease if they could be predicted, even though they are uncontrollable.

Control can be actual or potential. In the first case an individual is able to modify an event through some behavior initiated by himself. Potential control occurs when an individual believes that some controlling response is available to him but refrains from using it (Miller, 1979). In this case he is comforted by the thought that, if and when it becomes necessary to control an event, he will be able to do it; this is referred to as the "safety net" phenomenon. Other definitions of control and controllability are similar to those of Miller (1979). Averill (1973) and Lazarus (1966) include the notion of cognitive control, which can be analogous to presumed or potential control, although Miller (1979) argues that cognitive control is actually analogous to predictability, because it places a person in the presence of safety signals. Averill (1973) further distinguishes between behavioral control (taking direct action) and decisional control (the capacity to make choices among alternatives). Schulz (1976) argues that control in all instances is confounded by predictability since having control over a stimulus also means that it is predictable. The question of whether the ability to control adds anything over and above the ability to predict remains unanswered.

Fatalism and learned inflexibility have been studied in tandem and will therefore be discussed together. Both of these concepts are best understood within the framework of attribution theory (Heider, 1958), which postulates a relationship between *can* and *try*. Individuals are not likely to try something if they do not believe that they can do it. The relevance of attribution theory to locus of control can be stated simply. People who believe that they have some control over their lives are called "internals"; they believe that they can, and therefore they try. People who attribute life events to luck, chance, or fate are called "externals"; they do not try to control their lives because they do not believe that they can (MacDonald, 1971, p. 111). The notion of *can* is also referred to as *ability,* and *try* is sometimes referred to as *effort.*

Fatalism is a learned and persistent causal attribution tendency that directs an individual's perception of the causes of behavioral outcomes toward external factors, e.g., task difficulty or luck (Wheaton, 1980). Instrumentalism, the opposite concept, is a tendency to perceive the causes of behavioral outcomes as internal factors, e.g., one's own ability or effort. Fatalism increases one's vulnerability to stress by impairing and undermining effort in coping situations (that is, the intensity of performance of any behavior) and does not affect ability (Wheaton, 1980, p. 106).

"Learned inflexibility" is a summary term denoting a complex of orientations to social reality, including a strong belief in external conformity, rigidity, mistrust, and a limited range of available behaviors to use in coping situations (Kohn, 1972; Wheaton, 1980). Learned inflexibility is relevant to coping ability (range and flexibility of coping behaviors) and not directly related to effort. However, individuals with restricted ability may respond with minimal effort in stressful situations. The twin concepts of fatalism and learned inflexibility have considerable relevance in chronic illness. However, there has been little empirical work in this area.

SOCIAL CORRELATES OF PERSONAL CONTROL

The concept of personal control, or some variation of it, has been used in many research studies in an attempt to predict its effect on health and illness. Much of this research has focused on the relationship between age, socioeconomic status, ethnicity, or other demographic variables and personal control.

Life Stage and Personal Control

Age is perhaps the most common demographic variable in this research. Although age is important, it is often more useful to consider development stage (a range of ages) as a key factor in personal control and health.

In infancy, the development of personal control begins as a response to contingencies experienced in the environment. When an infant perceives a reliable response to his behavior, there is an increase in responding and emotional expression (Chapter 3). As the child grows, personal control becomes the means by which he learns about himself in relation to the environment (Brazelton, Koslowski, & Main, 1974; Fraiberg, 1974).

As the child reaches the concrete-operational phase of cognitive development, cause and effect relationships predominate in describing the environment. During this stage, every event is seen to be the product of a cause, and most causes are internal or egocentric (Minuchin, 1977). For example, children from 5 to 12 years of age are likely to believe that illness is a consequence of some wrongdoing by the sick person. The older children will identify more health-specific behaviors as causes of illness but, like younger children, blame the sick person for his own illness. The attribution of deserved outcome as an explanation for misfortune is consistent with both the egocentrism stage of development described by Piaget and the magical thought processes described in psychodynamic theory of development: every event must have a cause, and the power the child feels over the environment is supreme but unharnessed and nondirected.

In adolescence, the development of abstract thought processes result in the recognition of chance, randomness, and uncontrollability. The adolescent sees himself not as all-powerful but as capable of producing directed effects. Adolescence has been described as the age in which one believes that "I can do anything I put my mind to, if I choose to put my mind to it and if others would stop interfering". During this time, selective attention is paid to controllable events; uncontrollable events are ignored, or attention to them is deferred. The concept of blame is still a prevalent feature of interpretation of the environment. The adolescent feels strongly that other people can and should control their destiny but at the same time feels unable to control his own, being at the mercy of others' errors and poor judgment (White & Speisman 1977). The sense of personal control is strong in adolescence, yet the adolescent feels insecure and ambivalent about his growing independence.

The middle years are a time of growth and peak performance in life work. They are also a time of heavy demands and responsibilities for younger generations (offspring), older adults (usually parents/in-law), and career or occupational achievements. Kobasa's (1979) study is an example of research that focuses on personality and the ability to manage high levels of occupational responsibility. He developed a construct of "hardiness," which includes a component of belief in one's ability to control or influence life events. The middle-aged executives in Kobasa's study who were highly stressed but had few illnesses were more likely to score higher on hardiness than were highly stressed, frequently ill executives. Hardiness, and therefore personal control, appears to be an important mediating variable in this instance.

Kivett, Watson, and Busch (1977) used locus of control as a dependent variable and investigated the predictors for it among middle-aged adults. Three classes of predictors were used: physical variables (self-rated health, race, sex, and age); psychological variables (several dimensions of self-concept: actual, ideal, and appearance to others); and social variables (education, occupation, and religious motivation). These investigators found that self-concept, religious motivation, and occupation had the strongest relationship to perceived control. Occupations that allowed for control of people or machines, positive (actual) self-concept, and intrinsic religious motivation were predictive of internally oriented adults.

With the increasing recognition of the importance of understanding the life stage of *older adults,* more and more research into the problems of aging is being carried out. A major feature of aging in American society is the gradual, but persistent loss of influence over one's life and community. The psychological impact of the social and physical losses incurred by the aging has been shown to be related to one's sense of personal control. There is evidence from studies of personal control and aging that personal control is associated with higher activity levels (Kuypers, 1971), greater life satisfaction (Palmore & Luikart, 1972; Wolk & Kurtz, 1975), and positive self-concept (Reid et al., 1977; Wolk, 1976). Cicirelli (1980) has shown that a family variable, namely, sibling and child cohesiveness, is positively related to an internal locus of control among noninstitutionalized elderly persons.

Ethnicity, Socioeconomic Status, and Personal Control

Ethnic minorities and individuals of low socioeconomic status are frequently in situations of little personal control. There is reason to suspect that externality, fatalism, and learned inflexibility may be particularly dominant among these groups of people (Kohn, 1972; MacDonald, 1971; Varghese & Medinger, 1979; Wheaton, 1980).

Wheaton (1980, p. 101) has argued that low socioeconomic status socializes individuals to be more fatalistic in their casual perceptions and that fatalism increases that vulnerability to psychological disorder primarily because it undermines persistence and effort in coping situations. In other words, fatalism is an intervening or modifying factor in the relationship between social class and psychological disorder.

A model to explain schizophrenia among the socially disadvantaged suggests that learned inflexibility is a major factor (Kohn, 1972). According to Kohn (1972, p. 302), the constricted conditions of life experienced by people of lower social classes foster conceptions of social reality so limited and so rigid as to impair these people's ability to deal resourcefully with problems and with stress.

The arguments of Wheaton (1980) and Kohn (1972) imply that externality is a negative and maladaptive personality characteristic. Varghese and Medinger (1979), in contrast, propose that fatalism may be a very powerful buffer against depression and anxiety for aging ethnic minorities. They point out that aging is a problem of decreasing power resources. For individuals with decreasing personal, physical, and social resources and thus decreasing ability to intervene in the environment (a situation of high constraint), fatalism is an accurate assessment of reality and as such indicates strong mental health (Varghese & Medinger, 1979, p. 108). MacDonald (1971) reminds us that locus of control is not a motivational variable but an expectancy variable. Many disadvantaged persons may want to change their status but do not try to do so because they do not have any expectations of success. Motivation plus negative expectation may lead to despair. Thus, Varghese and Medinger's assertion that fatalism is a protection against depression and anxiety makes sense.

PERSONAL CONTROL AND HEALTH: EMPIRICAL EVIDENCE

The concept of personal control is particularly important in the management of long-term illness. Perceived control may mean the difference between living with chronic illness with a modicum of equanimity or surviving in a state of discouragement, increasing invalidism, and despair. A growing body of literature supports the idea that both actual and perceived control facilitate an individual's ability to cope with difficult, distressing, or frightening situations. In this section we review some of the literature that shows the important role of personal control in three areas, each of which has relevance to chronic illness: compliance, depression, and the management of tension.

Personal Control and Compliance
One of the most critical factors in chronic illness is compliance. The literature is replete with evidence that deviation from prescribed medication or treatment regimens is common. However, there are relatively few published reports on the role of personal control as a factor in compliance. Thus, one can only speculate about the relationship between factors affecting compliance and personal control. One such factor may be the acquisition of information about the nature of the illness and the nature of the treatment regimen, retention of that information, and its utilization. Seeman and Evans (1962) found that internally oriented tuberculosis patients possessed more information about their illness than did externally oriented patients. Davis and Phares (1967) demonstrated differences between internally and externally oriented college students in the active seeking of information. When available information was ambiguous, internal students sought more information than external students; under conditions requiring skill, external students sought significantly less information than internal students. Phares (1968) showed that internally oriented individuals are superior to the externally oriented in the utilization of information.

Wallston, Maides, and Wallston (1976) tested the hypothesis that health-related information seeking is a joint function of locus of control and the value of health. Specifically, these investigators proposed that "given the opportunity to gather information about a health problem which may or may not affect him/her, the internal who values health highly will seek more information than one who does not value health or who holds external beliefs." Their data supported this hypothesis (Wallston et al., 1976, p. 217).

In a review of the literature on locus of control and health, Wallston and Wallston (1978, pp. 108–111) report the following about control and compliance issues:

- Internal individuals are more likely than external individuals to change their smoking behavior or quit smoking (Platt, cited in Strickland, 1973) (some studies do not support these findings: Best & Steffy, 1971; Lichtenstein & Keutzer, 1967).
- In weight loss studies, external individuals generally weighed more but lost less weight; however, in treatment groups there

was no difference in locus of control and weight loss (Manno & Marston, 1972).

- In weight reduction programs *tailored* to the clients' tendencies toward internality or externality, internally oriented clients lost more weight in internally oriented, self-directed programs; external subjects did better in programs oriented to external factors, e.g. groups (Wallston et al., 1976).

- Among MI patients, return to hospital and/or death within 12 weeks of discharge has been related to the kind of self treatment intervention program established; that is, individuals in congruent treatment groups (internal individuals in high-involvement groups and external individuals in low-involvement groups) did better after hospitalization than did those in noncongruent treatment groups (Cromwell, Butterfield, Brayfield, & Curry, 1977). In other research no differences have been shown between internal and external individuals in various compliance measures post-MI (Marston, 1970).

- Internally oriented new diabetics know more about their disease than do external diabetics (Lowery & Ducette, 1976). Long-term diabetics did not differ in knowledge by locus of control. Internally oriented long-term diabetics became increasingly noncompliant in diet and clinic appointments.

- Internally oriented dialysis patients are more likely to comply with diet restrictions (Weaver, 1972), as well as medication regimens (Wenerowicz, Riskind, & Jenkins, 1978).

- Using a case study (no structured measures) approach, Viederman (1978) concluded that dialysis patients who believed themselves to be in control of their situation were better adapted to their disease and its requirements (i.e., complaint, minimal depression or anxiety).

- Externally oriented black women with hypertension were more compliant with diet and medication regime, but there were no differences in clinical appointment keeping by locus of control (Key, 1975).

- Children of mothers who perceive control over factors related to the children's weight problems are more likely to achieve weight loss than obese children whose mothers do not perceive such control (Becker, Maiman, Kirscht, Haefner, & Drackman, 1977).

It is clear from these research findings that compliance is a multifaceted phenomenon. Much of the research is contradictory, and there is no clear-cut pattern in the findings on personal control in situations requiring compliance. Svarstad (1976) reviewed much of the literature on factors relevant to compliance and concluded that one of the most important (although infrequently studied) is the interpersonal style of the physician. In general, clients are dissatisfied with the failure of physicians to reassure, explain, and invite questions (Kasl, 1975). As indicated in Chapter 2, participation in decision making about treatment plans is critical for a chronically ill person. If physicians, or nurse practitioners, counselors, and/or rehabilitation specialists, take the time to explain regimens, learn how these regimens fit into the client's life-style and goals, discuss variations and alternatives, and finally arrive at mutually agreeable methods of treatment, it is more likely that clients will comply. This kind of interaction between client and caregiver is the basis for the formation of an alliance or coalition of equal participants rather than merely compliance, which implies passive adherence by the client to the orders and recommendations of the caregiver (Barofsky, 1978).

Janis and Rodin (1979) noted one caveat in the methods that health care providers use to induce feelings of personal control in clients. Health professionals have very strong ideas about the effectiveness of treatment regimens and sometimes, in their zeal to influence clients, may overemphasize the "shoulds" and "musts." When the regimen being discussed involves difficult life-style changes (giving up smoking, omitting salt from diet, increasing exercise, or monitoring sexual activity), one response by the client might be what Brehm (1966) calls "reactance." This response occurs when individuals who perceive that their choices are restricted become motivated to restore their lost freedom and regain control. Janis and Rodin (1979 p. 502) indicate that this reaction may explain why some clients act in ways that seem not to be in their best interest, e.g., quitting treatment and excessive violations of diet or medication regimen. These clients may be trying to restore their sense of control, which they perceive to have been taken away by the health professional. Thus, noncompliance becomes an active coping strategy, but the consequences are likely to be negative.

In addition to increasing compliance by increasing client control through careful attention to interpersonal style, it has been suggested that treatment programs be tailored to the locus of control orientation of clients (Phares, 1976). For example, an externally oriented person may do much better in group situations where advice and counsel come from others (some of whom may be professionals). An internally oriented person might do better in a situation in which there are multiple options for treatment, a large degree of participation in decision making, and strong emphasis on personal responsibility and accountability for treatment outcomes (Wallston & Wallston, 1978, p. 114).

It is important for health care providers to recognize that, although many clients benefit from opportunities to exercise control, not everyone benefits from such opportunities. It would be foolish, if not dangerous, to attempt to make the orientation of all clients internal. Personal control can be so stress producing as to outweigh the benefits that may accrue from such control. In addition, attempts to control uncontrollable conditions are likely to induce self-blame, depression, or despair. Care must be taken to develop a plan of treatment for the chronically ill that will enhance an individual's personal resources and maximize the positive outcomes.

Personal Control and Depression

Personal control has been proposed as a factor in depression, a significant potential problem in chronic illness. Using the notion that depressed individuals perceive themselves to be relatively ineffective in exerting control over significant life events and their outcomes, Donovan, O'Leary, and Walker (1979, p. 461) developed and tested a measure of subjective helplessness for use in clinical assessment and counseling. They had previously shown that Rotter's (1966) I–E Scale was incapable of predicting levels of depression among alcoholics (O'Leary, Donovan, Cysewski, & Chaney, 1977). However, externally oriented subjects who had experienced minimal control over their health problem were significantly more depressed than other groups within the study. The combination of external locus of control and the experience of minimal influence over a life event was a better predictor of depression than was locus of control alone. Reasoning that the experience of minimal control produces a negative expectancy in future situations, Donovan et al. (1979) extended this line of investigation to show that alcoholic subjects who report high levels of perceived helplessness are significantly more depressed than those who report low levels of helplessness. The authors suggest that clients' reports of helplessness may be clinically useful in the understanding and treatment of depression among the chronically ill.

The perception by chronically ill individuals of a decreasing ability to master the environment may be due to any number of biological, psychological, or social assaults attending the long-term condition. Solomon (1981) has analyzed the process leading to depression among the elderly, a process in many ways analogous to that among persons with chronic diseases. Multiple stressors create an immediate sense of loss of mastery and competence; normal and expected (but intolerable) dependencies follow the onset of chronic illness, which engenders a sense of helplessness accompanied by fear, anger, and sometimes panic. An important intervening factor, according to Solomon (1981), is the individual's previous experiences and his style of coping. In the presence of adequate and appropriate coping skills the outcome of stress is problem solving and a renewed sense of mastery and adaptation. If there are no coping skills or if they are inadequate or inappropriate, the result is an ever-deepening and immobilizing depression.

Personal Control and the Management of Tension

The way in which individuals manage the stresses of chronic illness determines the extent to which their physiological, social, and psychological worlds remain intact and functioning. The question we have raised in this chapter is, What, if any, difference does a sense of personal control make in the management of chronic illness? We have seen that locus of control has a promising but mixed influence on individuals' compliance with treatment regimens, that client–caregiver interactions may influence the sense of personal control, and that perceived control and mastery may make a difference in warding off depression. Here, we selectively review the literature that addresses the role of personal control in the management of stress, tension, and/or crisis, all of which surface periodically in the lives of the chronically ill.

In a study referred to earlier, Kobasa (1979, p. 3) describes the concept of hardiness, the characteristics of which are a belief that one can control or influence life events, an ability to feel deeply involved in or committed to the activities in one's life, and the anticipation of change as an exciting challenge to further development. Kobasa (1979) considers personality to be one of several mediators of the influence of stress on health. The others are physiological predisposition, early childhood experiences (previous life experiences), and social resources. According to Kobasa (1979, p. 3), among persons under stress, those who have a greater sense of control over what occurs in their lives will remain healthier than those who feel powerless in the face of external forces.

Control has three dimensions (Averill, 1973): (a) decisional control, the capacity to choose autonomously among various courses of action to handle stress; (b) cognitive control, the ability to interpret, appraise, and seek information and to incorporate stressful events into an ongoing life plan and thereby deactivate their jarring effects (Foushee, Davis, Stephan, & Bernstein, 1980; Kobasa, 1979); and (c) behavioral control, the capacity to draw on a repertoire of suitable responses developed during earlier life experiences. Individuals without this repertoire of skills are powerless, nihilistic, and low in motivation (Kobasa, 1979). Kobasa's subjects were highly stressed executives, some of whom remained healthy and others of whom succumbed to illness. The highly stressed/low-illness executives; displayed greater hardiness than the highly stressed/high-illness executives; i.e. they had a strong commitment to self, a sense of meaningfulness, a vigorousness, and internal locus of control. Thus, Kobasa's hypothesis was supported.

Foushee et al. (1980) obtained slightly different results in a laboratory setting where some subjects had behavioral control and where cognitive control was manipulated by various feedback conditions (success, failure, no feedback). Behavior control had no effect on the subjects' abilities to perform. Subjects given feedback performed better on subsequent tasks than did those given no feedback. The investigators suggested that cognitive control (appraisal of performance) may be a better indicator of perceived control than is behavior control.

PERSONAL CONTROL AND THE IMPACT OF A CHRONIC ILLNESS

The two case studies in this section illustrate the concept of control in relation to stage of life development and the circumstances of a particular chronic illness. The life stages were selected to show how a chronic illness may affect the life of a toddler who is just beginning to achieve independence and an older adult who is struggling to maintain an independent life style.

Case Study I: Hemophilia

Brian Saddler is a 30-month-old white child who lives with his parents and 5-year-old sister, Elizabeth, in a small rural community near Bangor, Maine. His father works as a shipping manager for a large lumber firm and his mother, who was an elementary school teacher before she married, runs a small day-care center in their home.

Mrs. Saddler was the only child and grew up in a quiet family neighborhood in Boston. Mr. Saddler had a very different childhood, being the third of four sons who lived in the outback of Maine. He worked as a lumberjack until he sprained his back in a fall and was confined to a less strenuous office job. Mrs. Saddler had an easy pregnancy and delivery with Brian, and both parents eagerly welcomed the birth of their first son. Mr. Saddler especially looked forward to the rough-and-tumble activity he expected to have with his son.

Brian grew quickly and developed normally, even reaching some of the milestones ahead of his age group. By the time he was a year old he was walking with a stable gait, keeping up with many of the 2-year-olds who attended the day-care center. He followed his sister, Elizabeth, everywhere and tried to imitate her play. Because he showed a propensity for climbing and tumbling and the minor gymnastics his father engaged him in, both parents tended to overlook the bruises that he had almost continually on his arms and legs. Mr. Saddler considered these the "badges of boyhood," and the Saddler's family practitioner assured Mrs. Saddler that active children Brian's age always bruise when they learn to walk and run.

When Brian was 20 months old, he fell from a swing, bumping his head just above his left eye. Although he fell only a short distance, he quickly developed a large hematoma that increased in size even after Mrs. Saddler applied ice. By the time they reached the physician, the hematoma covered half of Brian's temporal and frontal region, closing his left eye. The physician suspected that the fall was more severe than Mrs. Saddler reported, and because of the eye involvement he transferred Brian to the medical center in Bangor. There the Saddler's learned that Brian had classical hemophilia. Because Mrs. Saddler had no brothers and only a vague recollection of an "uncle who died early with some blood disease," the family medical history had given no indication of this sex-linked inherited disorder.

The acute episode of bleeding was quickly controlled without surgical intervention; there was no damage to Brian's eye, and radiographic studies showed no joint involvement from earlier bleeding. The hematologist at the center told the Saddlers that it was to their credit that Brian had reached nearly 2 years of age without a major bleeding episode.

A week after admission Brian was discharged. The family physician was informed about the disorder and was involved in developing an emergency treatment regimen for future bleeding episodes. Although the physical consequences of Brian's first hospitalization were minor, the diagnosis had a major impact on the Saddlers. The family, in effect, left the center with a new child—they now saw their healthy, robust son as a fragile, vulnerable baby.

The psychological impact of any hereditary disease is often pervasive, affecting the relationship between parents and between parents and children. When the disorder involves overt and life-threatening manifestations (such as bleeding or seizures), the extent to which daily life is altered after diagnosis is often increased. Many extensive changes occurred in Brian's life after the diagnosis.

Mrs. Saddler, especially, tried to protect Brian from every harm. She no longer permitted him to climb or run or to play with the other children at the day-care center. She tried to keep him in an old playpen that he had long ago rejected, but he managed to climb out, nearly falling over the railing. Instead of using a playpen, Mrs. Saddler insisted on holding Brian's hand or keeping him in a carriage; when that failed, she carried him around in her arms. The more insistent she became about restraining him, the more resistant Brian grew. Temper tantrums became daily occurrences, often ending with Brian in his padded crib screaming until he fell asleep.

As Brian approached 2 years of age, the "I do Self" phase increased and grew more persistent. Brian was allowed to do some things such as dress or feed himself, but, typical of a 2-year-old's activity, most quiet, harmless action quickly evolved into some motor activity that Mrs. Saddler saw as threat to Brian's safety. Most of Brian's days were filled with struggle: his straining to be on his own, his mother's interference, and his frustrated resistence. Brian's interaction with the rest of the family also changed. Mr. Saddler no longer played with Brian for fear of hurting him. He realized that the bruises he had once noted with a sense of pride were really an indication of a dread disease, signs of weakness instead of strength.

Elizabeth was cautioned not to hurt Brian, to stay away from him, lest she accidentally fall on him or bump him, and not to let him see her play so that he would not try to imitate her and be injured. Mrs. Saddler closed the day-care center, partly because she needed full time to watch Brian and partly because she was afraid he would learn dangerous things from the other children.

Over the months, Brian's struggling slowly diminished. He became more passive, sitting by himself, crying, or sucking his thumb. He tried fewer and fewer new things and, instead of resisting his mother's restraint, clung to her. He did not seem to be learning much; his potty-training, which had been disrupted by the hospitalization, had never been resumed. He seemed to be talking less, learning fewer new words, and showing less spontaneity and interest in things around him.

Even with the protective bubble the family tried to provide, bleeding episodes occurred: Brian bumped his tooth on his high chair, cut his finger on broken glass, and closed a dresser drawer on his hand. Once he hit his head as he was trying to get away from his mother's grip. Each time he became bruised or bled, the Saddlers rushed him to the family physician, who gave him an intravenous injection of the clotting factor or treated him less aggressively with ice packs and observation.

On the last of these visits, Mrs. Saddler discussed her concern about the change in Brian's personality and development. She was particularly concerned with his decrease in speech. She wondered if these changes could be signs of undiagnosed bleeding, perhaps in the brain? To be certain and to reassure Mrs. Saddler, the physician again referred Brian to the medical center.

Brian had a diagnostic work-up that showed no cerebral organicity and no joint involvement, but the lag in development was a definite change from his earlier pattern of growth and maturation. The center had a large case load of young children with chronic illness; the changes in Brian and Mrs. Saddler's concerns were characteristic of a number of children who were patients there, not all with the same disorder, and of their families. Most of Brian's signs—his listlessness, irritability, and developmental lag—were a product of the management of the disorder rather than the disorder itself. There were no primary physical reasons for Brian's behaviors; they were a result of the disuse of developing abilities and an interruption of independence and interpersonal exchange. It was essential for Brian to try out things for himself in order to master each level of development. Because child development intricately involves all sensory–motor systems, restriction in one area interferes with maturation in another. When Brian was prevented from trying out his newly developing motor skills, his speech and social development suffered.

The question for the Saddlers was one of risk. Certainly they wanted Brian to develop normally, but did that require risking his life? This is the question faced by many parents of children with a chronic disease: how can one meet the demands of the disorder without interfering too heavily with the normal aspects of the child's life? The pediatric department at the medical center had a group of nurse practitioners and child-life workers who helped the parents of chronically ill children. A case worker assigned to the Saddlers introduced them to a group of parents who had hemophilic children. In the group, the Saddler's learned how other parents had worked with their children. They also learned that their all-or-nothing approach to Brian's developing sense of independence was giving them few options. For example, not every bump was life threatening, and so keeping Brian totally bump-free was an extreme that was both unnecessary and problematic. Similarly, Brian did not have to climb high trees to be independent, there were safer things that he could do on his own, perhaps risking minor injury but developing a sense of independence nevertheless. Mr. Saddler might not be able to play with Brian as vigorously as he had expected, but that did not mean he had to forego all contact with his son. Perhaps the whole family had to be much more careful, but at the same time it was important for Brian to learn that he could survive minor bumps and bruises and to learn what he could accomplish on his own.

The center influenced the Saddlers' response to Brian's illness in another way. By teaching them how to assess the extent of bleeding, how to administer the clotting factor, and how to anticipate the need for prophylactic medication, the center gave the Saddlers a greater sense of control over the consequences of the disease. Moreover, the center encouraged the Saddlers to become active members of the parents' group. Even though the center was over 50 miles from the Saddlers' home, the bimonthly meetings were an opportunity to exchange information with others who were handling similar problems. Parents of older children could provide guidance for the future. In turn, the Saddlers could provide information to new parents joining the group and feedback to older group members.

With the new support, instruction, and methods of care the Saddlers had received, they began to set more realistic limits for Brian, limits that were appropriate for the normal development of a 2½-year-old with hemophilia. As some of the restraints were relaxed, Brian began to recover his old energy and initiative.

Brian is now being disciplined, the process through which he can learn internal control, rather than externally restrained. He still wants to do things that would place him in jeopardy, and the disease is still threatening. As Brian grows, the Saddlers will be faced with the problem of balancing risks to his physical well-being against interference with normal development.

Discussion. The effects of a chronic illness on a child's development, specifically on the development of independence and personal control, are determined by many factors. Among these are the characteristics of the disease itself. Some chronic illnesses inherently limit development or activity. For example, a child with cerebral palsy or Down's syndrome may not reach developmental milestones, or a child with heart disease may not be able to keep pace with his companions. The achievement of independence or personal control for these children will have to fall within the limitations of the disease. However, other chronic disorders, such as hemophilia, epilepsy, and rheumatic fever, do not inherently affect development, energy levels, or motor maturation, they have an effect as normal development unfolds. In these cases, limitations are placed on a child's normal behavior to prevent him from suffering the consequences of the disease; hence, the child feels a struggle between his normally developing capabilities and the external restrictions that are placed on him.

A second factor that influences the impact of chronic illness on normal development is the role of independence or personal control in the child's maturation. Independence for a toddler is a medium for learning. The child learns by doing; he learns, for example, to walk, dress, and eat. By climbing, running, and playing, the child learns about himself in relation to the environment. By exercising his developing sense of personal control, the toddler learns about himself as "doer." The process of developing independence, therefore, lays the foundation for the child's later attribution of self-efficacy as well as personal vulnerability. In adults and older children, chronic illness often means a loss of independence; a state of dependency is often at odds with a person's sense of self (ego-dystonic). The individual struggles against the dependency or a resolution brought about by a new definition of self or of independence/dependence. For a toddler, the process of becoming independent is just beginning and normally occurs as motor, sensory, cognitive, and emotional capabilities unfold through development. To the extent that chronic illness interrupts this process, the child's definition of himself incorporates a sense of helplessness or ineffectiveness.

The last factor is the role of the family in the development of the child's sense of independence. To a large extent, a toddler's achievement of personal control depends on the confidence and effectiveness the family feels in dealing with the child and the illness. The child's exercise of personal control means that there will be unpredictable outcomes. The wider the parents' repertoire of coping responses and the more secure the parents feel with this repertoire, the more likely they will be to encourage the child's explorative and independent behaviors. Mrs. Saddler's sense of helplessness in dealing with injury once it occurred resulted in her restriction of Brian's activities. His independent behaviors carried the threat of injury, which Mrs. Saddler felt incapable of handling. Once she was given alternative coping actions, she felt more comfortable about allowing Brian to test his own limits.

The support from experts and peers (physicians, nurses, parents, etc.) enhanced the Saddlers' sense of personal control. In turn, the support they gave to Brian and the learning he shared with his peers (Elizabeth and the children in the day-care center) enhanced his sense of personal control. For the toddler (and probably throughout the life span) personal control develops most steadily when the environment is secure and supportive yet at the same time provides a challenge.

Case Study II: Osteoarthritis

Mrs. Elizabeth Cannon is a 75-year-old black woman who lives alone in a small home, which she owns. Her home is situated in an established neighborhood on the edge of a large midwestern city. Mrs. Cannon knows all of her neighbors; in fact, she knows several generations in each family. For years Mrs. Cannon served as the local "nurse" in the neighborhood; she delivered most of the babies and was consulted by most of the neighbors for advise in treating common ailments. She is a respected and valued member of the neighborhood.

Mrs. Cannon's husband died eight years ago. All of her grown children live in the same city but not in the same neighborhood. She has three daughters, two sons, fifteen grandchildren, and two great grandchildren. She is proud of her family and pleased with the way she brought them up—to be hard working and independent.

Recently Mrs. Cannon has become increasingly bothered by the "rheumatism" in her hips, knees, and back. She has had "aches and pains" for years, and the recent increase in pain and stiffness, she claims, is just due to old age. A week ago Mrs. Cannon fell in her home and sustained a serious blow to the head, which rendered her unconscious. When she awoke she was unable to get up because of a badly injured knee. She managed to crawl to the phone and call her oldest daughter, who had her mother taken to the nearest emergency room. Her sprained knee was wrapped in an ace bandage. Because she had been unconscious for an undetermined time, the physician admitted her to the hospital for observation. During Mrs. Cannon's hospitalization, the liaison community health nurse and the social worker made a careful assessment of her functional capacities and her living arrangements. They met with Mrs. Cannon and several of her children to develop a plan of posthospitalization care.

Mrs. Cannon's physical health status is of concern. Not only does she have extensive osteoarthritis in the hips, and lumbar spine, but she has failing vision due to senile cataracts and moderate hypertension. Mrs. Cannon's arthritis is exacerbated by obesity. She is five feet, three inches tall and weighs 192 pounds. The physician has ordered her to be on a diet of 800 to 1000 calories.

Of equal concern to her children is Mrs. Cannon's mental and emotional state. She has become very quiet and withdrawn and is frequently observed to be quietly crying. When asked what is wrong she replies, "It's okay; I'll take care of everything." Mrs. Cannon's thoughts, which she shares with no one, are about the way her life has changed in the past week. She cannot get around by herself; she does not think that she will be able to afford the kind of food necessary for her new diet; and she knows that the medicines will be expensive. She has never been able to lose weight before; how will she do it now? The physician has told her that her cataracts will have to be taken care of soon or she will be completely blind. How will she pay for an operation? She is supposed to see the physician once a month for the next few months. How will she get there? She cannot walk to the bus stop, she cannot afford a cab, and she has never relied on her children, although she knows that they will help if she asks. Besides, how can she pay for a monthly office visit? The worst thought of all, the one Mrs. Cannon tries not to think about, is the possibility that she will have to sell her home and move to an apartment or, worse, a nursing home. She would rather die first.

Discussion. Mrs. Cannon's situation is not unusual among older people who are able to manage their lives independently until an accident or illness occurs. Such an event often initiates a gradual loss of independence, a feature of most people's lives that they proudly and tenaciously cling to in the face of overwhelming odds.

Osteoarthritis is common among older adults. After the age of 60, 15 percent of men and 25 percent of women have symptoms of this disease (Grob, 1978). Since the weight-bearing joints are most affected by osteoarthritis, obesity aggravates the condition. The aching pain associated with osteoarthritis is relieved by rest and aspirin. Gait and posture are affected, and involvement of the hip and knee may cause instability, which, in addition to decreased visual acuity, probably caused Mrs. Cannon to fall.

Although osteoarthritis is not a particularly serious physical condition, Mrs. Cannon's situation illustrates a number of important aspects of personal control, which if not considered by caregivers can eventually result in incapacitating mental and emotional deterioration. During hospitalization, Mrs. Cannon is overwhelmed by the possible consequences of her recent accident. Because she does not share these fears with anyone, they seem insurmountable and cause her to become very depressed. After all, has she not been the source of strength of her family and the neighborhood for years? How can she ask them for help? Her sense of helplessness and worthlessness and her depression are acute.

The visiting nurse, social worker, and several of Mrs. Cannon's children discuss her situation in detail and outline a tentative plan of care that will preserve her sense of personal control. The plan is tentative because they will eventually discuss it with Mrs. Cannon and if necessary alter it to meet her goals and relieve some of her anxieties and fears. The six key objectives of the plan are as follows:

1. To acknowledge that Mrs. Cannon wants to maintain independence and control over her daily life.
2. To encourage Mrs. Cannon to express her fears and anxieties about the changes that have occurred in the past week.
3. To develop ways to ensure Mrs. Cannon's mobility around her home.
4. To work out a plan of meals that meet the caloric requirements of the new diet and ensure tastiness and economy.
5. To arrange transportation to the physician's office.
6. To ensure that all aspects of her care are economically possible (with minimal dependence on the family) and that they are worked out with her.

Mrs. Cannon and her children meet in her home on the day that she is discharged from the hospital to begin planning for the new situation. The children immediately assure Mrs. Cannon that she will be able to stay in her own home. This relieves Mrs. Cannon of a major, nagging concern. As Ebersole and Hess (1981) state, the home, is the "last strong bastion of independence" for an older adult. In the days that follow many aspects of Mrs. Cannon's new situation are explored, solutions suggested, and plans made. We shall note some of the solutions here to give the reader an idea of the scope of resources readily available within the family and neighborhood.

1. Mrs. Peabody lends Mrs. Cannon a walker. When Mrs. Cannon's knee improves, the walker will be very helpful to her in the house.
2. Mrs. Allen goes once each month to a general practice clinic that has several physicians who are known to take good care of older adults. The office nurse has agreed to schedule Mrs. Cannon's appointments on the same day as Mrs. Allen's so she can ride with Mrs. Allen.
3. The physicians at the clinic follow Medicare fee schedules, *listen* to their older clients, explain procedures, discuss plans and options for care, and prescribe generic drugs whenever possible. These features of the health care system are among the most important to an older client's sense of participation and control (Ebersole & Hess, 1981).
4. The clinic is next door to the senior center. The geriatric nurse at the senior screening center has agreed to initiate plans for a group of older "weight watchers" to meet and exchange problems, successes, and tasty, low-cost menus. Mrs. Cannon can also have her blood pressure checked here in between visits to the physician's office.

At present Mrs. Cannon is limited in her capacity to do something for others in the neighborhood; she must be content for a while to receive from others. However, she has been a participant in the decisions about her care; and her fears of loss of financial independence, loss of mobility, and loss of her home have been relieved. Her family is aware of how she feels, they respect her desire and ability to make decisions about her care, and the neighbors are pleased to have the opportunity to help their friend, who has always been such an important figure in the community. As soon as Mrs. Cannon's knee improves and she gets used to the walker, she plans to become involved in some of her previous activities. She has, with the intelligent assistance of family, neighbors, and health professionals, regained some measure of control in her life. Few people are completely self-sufficient, but mobility, the capacity to care for oneself, adequate financial resources, and a home of one's own constitute the major features of an older person's sense of competence, self-esteem, and independence.

REFERENCES

Arakelian, M. An assessment and nursing application of the concept of locus on control. *Advances in Nursing Science,* 1980, 3(1), 25–42.

Averill, J. R. Personal control over aversive stimuli and its relationship to stress. *Psychological Bulletin,* 1973, 80, 286–303.

Bandura, A. Self-efficacy: Toward a unifying theory of behavioral change. *Psychological Review,* 1977, 84, 191–215.

Barofsky, I. Compliance, adherence and the therapeutic alliance: Steps in the development of self-care. *Social Science and Medicine,* 1978, 12, 369–376.

Beck, A., Weissman, A., Lester, D., & Trexler, L. The measurement of pessimism: The hopelessness scale. *Journal of Consulting and Clinical Psychology,* 1974, 42, 861–865.

Becker, M. The health belief model and personal health behavior. In M. H. Becker (Ed.), *Health Education Monographs,* 1974, 2, 326–327.

Becker, M., Maiman, L., Kirscht, J., Haefner, D., & Drachman, R. The health belief model and dietary compliance: A field experiment. *Journal of Health and Social Behavior,* 1977, 18, 348–366.

Best, J. A., & Steffy, R. A. Smoking modification tailored to subject characteristics. *Behavior Therapy,* 1971, 2, 177–191.

Brazelton, T. B., Koslowski, B., & Main, M. The origins of reciprocity: The early mother–infant interaction. In Lewis M. & Rosenblum, L. (Eds.), *The effect of the infant on its caregiver.* New York: Wiley, 1974.

Brehm, J. W. *A theory of psychological reactance.* New York: Academic Press, 1966.

Cicirelli, V. Relationship of family background variables to locus of control in the elderly. *Journal of Gerontology,* 1980, 31, 108–114.

Coleman, J., Campbell, E., Hobson, C., McPartland, J., Mood, A., Weinfield, F., & York, R. *Equality of educational opportunity.* Washington, D.C.: U.S. Government Printing Office, 1966.

Cromwell, R., Butterfield, E., Brayfield, F., & Curry, J. *Acute myocardial infarction: Reaction and recovery.* St. Louis: Mosby, 1977.

Davis, W. L., & Phares, E. J. Internal–external control as a determinant of information-seeking in a social influence situation. *Journal of Personality,* 1967, 35, 547–561.

deCharms, R. *Personal causation.* New York: Academic Press, 1968.

Donovan, D., O'Leary, M., & Walker, R. D. Validation of a subjective helplessness measure. *Journal of Personality Assessment,* 1979, 43, 461–467.

Ebersole, P., & Hess, P. *Toward health aging.* St. Louis: Mosby, 1981.

Fabrega, H. Toward a model of illness behavior. *Medical Care,* 1973, 6, 470–484.

Foushee, H. C., Davis, M. H., Stephan, W. G., & Bernstein, S. M. The effects of cognitive and behavioral control on post-stress performance. *Journal of Human Stress,* 1980, 6(2), 41–48.

Fraiberg, S. Blind infants and their mothers: An examination of the sign system. In Lewis M. & Rosenblum L. (Eds.), *The effect of the infant on its caregiver.* New York: Wiley, 1974.

Heider, F. *The psychology of interpersonal relations.* New York: Wiley, 1958.

Janis, I., & Rodin, J. Attribution, control, and decision-making: Social psychology and health care. In G. Stone, F. Cohen, N. Adler (Eds.), *Health psychology.* San Francisco: Jossey-Bass, 1979.

Kasl, S. Issues in patient adherence to health care regimens. *Journal of Human Stress,* 1975, **1,** 5–17.

Key, M. *Psychosocial and education factors surrounding compliance behaviors.* Unpublished doctoral dissertation, George Peabody College, Nashville, Tenn. 1975.

Kivett, V. R., Watson, J. A., & Busch, J. C. The relative importance of physical, psychological, and social variables to locus of control orientation in middle age. *Journal of Gerontology,* 1977, **32,** 203–210.

Kobasa, S. Stressful life events, personality and health: An inquiry into hardiness. *Journal of Personality and Social Psychology,* 1979, **37**(1), 1–11.

Kohn, M. Class, family, and schizophrenia. *Social Forces,* 1972, **50,** 295–302.

Kuypers, J. A. Internal–external locus of control and ego-functioning correlates in the elderly. *Gerontologist,* 1971, **12,** 168–173.

Lazarus, R. *Psychological stress and the coping process.* New York: McGraw-Hill, 1966.

Lefcourt, H. M. Belief in personal control: Research and implications. *Journal of Individual Psychology,* 1966, **22,** 185–195.(a)

Lefcourt, H. M. Internal versus external control of reinforcement: A review. *Psychological Bulletin,* 1966, **65,** 206–220.(b)

Lichtenstein, E., & Keutzer, C. Further normative and correlation data on internal–external (I–E) control of reinforcement scale. *Psychological Reports,* 1967, **21,** 1014–1016.

Lowery, B., & Ducette, J. Disease-related learning and disease control in diabetics as a function of locus of control. *Nursing Research,* 1976, **25,** 358–362.

MacDonald, A. P. Internal–external locus of control: A promising rehabilitation variable. *Journal of Counseling Psychology,* 1971, **18,** 111–116.

Maier, S. F., & Seligman, M. Learned helplessness: Theory and evidence. *Journal of Experimental Psychology: General,* 1976, **105**(1), 3–46.

Manno, B., & Marston, A. Weight reduction as a function of negative covert reinforcement (sensitization) versus positive covert reinforcement. *Behavior Research Therapy,* 1972, **10,** 201–207.

Marston, M. Compliance with medical regiments: A review of the literature. *Nursing Research,* 1970, **19,** 312–323.

Mechanic, D. *Medical sociology* (2nd ed.). New York: Free Press, 1978.

Miller, S. M. Controllability and human stress: Method, evidence and theory. *Behavioral Research and Therapy,* 1979, **17,** 287–304.

Minuchin, P. *The middle years of childhood.* Monterey, CA: Brooks Cole Publishing Co., 1977.

Mischel, W. *Personality and assessment.* New York: Wiley, 1968.

Moos, R., & Tsu, V. Human competence and coping. In R. Moos (Ed.) *Human adaptation.* Lexington, Mass.: Heath, 1976.

O'Leary, M., Donovan, D., Cysewski, B., & Chaney, E. Perceived locus of control, experienced control, and depression: A trait description of the learned helplessness model of depression. *Journal of Clinical Psychology,* 1977, **33**, 164–168.

Palmore, E., & Luikart, C. Health and social factors related to life satisfaction. *Journal of Health and Social Behavior,* 1972, **13**, 68–80.

Phares, E. J. Differential utilization of information as a function of internal–external control. *Journal of Personality,* 1968, **36**, 649–662.

Phares, E. J. *Locus of control in personality.* Morristown, N.J.: General Learning Press, 1976.

Reid, D., Haas, G., & Hawkings, D. Locus of desired control and positive self-concept of the elderly. *Journal of Gerontology,* 1977, **32**, 441–450.

Rotter, J. B. *Social learning and clinical psychology.* Englewood Cliffs, N.J.: Prentice-Hall, 1954.

Rotter, J. B. Generalized expectancies for internal versus external control of reinforcement. *Psychological Monographs,* 1966, **80**(1), 1–28.

Rotter, J. B. Some problems and misconceptions related to the construct of internal versus external control of reinforcement. *Journal of Consulting and Clinical Psychology,* 1975, **43**(1), 56–67.

Schulz, R. Effects of control and predictability on the physical and psychological well-being of the institutionalized aged. *Journal of Personality and Social Psychology,* 1976, **33**, 563–573.

Seeman, M. On the meeting of alienation. *American Sociological Review,* 1959, **24**, 783–791.

Seligman, M. *Helplessness.* San Francisco: Freeman, 1975.

Soloman, K. The depressed patient: Social antecedents of psychopathologic changes in the elderly. *Journal of the American Geriatric Society,* 1981, **29**(1), 14–18.

Stotland, E. *The psychology of hope.* San Francisco: Jossey-Bass, 1969.

Strickland, B. *Locus of control: Where have we been and where are we going?* Paper presented at the meeting of the American psychological Association, Montreal, 1973.

Svarstad, B. Physician–patient communication and patient conformity with medical advice. In D. Mechanic (Ed.), *Growth of bureaucratic medicine.* New York: Wiley (Interscience), 1976.

Tolor, A. Some antecedents and personality correlates of health locus of control. *Psychological Reports,* 1978, **43**, 1159–1165.

Varghese, R., & Medinger, F. Fatalism in response to stress among the minority aged. In D. Gelfand, & A. Kutzik (Eds.), *Ethinicity and aging.* New York: Springer, 1979.

Viederman, M. On the vicissitudes of the need for control in patients confronted with hemodialysis. *Comprehensive Psychiatry*, 1978, **19**, 455–467.

Wallston, B., & Wallston, K. Locus of control and health: A review of the literature. *Health Education Monographs*, 1978, **6**, 107–117.

Wallston, K., Maides, S., & Wallston, B. Health-related information seeking as a function of health-related locus of control and health value. *Journal of Research in Personality*, 1976, **10**, 215–222.

Wallston, B., Wallston, K., Kaplan, G., & Maides, S. Development and validation of the health locus of control scale. *Journal of Consulting and Clinical Psychology*, 1976, **44**, 580–585.

Weaver, R. *Internality, externality and compliance as related to chronic home dialysis patients*. Unpublished masters thesis, Emory University, Atlanta, 1972.

Wenerowicz, W., Riskind, J., & Jenkins, P. Locus of control and degree of compliance in hemodialysis patients. *Journal of Dialysis*, 1978, **2**, 495–505.

Wheaton, B. The sociogenesis of psychological disorder: An attributional theory. *Journal of Health and Social Behavior*, 1980, **21**, 100–124.

White, R. Motivation reconsidered: The concept of competence. *Psychological Review*, 1959, **66**, 297–333.

White, K., & Speisman, J. *Adolescence*. Monterey, CA: Brooks Cole Publishing Co., 1977.

Wolk, S. Situational constraints as a moderator of the locus of control-adjusting relationship. *Journal of Consulting and Clinical Psychology*, 1976, **44**, 420–427.

Wolk, S., & Kurtz, J. Positive adjustment and involvement during aging and expectancy for internal control. *Journal of Consulting and Clinical Psychology*, 1975, **43**, 173–178.

Part 3

Major Issues In Chronic Illness

Chapter 9

Ethics and the Quality of Life in Chronic Illness

In this chapter we address two aspects of chronic illness that are interrelated, yet distinct: ethics of care and research and quality of life. Very little has been written specifically about either of these issues in chronic illness, although they have been dealt with in the context of acute or terminal illnesses. This chapter is not intended to be a substitute for bioethics texts. An increasing number of such texts have been published and the reader is urged to consult these for a solid base on this topic. The purpose of this chapter is to make the health care provider sensitive to a range of critical issues of ethics and life quality inherent in the care and treatment of the chronically ill. Questions relevant here include the following. Who decides what kind of care is necessary? How much information does the client have a right to? What criteria guide decisions about care? Do these criteria differ with the individual's life stage? When should the family participate in decision making? Does the client have the right to refuse care? Is technology inherently good, and should we use it in all cases simply because it is available and insurance will pay for it? How are decisions made regarding the allocation of scarce health care and technological resources? Who determines the issues of quality of life? Although we cannot address all of these questions, we will discuss some of them.

QUALITY OF LIFE AND HEALTH CARE TECHNOLOGY

The task of defining the quality of life of any individual is an impossible undertaking. For each of us the meaning and purpose of life are bound up in basic needs for material and spiritual sustenance, for health, for achievement of personal goals, and for a whole gamut of cherished hopes and expectations. For some the onset of a chronic illness means fundamental and profound changes in life style; For others less drastic changes are required. For none, however, does life retain precisely the same meaning or purpose it had before the illness, and thus for all there is some change in the quality of life.

Quality of life is thus an elusive concept at best and is defined largely in terms of personal or group preferences. Apart from any consideration of its relation to chronic illness, quality of life has been conceptualized at a macrosocietal level to include health, meaningful activity, freedom to choose among options, security and freedom from threat, stimulation, novelty and richness of life experiences, influence, affluence, affection, and friendship (Blumenfield, 1969; Katzner, 1979). The life quality of aggregate members of a society can be translated to reflect the quality of its individual members. As such, George and Bearon (1980) suggest that quality of life must be assessed both as objective measures of resources and as subjective evaluations of personal life experience. Quality of life thus includes both the conditions of life and the experience of life (Campbell, Converse, & Rodgers, 1976).

The subjective evaluation of life quality can be considered in terms of two dimensions: life satisfaction and self-esteem. Measures of life satisfaction cover a wide range of content related to past experiences, successes, and future prospects. Self-esteem is related to general life satisfaction and includes a sense of personal worth and self-love, acknowledging personal weaknesses and strengths. An important point for health care providers is made by Bloom (1975), who observes that the provision of services to a client may unintentionally result in lowered self-esteem by the client, who may perceive himself to be impotent, powerless, and needy. Paternalism, to which reference will be made later, may be unethical not only because it prevents client self-direction, but also because it damages self-esteem.

Objective conditions of life quality, according to George and Bearon (1980), are functional status and socioeconomic status. Functional status includes mobility, capacity for self-care, and enough energy to emerge in whatever activities one wishes. Socioeconomic status refers to material goods and financial security. Although income, tangible assets, and functional status can be objectively assessed, they are closely tied to perceived (subjective) assessment of adequacy. Thus, at the heart of the issue are personal values and judgments (Katzner, 1979).

With this brief overview of quality of life as background, we turn to the important consideration of medical technology. The use of highly advanced technology to sustain or maintain life in certain chronic conditions raises ethical questions that often are answered within the context of the quality of life. Let us first consider the philosophy of technology.

In an extremely perceptive discussion of technology, Jonas (1979, p. 35) outlines four traits of modern technology:

1. Every new step in whatever direction of whatever technological field tends *not* to approach an equilibrium or saturation point in the process of fitting means to ends (nor is it mean to), but on the contrary to give rise to further steps in all kinds of directions and with a fluidity to the ends themselves.
2. Every technical innovation is sure to spread quickly through the technological world community.
3. In relation of means to ends is not unilinear but circular. Familiar ends may find better satisfaction by new technologies ... but equally, new technologies may ... impose new ends, never before conceived, simply by offering their feasibility.
4. Progress, therefore, is not just an ideological gloss on modern technology, but an inherent drive.

If we accept Jonas's description of technology, we can anticipate that the explosion of technology in the field of health care will continue, perhaps even accelerate; that outcomes unknown at present will be upon us, even imposed upon us; that technological means of intervening in health and illness states will continue to permeate the medical marketplace, not only in the tertiary care setting, but in the primary care setting as well; and finally, that technology at an ever-increasing level of complexity, unless interfered with, will become, as Jonas (1979) says, our destiny.

Questions regarding the ethics of biomedical technology concern the means of gaining control over the process of technological advancement and using technology in a way that recognizes the human being in the maintenance of life and the relief of pain and suffering. As McCormick (1978, p. 30) notes, the availability of powerful new technologies that can sustain life almost indefinitely has forced us to ask what we are doing when we intervene to forestall death. What values are we seeking, and how can we maintain our grasp of the basic values that define well-being? These questions bring us once again to the issue of quality of life. What kind of life will be preserved by intervention with medical technologies? Life can mean two things: a state of *human* functioning and *human* well-being, or the existence of vital, metabolic processes without human capacity (McCormick, 1978). Although life in the latter sense is a necessary condition for human life, the concerns we address in this chapter have to do with the chronically ill person's capacity to function as a human being.

The use of advanced medical technologies generally brings mixed blessings to the recipients. A good example of this is the situation of an individual with advanced renal disese. Should the decision be made to remain on dialysis or to risk a transplant? A person on dialysis is not as likely to die but is quite likely to develop, in time further medical and psychological problems. Children on dialysis may have considerable difficulties, including severely retarded physical growth as well as diminished social development. An individual who has a successful transplant has some advantages in terms of generally good health and freedom from the regimen of dialysis treatments. However, immunosuppressant drugs, a lifelong requirement, have effects on the individual's appearance and render him extremely susceptible to infection. The technology of either dialysis or transplantation, although life sustaining, brings mixed blessings in its stead.

The use of advanced biomedical technologies to maintain life in conditions of chronic illness is inextricably tied to issues of life quality. In the next section we discuss a framework for decision making that ensures the inclusion of life quality concerns.

DECISION MAKING IN CHRONIC ILLNESS

All clinical decisions rest on (or should rest on) careful examination of the facts of the case and the consequences that can be expected when a particular course of action is taken. This is no different in cases of chronic illness, but recent emphasis on the ethical implications of the use of advanced technologies has heightened interest in and concern for the decision-making processes in clinical settings. Two basic questions are asked: who decides, and what are the criteria used to arrive at decisions?

Clinical decisions involve at least two individuals: the client and the professional caregiver (physician, nurse, soical worker, or other therapists). As indicated in Figure 1 each of these actors is influenced by a set of facts and values, which when interpreted give meaning to the situation. Ideally, there is open communication between client and caregiver that results in an accurate diagnosis and shared treatment goals, which from time to time are reviewed and revised when appropriate.

Both actors are confronted with facts, which in this case are signs and symptoms indicative of some deviation from a previously existing

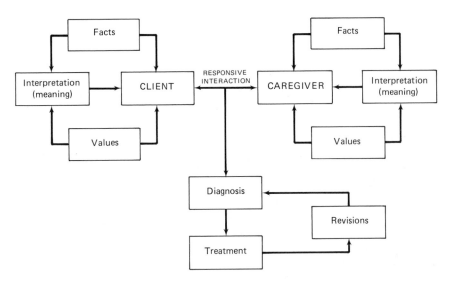

Figure 1. Model for clinical decision making and action. *Adapted from Martin (1978(a), p. 209)*

state of health. The caregiver (physician, for example) interprets these symptoms by conducting an examination and diagnostic procedures. The client may interpret them by reading and consulting with family and friends. Both actors have a set of values that permeate and influence their actions. They may include moral, religious, and cultural views of the world and personal goals and interests. For the physician these values include professional norms and codes of action (Martin, 1978 (a)). If, throughout the assessment and interpretive phase, each actor shares his viewpoint and listens to that of the other, the diagnosis is likely to be not only accurate, from a clinical perspective, but understood by the client. Such an understanding is critical to the decisions regarding treatment. Mutually shared goals are likely to result in greater adherence of treatment plans. Since chronic conditions change over time, this entire process recurs as revisions in treatment become necessary.

The model presented here requires caregivers to be cognizant of the clients' value system and personal definitions and to respect and incorporate the clients' wishes in the plan of care. The ideal situation, however, is rarely achieved. Writing on bioethical decision making, Holmes (1979) notes that distinctions must be drawn between ethical decisions and technical decisions. Frequently, technical jargon blurs the distinctions between these two kinds of decisions and reinforces the idea that lay people are unable to participate in the process (Holmes, 1979, p. 1132). When biotechnical reasoning is involved,

Holmes claims that the physician is the appropriate determiner, but when the decisions are mainly normative—religious, legal, or ethical—the lay person's reasoning should have as much weight as that of the physician (or other health care provider). Table 1 provides selected examples of technical versus ethical components in decision making. Holmes (1979, p. 1133) distinguishes between biotechnical and bioethical decisions in the following way. If the answer to a question can be confirmed by observation or experimentation, the decision is principally biotechnical. If the answer must rely on an appeal to a set of values, the decision is primarily bioethical.

In order for a lay person (client or family) to participate in decision making regarding care, be it "routine" or involving advanced medical technology, it is essential that the client be given adequate information at a level that he can understand. Only under informed conditions can a client determine whether to consent to treatment. In the following section we discuss the issues of self-determination and informed consent.

FACTORS IN SELF-DETERMINATION

In some chronic illnesses the patient's survival depends on exotic technologies, e.g., the artificial kidney. In other chronic conditions, the client may be required to make radical changes in life activities, e.g., change employment from heavy physical labor to something less demanding. In other situations, the chronically ill person must make changes that on the surface may seem quite simple, such as omitting salt from the diet or giving up smoking. Although these examples appear to form a continuum from the extreme to the simple, in each instance (and in every other conceivable instance) the individual has the right to decide whether to comply with the required changes or treatment, and the health professional has the obligation to facilitate that decision. The decision to participate in a plan of treatment must be voluntarily made by a competent client who has all the necessary information regarding the risks and benefits of the treatment. In short, the criteria for informed consent (information, voluntariness, and competence) must be operative. Although the conditions may be slightly different when consent is given for research rather than treatment, the criteria are the same. A complete review of ethical principles inherent in client self-determination is beyond the scope of this chapter. Numerous excellent treatises on bioethics are available for the interested reader (Aroskar, 1979; Bandman & Bandman, 1978; Beauchamp & Childress, 1979; Benjamin & Curtis, 1981; Davis &

TABLE 1. CRITERIA FOR DIFFERENTIATING BETWEEN THE TECHNICAL AND ETHICAL COMPONENTS OF BIOETHICAL DILEMMAS

Technical Criteria	Ethical Criteria
1. What is the most likely prognosis if treatment is offered?	1. Is a moral issue of rightness or wrongness involved in the treatment decision?
2. What is the most likely prognosis if treatment is withheld?	2. Is a legal issue rightness or wrongness involved in the treatment decision?
3. What is the probability of complications occuring if treatment is offered?	3. Is a religious issue involved in the treatment decision?
4. What is the probability of side effects occuring if treatment is offered?	4. Is the treatment decision acceptable to the patient and the family?
5. How effective is the treatment?	5. Is the treatment decision acceptable to society in general?
6. What are the direct costs of the treatment?	6. Who should bear the financial costs of the treatment?
7. What are the indirect or hidden costs of the treatment?	7. What should be the relative importance of various individuals and agencies in the decision-making process (e.g., the individual involved, the family physician, other family members, religious leaders, government agencies, professional societies, hospital ethics committees)?
8. What is the cost/benefit ratio of the treatment?	
9. What is the best treatment setting (e.g., hospital room, operating room, outpatient clinic, physician's office, patient's home)?	
10. What is the best combination of personnel to carry out the treatment?	8. Does the treatment have limited availability, such that its use for one patient will deprive someone else of it?
11. What equipment is necessary to carry out the treatment?	9. Is the individual involved sufficiently competent to represent himself? If not, who should represent him?

Reprinted with permission from Holmes (1979, p. 1134)

227

Aroskar, 1978; Fromer, 1981). In the following discussion we address the major aspects of informed consent.

The first condition of informed consent is information. Clients have a right to know what treatment is proposed, what the consequences of the treatment are, and what the side effects are likely to be. In research language, this is referred to as the risk/benefit ratio and, although it may seem to be a straightforward component of informed consent, it is often problematic. How much information is sufficient? The recent trend has been toward providing more rather than less information, a result, in part, of the lay public's closer scrutiny of the health care system and the emphasis on consumers' rights (Ratzan, 1980). Too much detailed information may be frightening to a client who is already experiencing the vulnerability of illness and may, in fact, be considered to be manipulative behavior on the part of the informant either to encourage or to discourage the client from consenting to treatment. Too little information may deny the client the right to make a reasonably informed decision. If the provider has established a sufficient degree of knowledge about the client (values, goals, responsibilities, etc.), this may facilitate a determination of how much information to provide. Involving a family member who can interpret the information for the client may also be a useful strategy. Unless the situation is an emergency, a good rule of thumb is to allow the client time to consider the alternatives and options before requesting consent.

A second condition of informed consent is voluntariness. The decision of the client must be his own rather than that of someone else (physician, nurse, or family member). In the course of making a decision, the client may seek advice and counsel from his family, his friends, and other health care providers in order to ensure that he has adequate information. The client has the right to a second professional opinion, and the health provider has some obligation to help him obtain this opinion. The final decision, however, must be freely made by the client.

The concept of autonomy is closely related to voluntariness. Autonomy, a form of personal liberty, is the exercise of free choice in following one's own plan of action (Davis, 1981). One of the most insidious forms of loss of the freedom to choose results when others (often the health care provider) use subtle coercive tactics to induce the client to choose what the professional believes is best. Paternalism, as this behavior is called, although supposedly for the good of the client, is a denial of the client's freedom of choice. Once a professional has made certain that a client has the necessary information and understands the nature and consequences of a given treatment, the client's decision must be respected even though it may not be the decision the professional thinks is best.

The third dimension of informed consent is competence. Competence is not an all-or-nothing concept, an individual may be competent in one area and incompetent in another. In clinical situations requiring the decision to participate in treatment or not, Beauchamp and Childress (1979, p. 69) offer the following advice:

> A person is competent if and only if that person can make decisions based on rational reasons. In biomedical contexts this standard entails that a person must be able to understand a therapy or research procedure, must be able to weigh its risks and benefits, and must be able to make a decision in the light of such knowledge and through such abilities even if the person chooses not to utilize the information.

Unfortunately, some health professionals make decisions about the competence or incompetence of a client on the basis of client characteristics that have nothing to do with intellectual capacity. For example, old people are often assumed to be incompetent without having had the opportunity to enter into dialogue with a health professional. Fromer (1981, p. 325) gives additional examples of individuals who are assumed to be incompetent: unkempt clients; emotional, boisterous clients; and clients with radical or deviant opinions. Katz (1977, p. 148) claims that many physicians believe that patients are neither emotionally nor intellectually equipped to play a substantial role in making decisions about their medical fate. Thus, significant discussion with clients is not standard practice for the vast majority of physicians.

Competence, according to Barber (1980), is determined in part by what is communicated. If physicians (or other health professionals) use esoteric, technical jargon, it is likely that clients will not be able to make a competent decision. However, if physicians use language that a lay person can understand, a competent decision will probably be made. Barber (1980, p. 79) accuses physicians of creating a "self-fulfilling prophecy"; that is, when information is communicated in a language that the client cannot understand, the assumption of incompetence is fulfilled.

In the abstract, the issue of informed consent may appear to be straightforward. One need only ensure that sufficient information is provided to a competent client, who must then be allowed to make a voluntary decision. In reality, informed consent is very complex. Health professionals must, however, make reasonable efforts to ensure that lay people have sufficient understanding to make a prudent decision for their own good (Barber, 1980). In the following discussion, we review selected instances involving conformed consent in which an individual developmental stage may be at issue.

Informed Consent and Life Stage

It is rarely possible to resolve issues of quality of life or to determine the most appropriate bioethical action without encountering uncertainty, ambiguity, and moral dilemmas. This is particularly the case, although for different reasons, in situations requiring the informed consent of children and the elderly.

Children. The National Commission for the Protection of the Human Subjects of Biomedical and Behavioral Research, (1977, p. 3) has provided the following definition: "*Children* are persons who have not attained the legal age of consent to general medical care as determined under the applicable law of the jurisdiction in which the research will be conducted." Although this definition applies specifically to children as subjects of research, it is also applicable to children undergoing treatment for medical problems.

Until recently, children were defined by common law as possessions of parents or, in the absence of parents, as wards of the court. Thus, medical treatment of minors merely required parental or court permission. The following have been exceptions to this general rule: (a) emergencies—in life-threatening situations, proxy consent may be obtained from people acting on behalf of parents; (b) "emancipated minors"—individuals under 18 years of age who are married or managing their own finances or living in their own residence may give legally valid consent for their own medical care; and (c) "mature minors"—individuals under 18 (not legally emancipated) who are able to understand the consequences of treatment may give consent for care. (In some states the "mature minor" concept is being battled in the courts. Health care workers should be aware of the legal variations operative in their place of practice.)

More recently, the definition of "child" has come to include a stronger emphasis on the child's "personhood," i.e., the child's autonomy. The developmental stages of infancy, childhood, and adolescence involve an increasing ability to understand. The process of informed consent must acknowledge this evolving maturity (Barber, 1980). The national commission (1977, p. 16) recognizes this by stating that "children who are seven years of age or older are generally capable of understanding the procedures and general purposes of research [treatment] and of indicating their wishes regarding participation." Although 7-year-old children may not be legally competent to give consent, they are able to give their assent to treatment. Barber (1980, p. 171) paraphrases the national commission's comments on this subject:

> Informed consent must be a mixture of different amounts of "assent" from the child depending upon his maturing moral capacities, and of "permission" from the parent. There should be more "assent" from the age of seven on and less permission.

Health care providers have a moral, if not legal, obligation to discuss treatment options, risks, benefits, and expected outcomes of treatment with children as well as with parents. Achieving the appropriate mix of assent and permission will depend on factors peculiar to each case. The health care providers' effort to achieve this balance is a good indication of their respect for the child's personhood.

Elderly. Informed consent in the case of older adults involves the same three dimensions discussed above (information, voluntariness, and competence). As indicated earlier, the current trend is toward providing more information about procedures and consequences. Because of physiological changes in most organ systems in the elderly, a reorientation of emphasis on information giving is necessary. What may seem to be a small risk for a younger client may be an enormous risk for an older client and must therefore be precisely and accurately outlined. For example, if there is a 1 percent chance that a certain drug will cause impaired hearing, that information is critical to the consent process for an 85-year-old who probably has impaired hearing already. The same information may seem trivial or irrelevant to a 30-year-old.

In addition, the format of the information being presented to an older client must be considered. It has been shown that the longer the form to be read or filled out, the less likely it is that an older person will comprehend or consent (Epstein & Lasagna, 1969). Because of the complexity of detailed information as well as the client's assumption that a decision must be made quickly (not because of the emergent nature of the situation, but because clinics are routinely overbooked and behind schedule), it is strongly recommended that simple explanations and short forms be used whenever possible (Ratzan, 1980).

The question of who provides the information cannot be simply answered. It is true that the health care provider (generally the physician or nurse) is obligated to see that the client is informed. However, it is sometimes difficult for a client to say no to a prestigious physician or a kind and caring nurse. Thus, without intending to, the physician or nurse may be coercive. Perhaps a well-informed advocate would be more effective; such an individual might not only provide accurate information without subtle coercion, but also have the time to ensure that the information is understood.

Many older people experience a loss of autonomy as a result of the gradual deterioration of their physical and/or mental capacities. This increases their dependence on family, neighbors, and local, state, and federal resources. It is particularly important that the decision made by an older person about treatment or research be truly voluntary and not simply acquiescence. This is true not only for the institutionalized elderly, but also for noninstitutionalized older adults. Paternalism, as earlier noted, can be a serious, but insidious threat to the autonomy of older people. In the name of kindness and concern, health care workers often take over and make decisions that they believe are best. Preempting older adults' responsibility for their own decisions, even with the best of intentions, is a serious infringement of their rights (Davis, 1981, p. 271).

Perhaps the most ambiguous component of informed consent in the case of older clients is the determination of competence. Certainly this issue has raised considerable controversy in the courts. Fortunately, the majority of older people are sufficiently competent to enter into discussions and make their own decisions about care. The situation is much more complicated when an individual is incompetent or not fully competent. The decision to be reached in such cases is very difficult, and no unequivocal solutions exist (Reiss, 1980). Reiss (1980, pp. 74–75) suggests three general guidelines for determining treatment for an incompetent older person:

1. Consideration of the functional status of the person prior to the onset of the problem.
2. Use of multidisciplinary consultation, sharing the responsibility with a gerontologist, psychiatrist, appropriate medical specialist and other relevant specialists.
3. Consultation with family members to determine their wishes.

In addition, an attempt should be made to determine what the client's wishes would have been had he been able to enter into the discussion. Older people often tell family or friends what course of action they would like to be followed in the event of serious illness. Their wishes should be considered in the decision about treatment or care. "Formerly competent patients' wishes clearly expressed while competent should be determinative when the patient is no longer competent" (Veatch, 1978).

Some older people draw up and sign a living will before the onset of illness or cognitive difficulties. A living will is a document stating that, in situations in which the individual is incapable of making a decision, extreme measures to prolong his life should be avoided (Olson, 1981). Several states now recognize the living will as a legally binding document under certain conditions. None of these guidelines make the decision-making process simple in the case of an incompetent client. The issues of determining competency, intermittent competence, ordinary versus extraordinary treatment, quality of human life versus biological life, cost to society or to family (both economic and psychological cost), allocation of scarce resources as in the case of organ transplants, and other complex moral and ethical issues enter into the problem of deciding treatment for the incompetent (as well as the competent in many cases). The reader is referred to further readings in philosophy and ethics for a comprehensive treatment of these issues (Annas, 1980; Bandman & Bandman; Burder, 1980; Beauchamp & Childress, 1979; Curtain, 1979; Eisenberg, 1975; Gadow, 1979; Imbus & Zawacki, 1977, Kuhse, 1981; Levine, 1978; Martin, 1978(b); McCloskey & Grace, 1981; Parsons & Lock, 1980; Veatch, 1980).

In conclusion, we offer two general comments regarding informed consent and the treatment of older clients. First, it is unethical and discriminating to withhold treatment from older patients simply on the basis of age when the same treatment is routine for younger clients (Reiss, 1980). Second, "insofar as the elderly do have different values, strengths and weaknesses from those of younger adults, these differences must be considered and respected when the elderly are asked to volunteer for research *or treament*" (Ratzan, 1980; emphasis added).

SUMMARY

Ethical dilemmas and decisions about quality of life abound in situations of chronic illness. In this chapter we have pointed out some of these dilemmas and the implications of certain decisions for quality of life. There are no simple answers. Every advance in biomedicine creates a greater need for moral responsibility and adds to the ethical quandries: who lives, who dies—and who decides? ("When Doctors Play God," 1981; Fuchs, 1974).

Decisions about treatment are, or should be, based on a composite of the values, beliefs, knowledge, and goals of both the client and the health care provider. Collaboration between client and caregiver is the sine qua non of ethical decision making. Only rarely should it be the right or responsibility of a caregiver to decide treatment in the absence of input from the recipient of that treatment.

Self-determination in health care is the right of every client, and it is the responsibility of every caregiver to ensure that the client exercises this right. The criteria for self-determination consist of having at one's disposal appropriate and adequate information about the proposed treatment, complete freedom to choose or refuse treatment (voluntariness), and sufficient competence to participate in the decision. The issue of competence is especially complex when the client is a child or a cognitively impaired older person. In this chapter, we offer basic guidelines for the care provider to consider when dealing with either a child or of a cognitively impaired adult. We are well aware that there are rarely unequivocal answers in the area of bioethical decision making. It is our hope that every health professional will recognize the dilemmas involved in deciding on a course of treatment, will be wise enough to seek advice when in doubt, and will have the insight to recognize that technology is not an end in itself. The goal of care in all cases is to maximize the quality of life for the recipient of care.

REFERENCES

Annas, G. J. Quality of life in the courts: Earle, Spring in fantasy land. *Hastings Center Report*, 1980, **10**(4), 9–10.

Aroskar, M. Ethical issues in community health nursing. *Nursing Clinics of North America*, 1979, **14**(1), 35–44.

Bandman, E., & Bandman, B. (Eds.). *Bioethics and human rights.* Boston: Little, Brown, 1978.

Bandman, E., & Bandman, B. The nurses' role in protecting the patients' right to live or die. *Advances in Nursing Science*, 1979, **1**(3), 21–35.

Barber, B. *Informed consent in medical therapy and reserach.* New Brunswick, N.J.: Rutgers University Press, 1980.

Beauchamp, T., & Childress, J. *Principles of biomedical ethics.* New York: Oxford University Press, 1979.

Benjamin, M., & Curtis, J. *Ethics in nursing.* New York: Oxford University Press, 1981.

Bloom, M. *The paradox of helping: Introduction to the philosophy of scientific practice.* New York: Wiley, 1975.

Blumenfield, H. Criteria for judging the quality of the urban environment. In W. Bloomberg, & H. Schmandt, (Eds.), *The quality of urban life.* Beverly Hills: Sage, 1969.

Campbell, A., Converse, P. E., & Rodgers, W. L. *The quality of American life.* New York: Russell Sage Foundation, 1976.

Curtain, L. The nurse as advocate: A philosophical foundation for nursing. *Advances in Nursing Science*, 1979, **1**(3), 1–10.

Davis, A. Ethical considerations in gerontological nursing research. *Geriatric Nursing*, 1981, **2**, 269–272.

Davis, A., & Aroskar, M. *Ethical dilemmas and nursing practice.* New York: Appleton, 1978.

Eisenberg, L. The ethics of intervention: Acting amidst ambiguity. *Journal of Child Psychology and Psychiatry,* 1975, **16**, 93–104.

Epstein, L., & Lasagna, L. Obtaining informed consent: Form or substance. *Archives of Internal Medicine*, 1969, **123**, 682–688.

Fromer, M. J. *Ethical issues in health care*. St. Louis: Mosby, 1981.

Fuchs, V. *Who shall live? Health, economics and social choice*. New York: Basic Books, 1974.

Gadow, S. Advocacy nursing and new meanings of aging. *Nursing Clinics of North America*, 1979, **14**(1), 81–91.

George, L., & Bearon, L. *Quality of life in older persons*. New York: Human Sciences Press, 1980.

Holmes, C. Bioethical decision-making: An approach to improve the process. *Medical Care*, 1979, **17**, 1131–1138.

Imbus, S., & Zawacki, B. Autonomy for burned patients when survival is unprecedented. *New England Journal of Medicine*, 1977, **297**, 308–311.

Jonas, H. Toward a philosophy of technology. *Hastings Center Report*, 1979, **9**(1), 34–43.

Katz, J. Informed consent—A fairy tale? Law's vision. *University of Pittsburgh Law Review*, 1977, **39**, 137–174.

Katzner, D. *Choice and the quality of life*. Beverly Hills: Sage, 1979.

Kuhse, H. Debate: Extraordinary means and the sanctity of life. *Journal of Medical Ethics*, 1981, **7**, 74–82.

Levine, C. Dialysis or transplant: Values and choices. *Hastings Center Report*, 1978, **8**(2), 8–10.

Martin, R. A clinical model for decision-making. *Journal of Medical Ethics*, 1978, **4**, 200–206.(a)

Martin, R. Some ethical issues in the disclosure of progressive diseases of the nervous system. *Southern Medical Journal*, 1978, **71**, 792–794.(b)

McCloskey, J., & Grace, H. *Current issues in nursing*. Boston: Blackwell, 1981.

McCormick, R. The quality of life, the sanctity of life. *Hastings Center Report*, 1978, **8**(1), 30–36.

National Commission for the Protection of Human Subjects of Biomedical and Behavioral Research. *Research involving children: Report and recommendations* (2 vols.). Washington, D.C.: U.S. Government Printing Office, 1977.

Olson, J. To treat or to allow to die: An ethical dilemma in gerontological nursing. *Journal of Gerontological Nursing*, 1981, **7**, 141–147.

Parsons, V., & Lock, P. Triage and the patient with renal failure. *Journal of Medical Ethics*, 1980, **6**, 173–176.

Ratzan, R. Being old makes you different. The ethics of research with elderly subjects. *Hastings Center Report*, 1980, **10**(5), 32–42.

Reiss, R. Moral and ethical issues in geriatric surgery. *Journal of Medical Ethics*, 1980, **6**, 71–77.

Veatch, R. Three theories of informed consent: Philosophical foundations and policy implications. The National Commission for the Protection of

Human Subjects of Biomedical and Behavioral Research. *The Belmont Report: Ethical Principles and Guidelines for the Protection of Human Subjects of Research.* (3 Volumes), Washington, D.C.: U.S. Government Printing Office, 1978.

Veatch, R. Voluntary risks to health. *Journal of the American Medical Association,* 1980, **243**(1), 50–55.

When doctors play God. *Newsweek,* August 31, 1981, pp. 48–54.

Chapter 10

Research Issues in Chronic Illness

The primary focus throughout this text has been on two concepts: chronicity and life span. These concepts have provided the framework for discussions of family, career, social support, identity, personal control, and ethical issues in chronic illness. Basic to the study of chronic illness throughout the life span are the distinctions between disease, illness, and sickness: disease is a biological concept, and illness and sickness are social-psychological and sociological concepts, respectively (Chapter 1). Since no one is in perfect health but not everyone is ill, it is also necessary to define the concept of health in relation to disease, illness, and sickness (Chapter 1).

When disease, illness, and sickness are considered in the context of chronic illness, three definitional perspectives are apparent. Disease is a clinical definition, illness is a personal definition, and sickness is a social definition. The interaction of these perspectives influences the behavior of a person with a chronic illness (Chapter 2).

Similarly, an individual's developmental stage has a major influence on his behavior. The developmental tasks of each life stage differ significantly, and therefore the impact of a chronic illness also differs at each stage (Chapter 3). In this chapter, we discuss research issues in relation to each of these definitional perspectives and examine some of the methodological issues involved in the study of chronic illness throughout the life span.

As a framework for this discussion we use the typology of studies described by Diers (1979): factor-searching, relation-searching, association-testing and causal-hypothesis-testing.

The goal of *factor-searching* studies is to describe a phenomenon (an event or situation), identify factors, and determine how to categorize or conceptualize the phenomenon. Factor-searching studies are descriptive and exploratory. In general, they are done when little is known about the topic or when an investigator wishes to study a subject from a unique perspective or within a unique context. Observational techniques (participant and non-participant), and ethnographic interviews are good methods of data collection for factor-searching studies. These methods are particularly useful to ascertain the meaning of an event from the individual's perspective (Spradley, 1979, 1980).

Relation-searching studies are undertaken when the factors (variables) are known, but their relationships are not. Like factor-searching studies, these studies are exploratory and descriptive. Since the factors are known, operational and conceptual definitions are required. Comparisons are often made between groups of people or situations; for example, the phenomenon being investigated may be examined by age categories, socioeconomic levels, marital status, kinds of illness, or types of surgery.

The aim of *association-testing* studies is to test predicted relationships between factors. Hypotheses are tested, although cause-and-effect relationships cannot be determined. Association-testing studies rely on the natural variation of factors in a situation. No attempt is made to manipulate or change the condition of the phenomenon under study. Association-testing studies are referred to as correlational studies, which distinguishes them from purely descriptive, exploratory factor-searching and relation-searching studies.

The purpose of *causal-hypothesis-testing* studies is to make statements about cause and effect. In these studies the factors (variables) are labeled "independent" or "dependent." The important distinction between causal-hypothesis-testing and association-testing studies is that the former requires intervention by the investigator in the form of manipulation of the independent variable, whereas the latter are done in naturally occurring situations. Causal-hypothesis-testing studies require control over all factors that might influence the relationship between the independent and dependent variables. Thus, the appropriate design is experimental.

As Diers (1979) explains so well, experimental studies can be carried out only when there is sufficient knowledge of the variables to predict their relationships and design an appropriate intervention study. This implies that careful factor-searching/factor-relating and association-testing must be performed first. In many cases little is known about the critical factors that account for differences in the responses of individuals to chronic illness. Sometimes these factors may be the characteristics or clinical manifestations of the disease itself; in some cases, the critical factor may be developmental stage; and in some cases, the factors may include those discussed in this text—family, career, social support, personal identity, and personal control. Complex interrelationships exist among and between each of these factors, and it is therefore important to advance our knowledge through careful, systematic investigative efforts.

Having briefly reviewed the major types of research studies (we strongly recommend that the reader refer to Dier's excellent treatment of this topic for more detail), we present a series of suggested research questions for each definitional perspective of the study of chronic illness across the life span. This series is not intended to be exhaustive, but merely to show selected ways of approaching research in this area.

CLINICAL DEFINITIONS OF DISEASE

Clinical definitions of long-term disease are made on the basis of anatomical or physiological malfunction. Since objective biological deviations form the basis of these definitions, they are generally made by physicians, nurse practitioners, and other health care professionals where expertise lies in the biological sciences. As noted in Chapter 1 the clinical diagnosis of disease is complicated by the fact that not all bodily functions are observable. The diagnostician must also rely on unobservable indicators reported by clients. Herein lies the first instance of interaction between clinical definitions (disease) and personal definitions (illness), and the issue of congruence becomes important. Incongruent definitions, as described in Chapter 1, apply to instances in which the signs and symptoms do not match; e.g., observable physiological deviations may be present, yet the client feels no symptoms (as in the case of hypertension), and vice versa (as may be the case with certain kinds of headaches). Few health care providers take an entirely disease-oriented approach in practice. However, many are likely to emphasize this approach, and in some instances a disease-oriented perspective (sometimes referred to as the medical model) is required for legal purposes (Chapter 2).

As indicated in Chapter 3 chronic illness occurs among people in all age groups. However, the impact and consequences of long-term illness differ on the basis of the individual's developmental stage.

Thus, as we have argued throughout this text, it is necessary for health care providers and researchers to consider chronic illness in the context of life span. One concept that embodies both chronicity (long termness) and life stage is career (Chapter 5). In the most general sense, career refers to a strand or dimension of an individual's life over the course of time. The career experiences of chronically ill individuals differ not only on the basis of the characteristics of their disease, but also as a function of their developmental stage. For example, asthma may manifest similarly in both a child and an adult, but the impact of the disease on the child's life will be quite different from that on the adult. Treatment plans should reflect these differences, and investigative efforts should include the developmental stage variable.

Research Issues.
Clinical practice is based on systematic assessment, intervention, and evaluation techniques, which are known collectively as the assessment process. This process is founded on the biological and social sciences. It is our thesis that clinical problems common or unique to chronic illnesses are important topics for research. In this section we suggest a number of research questions and hypotheses that are derived from our discussions of clinical definitions of disease earlier in the text.

Several research questions related to the unifying concept of disease (clinical definitions) in the study of chronic illness throughout the life span are presented below.

Descriptive Studies (Factor Searching)

1. What are the similarities and differences in the career experiences of individuals with different clinical manifestations of chronic illness (e.g., abrupt versus insidious onset)?
2. How do the career experiences of individuals with an abrupt onset of chronic illness differ by life stage?

Discussion. In the first question the concept that varies is onset of the disease. Developmental stage or age grouping is constant. The investigator would select two disease conditions that have different onsets and that may occur among the same age groups. For example, multiple sclerosis has an insidious onset, whereas myocardial infarct is abrupt. Both conditions may be found in young or middle adult groups.

In the second question, on the other hand, the concept that varies is the developmental stage, and the disease is constant. In this case the investigator might select diabetes as the disease and compare the career patterns of adolescents with those of other adults, or one could describe the career experience of a young adult versus a school-age child with a spinal cord injury.

Descriptive Studies (Factor Relating)

1. What is the relationship between personal identity and changing clinical manifestations of diabetes and cystic fibrosis among adolescents?
2. What is the relationship among personal identity, visibility of a chronic condition, and progress in school among school-age children?

Discussion. In the first question the concepts are personal identity (see Chapter 7) and a chronic illness characteristic here referred to as "changing in clinical manifestations". The investigator chooses two disease conditions in which the clinical manifestations are likely to vary radically. By investigating the problem in a sample of adolescents, the researcher controls the variation that might occur because of developmental stage. Therefore, a stronger statement can be made about the relationship between personal identity and changing clinical manifestations.

In the second question there are three concepts: personal identity, visibility of symptoms, and school progress. Again, the developmental stage is controlled. The investigator must select chronic conditions in which the visibility differs markedly. This could be accomplished by choosing subjects with different kinds of limb amputations, e.g., below the knee versus below the elbow. School-age children with burn scars would also be appropriate, e.g., facial burns versus arm or hand burns. Subjects might also be selected with different chronic conditions and different visibility, e.g., muscular dystrophy versus asthma.

Correlation Studies (Association Testing)

1. There will be greater changes in personal identity among adolescents with cystic fibrosis than among adolescents with diabetes.
2. School progress will vary inversely by degree of leg amputation among school-age children.

Discussion. These two statements are hypotheses that can be tested in natural settings with no intervention or manipulation of the independent variable by the investigator. In both statements the developmental stage is controlled, and the disease condition is selected in such a way that one can make strong statements about the variation in personal identity and school progress.

Experimental Studies (Causal-Hypothesis Testing)

1. Young male adults with chronic kidney failure who participate in a social support group of peers will be significantly
   more likely to maintain employment than those who do not
   participate in a social support group.
2. Young female adults with multiple sclerosis who participate
   in assertiveness classes will be more likely to perceive themselves as in control of their treatment regimens than those
   who do not participate in assertiveness classes.

Discussion. These hypotheses can be tested only with an experimental design. Each requires intervention or manipulation of the
independent variable by the investigator. In the first statement the
independent variable is a social support group of peers with chronic
kidney failure, and the dependent variable is maintenance of employment. In the second statement the independent variable is perceived
control over the treatment regimens for multiple sclerosis. In both
hypotheses the developmental stage is controlled. However, some
researchers may wish to determine whether assertiveness classes are
differentially effective in enhancing perceived control for women of
different age groups who have the same chronic illness. In this case the
design would include, for example, young female adults and aged
women with diabetes randomly assigned to assertiveness classes.

PERSONAL DEFINITIONS

Personal definitions represent the existential experience of disease. As
indicated in Chapter 1, disease is an objective reality, and illness is the
subjective interpretation of this reality. The personal meaning of
disease is a key factor in the way in which chronically ill individuals
manage disease. Among the factors that influence personal definitions
are the stage in the life cycle at which disease occurs, the characteristics of the disease, the nature of the onset (abrupt versus insidious
and gradual), the visibility and stigma attached to the disease, and the
course, prognosis, and type of treatment regimen required (Chapter 2).

The help-seeking behaviors of chronically ill individuals are
reflections of their personal assessment of the disease and its meaning
to them. (Help-seeking behavior is a dimension of illness behavior;
refer to Chapter 1 for a discussion of illness behavior and to Chapter 2

for a discussion of illness behavior and chronic illness.) One of many factors that may enter into a decision to seek help is the belief that seeking help will make a difference in the outcome of the disease. As shown in Chapter 8, a sense of personal control and a belief in one's ability to manage difficult situations prompt an individual to adopt active coping strategies (e.g., help seeking). Thus, when investigating problems of importance to the management of a chronic illness, for example, clinic-visiting behaviors or compliance, the researcher would be wise to include an assessment of the meaning of the disease to the client and his perceived ability to manage the regimen.

Like clinical definitions (disease), personal definitions (illness) can be used as a unifying concept for exploring research approaches. These are discussed below.

Descriptive Studies (Factor Searching and Relating)

1. What factors enter into the personal definition of chronic illness among children?
2. What are the major variations in help-seeking behavior among older adults with arthritis and adolescents with arthritis?

Discussion. The first question is a factor-searching question, and the second is a factor-relating question. In the first instance the study is intended to identify, name, and perhaps categorize the variables that seem to be a part of the definitional process. The investigator must determine which chronic illnesses to include. Life stage is controlled.

In the second question the variable, help-seeking behavior, is named. The investigator compares this behavior at two different developmental stages for a similar chronic condition.

Correlational Studies (Association Testing)

1. Middle-aged women who perceive themselves to be ill are more likely to comply with treatment for hypertension than those who do not perceive themselves to be ill.
2. The greater the perceived ability to control symptoms the greater the likelihood of participation in social events by young male adults with ulcerative colitis.

Discussion. In both of these hypotheses the notion of perception is critical: in the first case, the perception of the disease condition of hypertension as an illness and, in the second, the perception of ability to control symptoms. It is important for the investigator of the first hypothesis to distinguish between severity of hypertension (the disease) and self-identification of illness by the women in the study. The disease process is not the focus. Similarly, in the second hypothesis the issue is not whether the symptoms *can* be controlled, but whether the young men in the study believe that they can control the symptoms.

Experimental Studies (Causal-Hypothesis Testing)

1. Adolescents with juvenile diabetes who are given options in their treatment regimens will have more positive attitudes toward themselves than adolescents who follow rigid regimens with no options.
2. Middle-aged men who participate in MI rehabilitation programs especially tailored to their locus of control (internal or external) will be more compliant than middle-aged men who receive standard, routine post-MI instruction.

Discussion. These two hypotheses emphasize the importance of personal definitions of chronic illness at different stages of the life span and the effect of these definitions on the outcome of a chronic illness. In the first hypothesis it is recognized that adolescence is a life stage in which one attempts to gain control (Chapter 3). In the medical regimen for an adolescent this need for control of one's life has to be taken into account. In the second hypothesis it is recognized that a more stable identity has developed by middle age and that an individual's personality characteristics influence the treatment regimen. A major personality characteristic to consider is internal versus external locus of control, since research studies have found these variables to be associated with compliance to specific treatment regimens.

SOCIAL DEFINITIONS

Social definitions are those made, either implicitly or explicitly, by others: family, friends, employers, health care workers, "people on the street," or society in general (Chapter 2). The fact that others make definitions implies a social awareness of the presence of either disease or illness. Once illness becomes a social phenomenon, the social interactions of an ill person with his associates is modified, and in time the associates usually come to redefine or legitimate behaviors that differ from those people who are not ill. The most common contexts in which legitimation occurs are the family, school, and work. The kind and extent of legitimation depend on the ill person's life stage, the characteristics of the chronic disease, and the nature of the relationship between the ill person and the associate. For example, in intimate relationships such as those found in the family, greater deviations from normal may be tolerated than at school or at work.

We know relatively little about the impact of social definitions on the chronically ill. In the following section we suggest several research problems related to social definitions.

Descriptive Studies (Factor Searching and Relating)

1. What is the role of the family in defining whether symptoms of gender dysphoria require professional treatment?
2. How does the family compare with the work group in defining or interpreting the symptoms of a post-MI man?

Discussion. The first question is a factor-searching question. As noted in the case study of transsexualism in Chapter 5 there are many symptoms indicative of gender identity problems. The investigator is interested in identifying the specific symptoms which family members perceive as sufficiently troublesome to require professional treatment. In the second factor-relating question the investigator is interested in comparing the interpretation of symptoms by two important social groups: the family and work group. In both questions the focus is on "other-definitions" rather than self-definitions.

Correlational Studies (Association Testing)

1. The greater the congruence of definitions of symptoms between a chronically ill person and his spouse, the greater will be marital harmony and mutual satisfaction with adjustment to the disease.
2. Incongruence among definitions of symptoms made of self, physician, and parents increases the likelihood of noncompliance among adolescents with hemophilia.

Discussion. Although social definitions are the focus, these hypotheses are intended to test the important concept of congruence. In the first case the investigator could select any chronic illness as long as the ill person had a spouse. The age grouping could thus range from adolescent through old age. The second hypothesis focuses on the adolescent and the effect of incongruence among the definitions of significant others (the physician and parents) and the adolescent's definition.

Experimental Studies (Causal-Hypothesis Testing)

1. Dialysis patients who are accompanied by their spouses to instructional classes in meal preparation will be more compliant with dietary restrictions than those who attend classes alone.
2. Adults who participate in planned information and support group sessions will be less likely to institutionalize an aged parent with Alzheimers' disease than adults who do not participate in such groups.

Discussion. Although these hypotheses do not directly test the definitions made by others, they address another critical aspect of managing chronic illness: the support provided by others (Chapter 6). There are several design options in both cases. In the first case dialysis patients would be randomly assigned to an instructional class made up of couples or to one of singles. Since dietary instruction is routine in most dialysis units, it would be unethical to withhold this information; thus, there would be no control group receiving no instructions. Since Alzheimers' disease support groups are relatively uncommon, it is possible that a no-treatment group could be used. In all instances of experimental design, the no-treatment situation must be carefully assessed for its ethical implications. In most instances the no-treatment group is actually the routine-treatment group. In the following section we discuss several methodological issues that confront the investigator who wishes to study chronic illness throughout the life span.

METHODOLOGICAL ISSUES IN THE STUDY OF CHRONIC ILLNESS THROUGHOUT THE LIFE SPAN

Although the basic features of the research process used in the study of chronic illness throughout the life span do not differ from those of any other research process, there are several methodological issues to which attention must be drawn. The first is the use of *longitudinal designs*. Since by definition chronic illness occurs over time, it is logical to study it over time. This is particularly true of descriptive studies, in which one is looking for key factors or trying to ascertain whether and how important factors relate to one another. For example, in an investigation of the role of the family in defining symptoms of gender dysphoria, it is probable that with time the manifestations of the condition would change as the individual developed and that family definitions regarding the seriousness of symptoms would also change. Thus, in the descriptive phase of investigation, a full understanding of the role of the family would be possible only with a longitudinal design.

The goal of most studies of illness is eventually to intervene in some way to ameliorate the effects of the illness. We have shown that some chronic illnesses have distinct stages and that the experience of the ill person may vary from one stage to another (Chapter 5). Thus, the type of intervention and its timing must vary as well. For example, the type of social support most appropriate for an individual with a chronic illness is likely to vary depending on whether the situation is in a crisis or stable state (Chapter 6). Longitudinal designs are the most effective for studying the stages of chronic illness in order to plan intervention strategies.

A second methodological issue is the use of *cohort studies*. Only very rarely can an investigator establish a sample in infancy, early childhood, or adolescence and follow that sample into old age, yet it has been a theme of this text that illness is experienced differently at various developmental stages. One way to analyze the variations in this experience by life stage is through the use of cohort studies. For example, the investigator can select a specific disease, such as diabetes, and describe the way in which it is experienced by young, middle, and older adults. Each of these three life stages place different demands and expectations on individuals, and the added demand of a chronic illness is likely to be experienced differently by each group. The investigator can gather data at one time and compare them across cohorts. However, by combining the cohort approach with a longitudinal design and gathering data at several times, the investigator can make comparison from a significantly richer data base and thus enhance the significance of the study.

The third methodological issue is the clear specification of the *unit of analysis*. This is important in all research, but it has particular significance in chronic illness. The experience of chronic illness has three levels: disease, illness, and sickness; and, as we have shown, there are three general definitional perspectives: clinical, personal, and social. It thus becomes apparent that the unit of analysis must be clearly defned at the outset of any research study. One of the implications of this is that one must decide whether to adopt an *a priori*, or deductive research method or an inductive method. If a researcher wishes to study the personal experience of a disease, he selects a method of data generation that ensures a phenomenological or "personal experience" account, which permits him to take an inductive approach, e.g., unstructured interviews with the ill person or some method of observation. The investigator must bear in mind that the ill person's definition of the situation is the focal point. The actual progress of the disease or the definitions of others are important only as covariants of the personal experience and interpretation of events. In the terminology of Diers (1979) this kind of study is either a factor-searching or a factor-relating study.

Conversely, the investigator may wish to investigate the course of a disease over time. In this case he might select a deductive approach in which predictive statements are made about the factors related to or causing change in objective clinical outcomes. The focus in this kind of study is the disease process, and personal or social definitions of the situation are covariants or explanatory factors. The researcher in this instance conducts either an association-testing or causal-hypothesis-testing study. Clearly, it is possible and important (depending on the state of knowledge about any given factor) to use a combination of research approaches in a single study. However, the investigator must be very clear about the unit of analysis so that data are not generated from a perspective that fails to address the research questions or does not allow one to test the hypotheses.

SUMMARY

To be fully understood, chronic illness must be considered from a clinical, personal, and social point of view, and it must be considered at various stages of the life span. In this chapter we have presented examples of research questions that can be asked using different definitions of chronic illness at different stages in the life span. We have also presented what we consider some methodological imperatives related to research in chronic illness with a developmental perspective.

SUGGESTED READINGS

Bogdan, R., & Taylor, S. *Introduction to qualitative research methods.* New York: Wiley (Interscience), 1975.

> A good text for the beginning investigator on the use of participant observation, unstructured interviewing, and personal documents. Particularly good discussion of data analysis.

Campbell, D., & Stanley, J. *Experimental and quasi-experimental designs for research.* Chicago: Rand McNally, 1963.

> The original bible of experimental design. Still timely; succinct and understandable.

Cook, T., & Campbell, D. *Quasi-experimentation: Design and analysis issues for field settings.* Chicago: Rand McNally, 1979.

For the advanced student and mature investigator, this text is a particularly lucid analysis of designs intended for use in hypothesis-testing studies. Special emphasis is given to issues of internal validity.

Diers, D. *Research in nursing practice*. New York: Lippincott, 1979.

An excellent text for the advanced student and mature investigator. In addition to the organizing framework referred to in Chapter 10 of the present text, this book has an outstanding bibliography. For each type of research (factor searching, factor relating, etc.) the author provides a comprehensive reference list of examples.

Glaser, B., & Strauss, A. *The discovery of grounded theory*. Chicago: Aldine, 1967.

Although somewhat dated, this is still the most comprehensive text on the philosophy and methods of grounded theory.

Lofland, J. *Analyzing social settings*. Belmont, Calif.: Wadsworth, 1971.

Excellent guide for the beginning researcher in qualitative observation and analysis techniques and strategies.

Lofland, J. *Doing social life*. New York: Wiley (Interscience), 1976.

Strategies for approaching the study of human interaction in natural settings. Includes complete reprints of examples of qualitative research studies.

Polit, D., & Hungler, B. *Nursing research: Principles and methods*. New York: Lippincott, 1978.

Excellent text for the beginning investigator. Steps in the research process are clearly identified and carefully explained. Particularly well written discussions of types of research designs and considerations necessary for selecting a design.

Spradley, J. *The ethnographic interview*. New York: Holt, Rinehart, 1979.

Outstanding reference for qualitative research techniques. Particularly fine example of how to organize, manage, and make sense of a large amount of unstructured data. Examples of real data are used to illustrate techniques.

Spradley, J. *Participant observation*. New York: Holt, Rinehart, 1980.

A companion text to *The Ethnographic Interview*. The emphasis is on participant observation. Excellent examples of analytic techniques for use with unstructured data.

Index

Activity theory, 81
Adams' theoretical model of family,
    94, 98–104, 109
Adjustment, and family, 153–154
Adolescence, 69–73
  cognitive development in, 71
  and help-seeking behavior, 243
  and identity, 172, 173, 181–184,
      241–242
  and illness, 243, 244
  and personal control, 199–200
  physical development in, 70
  psychosocial development in, 71–72
  and research issues, 241–242, 243,
      244
  and treatment options, 244
Adulthood. *See* Early adulthood;
    Late adulthood; Middle
    adulthood
Affective self, 166–167
Aging
  biological theories of, 76–78
  and identity, 170, 171
  negative image of, 170
Alcoholic patient, and family,
    153–154
Alienation, in adolescence, 72
Alliance, reliable, 146
Ambiguous human beings
  impact of professional reactions on

  identity of, 178–181
  reactions to, 176–179
Ambiguous identity, development of,
    173–176
Ambivalence, as reaction to
    ambiguous and stigmatized
    human beings, 176–177
Association-testing studies, 238,
    241–242, 243-244, 245
At-risk role, 47–49
Attachment, 146, 161
Attribution theory, 198
Autogenic theories, 55–56
Autonomy
  as condition of informed consent,
      228–229, 230, 231–232
  as developmental task, 66
Aversion reaction, to ambiguous and
    stigmatized human beings,
    176–177
Avoidance, of ambiguous and
    stigmatized human beings,
    177–179

Bargaining, in career, 119, 120,
    121–124, 125, 126–127, 129,
    132–133, 136, 139
Behavioral control, 198, 206, 207
Blindness, 63, 179–180

251

Career, 115–143
  continuous, 118
  declining, 124–127
  determinate, 120–121
  episodic, 118
  fatalistic, 117
  humanistic, 117
  indeterminate, 120–121
  of mental patient, 127–131
  and myocardial infarction, 134–142
  of nursing home patient, 124–127
  and pace norms, 118–120
  of polio patint, 121–124
  and research issues, 240–241
  regressive, 125–127
  and sequence norms, 118–120
  of stroke patient, 124
  and time, 115–121
  and transsexualism, 131–134
  of tuberculosis patient, 116,
      118–121
Career contingencies, 129
Career failure, 120, 125, 129, 132
Career timetable, 116, 120
Causal hypothesis testing studies,
    238, 242, 244, 246
Cerebrovascular accident
  and career, 124
  and social support, 160–162
Child-rearing customs, 56
Childhood, 64–68
  cognitive development in, 64–66
  physical development in, 64
  psychosocial development in, 66–68
Children
  effects of chronic illness on
      development of, 211–212
  and identity, 184–189, 241
  and illness, 243
  and informed consent, 230–231
  and personal control, 199, 207–212
  and research issues, 241–242
Chronic disease, classic definition of,
    33–34
Chronic illness
  vs. acute illness, and behavior,
      41–42
  at-risk role in, 47–49
  historical perspective on, 31–33
  illness behavior in, 45–47
  terminology of, 33–35
  theoretical perspectives on, 38–49

Chronic renal failure, and social
    support, 156–160
Clinical definitions, 36, 239–242
Cognitive control, 197–198, 206, 207
Cognitive development
  in adolescence, 71
  in childhood, 64–66
  in infancy, 56–58
  in late adulthood, 78–79
Cognitive self, 166–167
Cohort studies, 247
Communication
  between chronically ill patient and
      family, 183–184
  between family and provider,
      159–160
  lack of, and nursing home patient,
      125–126
Compartmentalization, in reducing
    role strain, 39
Competence, 196–197
  as condition of informed consent,
      229
  determination of, 232–233, 234
  perceived, 169
Compliance
  and chronically ill person, 48
  and incongruence, 105
  and personal control, 202–205
  and research issues, 243–244, 246
  and sick role, 41–42, 48
Concrete operational stage, 65, 199
Conditionality, in late adulthood, 78
Continuous career, 118, 121
Control. See Locus of control;
      Personal control
Creativity, in late adulthood, 79
Crisis concept, 83–84
Crisis situation, and social support,
    151, 152
Culture
  and child-rearing, 56
  and concept of health, 11
  and disease, 11
  and expression of emotional
      distress, 5

Decentering, 71
Decision making, 42, 47–48, 204,
    224–226, 227t, 233
Decisional control, 198, 206

Declining career, 124–127
Deficit situations, and social support, 151, 152
Definitions
    clinical, 36, 239–242
    implications of, 35–38
    incongruent, 239, 245
    interactions of, 37–38
    personal, 36, 242–244
    social, 36, 244–246
Delegation, in reducing role strain, 39
Denial, as reaction to ambiguous and stigmatized human beings, 176, 177–179
Dependence, in spinal cord injury, 182
Depression, and personal control, 205–206, 214
Determinate career, 120–121, 126, 128
Developmental theory, 53–54, 82–87
    of family, 97–98, 99, 109
Deviance
    primary, 23, 24–25
    secondary, 23, 25
    sick role as, 21, 23, 24–25
Disabled
    factors influencing societal response to, 31–33
    roles of, 39–40
Disability
    advantages of concept of, 35
    beliefs about origin of, 32
    definition of, 35
Discontinuity, in stressful situation, 151
Discrimination, as isolation, 43
Disease
    concept of, 304, 23–24
    diagnosis of, 4
    without illness, 5
    and normalized situation, 176
    and research issues, 239–242
    and stress, 6
Disengagement theory, 80–81
Diversion, as reaction to ambiguous and stigmatized human beings, 178

Early adulthood, 73–74
    and illness, 243–244
    and personal control, 242, 243–244

and research issues, 242, 243–244
and social support, 158–160, 242
Ecological theory, 67
Economic compensation, and clinical definition, 36.
Ego integrity, 74, 80
Egocentrism, 57–58, 199
Elderly. See Late adulthood
Emotional isolation, 146
Emotional support, 147, 151–152, 161
Employers, discrimination of, 43
Employment policies, flexibility in, 42
Environment
    and Eriksonian theory, 67
    in infancy, 56, 57, 60
    and self-esteem, 68
Episodic career, 118, 121
Eriksonian theory, 60, 66–67, 69, 70, 71–72, 73, 80, 83, 84
Esteem support, 147
Ethics, 221–236
Ethnic minorities
    and fatalistic career, 117
    and personal control, 201
Expectancy
    generalized, 194, 195, 196
    and locus of control, 194
    outcome, 196
    situational, 194, 195
Extension, in reducing role strain, 39

Factor-relating studies, 241, 243, 245
Factor-searching studies, 238, 240–241, 243, 245
Family
    Adams' theoretical model of, 98–104
    as causative agent in illness, 94, 104–105
    and communication with chronically ill patient, 183–184
    and communication with provider, 159–160
    and development of child's sense of independence, 212
    effect of illness on, 108–109
    and illness behaviors, 105–106
    life-cycle stages of, 97, 98, 106
    and mental health and illness, 93–94

Family (continued)
  and rehabilitation, 183
  and sick role behaviors, 106–108
  as source of support, 42, 48–49,
      152–156, 159, 161–162
  theories of, 94–98, 108–109
Family assessment guide, 109–112
Family formation continuum, 99–100
Family therapy, 93–94
Fatalism, 198, 201
Fatalistic career, 10, 117
Formal operational stage, 65, 71
Freudian theory, 59–60, 66, 69
Friends, as source of support,
    156–158, 161–162
Functional limitations, 34–35
Functional status, 222

Gender, vs. sex, 131
Generalized expectancy, 194, 195,
    196
Generalized other, 168
Guidance, obtaining, 146–147

Handicap, 35
Hardiness, 200, 206
Health, conceptualizations of, 7–12
Health behavior, 12
Health belief model, 16–18
Health care services, utilization of,
    18, 106
Health care technology, 222–224
Health/disease status, 12–28
Health-illness continuum, 8
Help-seeking behavior, 242–243
  and illness, 6
  models of, 13–22
  and sickness, 6
Hemodialysis, and social support,
    158–160
Hereditary diseases, 104, 105
Home treatment, 106
Hopelessness, 197
Human development. See
    Developmental theory; specific
    stages; theories
Humanistic career, 117
Humanitarianism, as reaction to
    ambiguous and stigmatized
    human beings, 178
Ideal self, 167

Identicality, 72
Identity, 165–191
  in adolescence, 71–72
  ambiguous, 173–176
  and chronic illness, 173–181
  components of, 166–167
  definition of, 166–167
  development of, 167–170
  impact of professional reactions to
      ambiguous and stigmatized,
      179–181
  and juvenile diabetics, 184–189
  and research issues, 241–242,
      243–244
  sex differences in, 170, 171–173
  and spinal cord injury, 181–184
Identity spread, 175–176
Illness
  concept of, 5–6, 23–24
  defining, in family, 105
  without disease, 5
  effect of, on family, 108–109
  family as causative agent in, 94,
      104–105
  and help-seeking, 5–6
  and normalizing a situation, 176
  and research issues, 242–244
  self-defined vs. other-defined, 15–16
  social construction of, 22–26
Illness behavior, 12–13
  in chronic illness, 45–47
  definition of, 12, 45
  and family, 105–106
Impairment, 34
Impulsive reaction, to ambiguous and
    stigmatized human beings,
    177
Incorporate stage, 60
Independence
  development of, 211–212
  loss of, 213
  retaining, 214–215
Indeterminate career, 120–121, 124,
    125, 126, 132, 133–134
Indifference, as reaction to
    ambiguous and stigmatized
    human being, 179
Individual dominance, 103
Individuation, 72
Induration, as reaction to ambiguous
    and stigmatized human being,
    179
Industry, 66

Infancy, 54–63
  autogenic theories of, 55–56
  cognitive development in, 56–58
  interactive theory of development
      of, 61–63
  and personal control, 199
  social and personality development
      in, 58–61
Infants, blindness in, 63
Infectious disease, 105
Information
  and compliance and personal
      control, 202
  as condition of informed consent,
      228, 231
Informed consent, 226, 228–233
Initiative, 66
Institutional embeddedness, 102–103,
      104, 106, 107–108
Intelligence, in late adulthood, 78–79
Interactional approach to family,
      96–97, 98–99, 108, 109
Interactive theory of development,
      61–63, 84–87
Intermittent conditions, and illness
      behavior, 46
Intimacy, 74
Intrusion, barriers against, in
      reducing role strain, 39
Invalid behaviors, 44–45
Isolation. See Emotional isolation;
      Social isolation

Juvenile diabetes, 184–189

Kidney transplant, and family
      closeness, 153
Kin group embeddedness, 103

Labeling theory, 25–26, 68
Late adulthood, 76–82
  cardiovascular accident in, 160–162
  cognitive development in, 78–79
  and help-seeking behavior, 243
  and identity, 170, 172–173
  and informed consent, 231–233, 234
  losses in, 160–161
  and personal cintrol, 200, 201,
      212–215

physical development in, 76–78
  psychosocial development in, 79–82
  and research issues, 243
Lay referral system, 18–19, 105–106,
      116
Learned helplessness, 197
Learned inflexibility, 198, 201
Learning, in infants, 56–58, 61
Learning theory, 67
Legitimacy, and illness, 24–25
Legitimation
  dilemmas of, 43–44
  maladaptive behavior resulting
      from, 43–44
  uneven distribution of, 43
Life satisfaction, 222
Life transitions, 85–87, 151, 152
Living will, 232–233
Lobbying, 33
Locus of control, 193–198
  and compliance, 202–203
  concepts related to, 196–198
  and depression, 205
  in middle-age adults, 200
  misconceptions about, 195–196
  and socioeconomic status, 201
  and treatment programs, 204
Longitudinal designs, 246–247
Looking-glass self, 68, 167–168

Marital role structure, 101–102
M*A*S*H effect, 178–179
Mate selection, 99–100, 104
Material self, 166, 182
Maternal-infant attachment, 56,
      58–59
Maternal-infant relationship, 56,
      58–59, 61–63
Media coverage, 33
Medicine, 3, 4
Memory, in late adulthood, 78
Mental illness
  and family, 93–94
  and labeling theory, 25–26
  stigmatization of, 26, 128
Mental patient, career of, 127–131
Methodological issues, 246–248
Middle adulthood, 73–76
  and compliance, 243–244
  and identity, 172, 173
  and illness, 243–244
  and personal control, 200, 243–244

Middle adulthood (continued)
  and research issues, 243–244
Mutuality, 72–73
Myocardial infarction
  and career, 134–142
  and self-concept, 155

Normalization, as reaction to
    ambiguous and stigmatized
    human being, 178, 183
Normative adaptation, 42–44
Nursing home patient, career of,
    124–127
Nurturance, 146

Obscenity reaction, to ambiguous
    and stigmatized human being,
    177
Oral phase, 59–60
Orthopedically disabled, and family,
    154
Ostracism, of disabled, 32
Overprotection, 155

Pace norms, 118–120
Paternalism, 222, 232
Patient, management of illness by,
    42, 47–48, 204, 224–226, 233
Peers, 188
Personal definition, 36, 242–244
Personal control, 193–219. See also
    Locus of control
  actual, 197, 201
  behavioral, 198, 206, 207
  cognitive, 197–198, 206, 207
  and compliance, 202–205
  decisional, 198, 206
  and depression, 205–206
  and ethnic minorities, 201
  and hemophilia, 207–212
  and life stage, 199–200, 207–215
  and management of tension,
    206–207
  and osteoarthritis, 212–215
  perceived, 196, 201, 207
  potential, 197
  and predictability, 197, 198
  and socioeconomic status, 201
Personal embeddedness, 103–104, 107
Personal resources, 152

Personality development. See also
    Psychosocial development
  in infancy, 58–61
Pessimism, 197
Phantom limb, 166
Physical development
  in adolescence, 70
  in childhood, 64
  in late adulthood, 76–78
Physician, dependence on, 121–122
Physician-patient relationship, 41–42,
    47–48, 204
Piagetian theory, 57–58, 65, 69, 70,
    71, 83, 84, 199
Polio patient, career of, 121–124
Poverty, beliefs about, 32
Prejudiced reaction, to ambiguous
    and stigmatized human being,
    177
Preferential treatment, 155
Preoperational stage, 65
Procrastination, in seeking care, 18
Productivity, 74
Professional reactions, impact of, on
    identity of ambiguous
    individuals, 179–181
Progressive condition, and illness
    behavior, 46
Prognosis, 45, 46
Psychological self, 166, 182
Psychosocial development
  in adolescence, 71–72
  in childhood, 66–68
  in late adulthood, 79–82
Psychosomatic diseases, 6

Quality of life, 221–236
  and health care technology,
    222–224
  objective conditions of, 222
  subjective conditions of, 222

Reactance, 204
Reciprocity, 146, 148–149, 150, 153
Reference group theory, 168–169
Regressive career, 125–127
Rehabilitation, and family, 183
Rehabilitation industry, 32
Relation-searching studies, 238
Research issues, 237–249
Residual rule breaking, 25–26

Ritual separation, as reaction to
    ambiguous and stigmatized
    human beings, 177–178
Role analysis, 97
Role behaviors, in family, 97
Role discontinuity, 40
Role expectations, in family, 96–97
Role models, and stroke patient, 124
Role obligations, rededinition of,
    42–44
Role relations, elimination of, in
    reducing role strain, 39
Role responsibilities, 41
Role strain, 38–39, 40
Rotter's I-E Scale, 194–195, 205

Schizophrenia, 153, 201
Secondary gains, 22, 155
Self, 67–68. *See also* Identity
    active role of, 169–170
    "bad," 60
    cognitive and affective, 166–167
    "good," 60
    ideal, 167
    looking-glass, 68, 167–168
    material, 166, 182
    private, 132
    psychological, 166, 182
    public, 132
    social, 167
Self-concept, 67, 81, 155
Self-definition, of mental patient,
    128–131
Self-determination, 226, 228–234
Self-efficacy, 196
Self-esteem, 169, 170
    growth of, 67, 68
    and quality of life, 222
Sensorimotor stage, 65
Sequence norms, 118–120
Sex, vs. gender, 131
Sex differences, in identity, 170,
    171–173
Sex reassignment surgery, 132–134
Shopping, for medical care, 18
Sick people, factors influencing
    societal response to, 31–33
Sick role, 7, 18–19, 21–22, 39–40
    alternatives to paradigm of, 42–45
    in chronic illness, 38–42
    compared with at-risk role, 47
    as deviance, 21, 23, 24–25

and disability, 155
and role strain, 38–39, 40
Sick role behavior, 12–13
    and family, 106–108
Sickness
    concept of, 6–7
    and normalizing a situation, 176
    and research issues, 244–246
Significant others, and identity, 168
Signs, 4, 7
Situation
    normalizing, 176
    stressful, and social support,
        151–152
Situational expectancy, 194, 195
Social aging, 127
Social behavior, in response to
    symptoms, 12–22
Social construction of illness, 22–26
Social death, 125, 126, 127
Social definitions, 37, 244–246
Social development. *See also*
    Psychosocial development
    in infancy, 58–61
Social integration, 146
Social isolation, 146
    levels, of, 156
    of nursing home patient, 125
Social learning theory, 194, 195
Social network, 147–150
Social reconstruction syndrome, 81
Social relations, types of, 146–147
Social self, 167
Social support, 145–164
    in cerebrovascular accident,
        160–162
    in chronic renal failure, 158–160
    conceptualizing, 145–150
    and family, 42, 48–49, 152–156,
        159, 160–162
    and friends, 156–158, 161–162
    perception of, 159
    and research issues, 242, 246
    role and function of, 150–152
Socialization continuum, 99*f*,
    100–101, 104
Societal response, to sick and
    disabled, 31–33
Socioeconomic development, and
    response to sick and disabled,
    32
Socioeconomic status
    and fatalistic career, 117

Socioeconomic status (continued)
    and marital role structure, 101–102
    and personal control, 201
    and quality of life, 222
    and sick role, 107
Socioenvironmental theory, 81–82
Spinal cord injury, and indentity,
    181–184
Spiritual transcendence, as reaction
    to ambiguous and stigmatized
    human being, 178
Stable condition, and illness
    behavior, 46
Stigma, 43
    definition of, 174
    degree of, 32–33
    of mental illness, 28, 128
Stigmatized human beings, reaction
    to, 176–179
Stigmatized identity, development,
    173–176
Stress
    and disease, 6
    management of, and personal
        control, 206
    and social support, 151–152
    and symptoms, 5
Structural functional theory of
    family, 95–96, 97, 98, 109
Symbolic interaction theory, 68
Symptoms
    definition of, 4
    meaning of, to individual, 45, 46
    response to. See Illness behavior
    social behavior in response to,
        12–22
    and stress, 5

Taboo reaction, to ambiguous and
    stigmatized human being, 177
Tension, management of, and
    personal control, 206
Time
    and career, 115–121
    and polio patient's career, 121–124
    and transsexual's career, 133–134
    of tuberculosis patient, 116,
        118–121
    and social support, 152
Time tracks, 116
Transitions, 85–87
    and social support, 151, 152
Transsexualism
    career of, 131–134
    and research issues, 245
Tuberculosis, and career, 116,
    118–121

Unit of analysis, 247–248

Valid behaviors, 44–45
Value, and locus of control, 194, 195
Veterans, disabled, 33
Voluntariness, as condition of
    informed consent, 228

Wife-mother, 105–106, 107
Worth, reassurance of, 146

Youth, 72–73, 74